Religious Education Development

Images for the Future

Gabriel Moran

WINSTON PRESS

Cover design: Tom Egerman

Library of Congress Catalog Card Number: 82-51164

ISBN: 0-86683-692-6

Printed in the United States of America.

5   4   3   2   1

Winston Press, Inc.
430 Oak Grove
Minneapolis, Minnesota 55403

Contents

Introduction...*1*

PART ONE: A SURVEY OF DEVELOPMENTALISTS
1. Development and Its Theories...*9*
2. Psycho-Social Approach: Erikson and Others...*29*
3. Constructivist Approach: Piaget...*47*
4. Moral Reasoning: Piaget to Kohlberg...*67*
5. An Alternative Approach to Moral Development...*87*
6. Faith Development: Fowler...*107*

PART TWO: A PROPOSED THEORY FOR RELIGIOUS EDUCATORS
7. A Grammar of Religious Development...*129*
8. A Grammar of Educational Development...*157*
9. A Theory of Religious Education Development...*183*

Notes...*209*

Index...*227*

Introduction

In most of the educational world, developmental theory still seems to be a best seller. Nevertheless, I meet many colleagues these days who say they are skeptical about all theories of development. I share much of their skepticism, but I am also interested in specifying the problem as clearly as possible.

During several decades of writing on religious education I had never had a special interest in developmental theories. Of course, I had some acquaintance with Piaget, Erikson, and others, but I had no strongly held convictions about them. I think it was the work of James Fowler that forced me to confront the issue directly. Although I had been in conversation with Fowler since early in his work, I had refrained from writing any critical comments while he was still elaborating his theory. With the publication in 1981 of Fowler's *Stages of Faith,* development and faith development became omnipresent topics in church circles. I was invited to several symposia on faith development, and I had to ask myself what, if anything, did I think about the whole idea of development.

I tried to encounter the question of development as someone who had arrived from another planet might do. Can anyone say for sure what this idea of development means? Who spread the idea, and why? Is development a good idea, or a bad one?

My first conclusion was that I had to make a basic choice. I could fight against development as an ill-conceived idea, or else I could fight for a more adequate meaning of the term. When this choice had become clear I had no doubt that the second route was the one I found preferable.

As I listened closely for the word *development* I was surprised to find how frequently the term is used. The idea is all over the place; it winds through ordinary conversation and occupies a central place in nearly every field of study. Indeed, fighting against the term would be an almost quixotic undertaking. Instead, the question became: What tendencies in the use of the term do I wish to resist?

People use the word *development* to refer to many kinds of change or process. It can simply be one of those four-syllable words that government bureaucracies love to use. Nonetheless, most of the time the word carries the sense of progress or improvement. The phrase "research and development" suggests that the change at issue will be for the better. Development often means increased knowledge, more sophisticated machinery, or more powerful weapons.

One word that seems to have an especially close relation to development is *growth*. People often use the phrase *growth and development,* which I find somewhat puzzling. Grammatically, the words could refer to two distinct ideas, although I think that is seldom what is meant. Growth and development are thought to be almost but not quite synonymous. But to what extent is the meaning of development really tied to the image of growth? That strikes me as an important and seldom-investigated issue.

Many of my skeptical colleagues hear the phrase "growth and development" as a single idea. They therefore resist transferring what they see as a biological image to areas of morality, religion, or human life as a whole. We think we understand what it means to talk of growth. We have all seen a plant or a child grow. A child undergoes a process of growth from birth to some point in adolescence when we think of the child as "grown up." (Other kinds of growing, such as growing out at the waist line, we do not consider essential parts of growing up.)

Growth as a visible process of physical expansion serves us as an image we can use to talk about other things in life. We can say the likelihood of war is growing; we talk of growth stocks on Wall Street, or the growing skepticism about a theory. Generally we are aware that we have moved from a primary meaning to an analogous meaning. After all, if we think about it for just a moment, we can see that the likelihood of war does not grow in the same sense that a plant or a child grows.

An analogous as well as a primary meaning for growth does not entirely explain the contemporary usage of the term. Some modern psychologists claim that the child's powers of thinking slowly expand in a way that practically coincides with physical growth. This claim should probably not surprise us. Over the centuries, most thinkers have acknowledged that whatever autonomy might be claimed for the spiritual powers of rational thought and free choice, these powers are intimately connected to the physical organism while we are earthly creatures. Thus, a theory about growth in the capacity to use the mind is not necessarily materialistic. The slow growth of mental processes that is concomitant to physical growth simply says nothing about the origin or destiny of a spiritual realm.

The easy association of growth and development is therefore understandable when we speak about physical maturation and about mental change in a child's life. But outside these realms the image of growth becomes questionable. I am not suggesting we should never use the word *grow* outside this narrow range of meaning. Rather, we should just be aware of the comparison we are making. We surely can speak of "growing old," but it helps to remember that these words refer to something like—but not exactly like—a child's growing up.

The close association of growth and development needs careful scrutiny if one is to talk of moral development, religious development, and human development. The image of growth is limited in maneuverability and variety. Yet for discussing morality, religion, or life as a whole we need rich, flexible, multi-dimensional imagery. A general use of the word *development* requires a meaning that includes growth but also can connote other kinds of movement. One of the first dictionary meanings of *growth* is "increase by natural development." Logically, that implies there are other kinds of development besides growth.

Is it possible to imagine some facets of life as proceeding in some other way than pushing relentlessly upward and forward to bigger things? Anyone using the phrase "human development" should be prepared to answer that question. I will cite one example of what strikes me as deficient imagery for talking about human development. Gail Sheehy's *Passages* is a good journalistic summary of work done in recent decades on developmental theories.[1] The sale of *Passages* indicates there were millions of people waiting for a meaning of development that included them. These days, adults are encouraged to develop or, as it is often put, to keep growing. While I do not advocate that adults shrink, I think we should examine the imagery that floats loose in this literature.

Gail Sheehy's more recent book *Pathfinders* tries to document cases of what she calls "well being."[2] Her first example is a woman named Delia Barnes who has gone through a series of conflicts and depressions in fighting to be her own self. Sheehy leaves this woman at the age of 47 saying: "I'll never adjust downward."[3] I don't mean to belittle this woman's struggle to find her own way. Nevertheless, I think that Sheehy or someone should raise a question whether such a person is trapped by a rigid image of where life goes. Maybe, for example, the woman should try adjusting inward. Or maybe to adjust downward, far from being a sign of failure, means going in the direction of the depth many people lack today. So I find it strange that Sheehy offers this woman as her first case of well being.

In trying to approach the term *development* with an innocent attitude I noticed that two groups use the term very frequently: psychologists and economists. Both groups talk as if they had invented the idea and as if the real meaning of development is whatever they say it is. The two bodies of literature hardly ever impinge on each other. That makes for a somewhat humorous situation in that the real meaning of development in one journal on the library shelf apparently has nothing to do with the real meaning of development in the next journal on the shelf.

I used the word *apparently* in the preceding sentence because I suspect that in fact there is a hidden link between the personal development referred to in psychology and the economic development referred to in business and politics. Because the link between them is unconscious, the theories of development in both literatures are subject to powerful biases. Some day someone may be able to write the story of the development of *development*. Are theories of economic development written by individuals whose own development went up one narrow track? Are psychological theories of development a justification of the status quo issued by the well-to-do part of well-to-do countries?

I have suggested that in theories of personal development, all of us—including psychologists—probably start with some simple image of physical growth. However, when we use the word *growth* for many different aspects of adult life, then biology as the source of the term's meaning begins to fail us. We grope about for other images of "growth and development," and modern economics is all too ready to help us. The woman who would never adjust downward could have been talking about her stock investments rather than her personal life. We do not have to go looking for economic imagery because the economic concerns of buying, selling, saving, investing, and losing things affect our daily lives.

Until recently the notion of economic development seemed to be a simple idea, simpler even than expansion in the organic world. A nation's development or underdevelopment could be measured with a set of numbers, and countries could be ranked on a developmental scale. In recent years, however, the notion of economic development has been under challenge, so economists are now factoring in more numbers to improve the definition of development.

Financial interests around the world may still be missing the point of how their system is being challenged. What may be happening is that people in "developed," "developing," and "underdeveloped" nations are rebelling against the control of the term by one group. Some people may be asserting that the development of a people, a nation, or a culture has little to do with any of the figures that technologists and business interests have been using. Economists certainly deserve a hearing, but an adequate meaning of development on a world scale requires criteria that no individual or group knows for certain.

In a parallel fashion there may be a growing resistance to psychologists being the definers of development at the level of individual life. Who assigned the course called Human Development to the psychology department? It seems that in the twentieth century if we want to know how our lives are developing, we expect psychology to give us the answer. Persons who are rebelling against developmental psychology may be doing something other than offering another school of psychology or rejecting the idea of development.

Two conclusions can be drawn from these comments on economics and psychology. First, we should always speak with appropriate modesty when referring to "human development" or "the development of peoples." Second, with all due deference to the two disciplines in question, human development is too important to be left to psychologists and economists. If the human race is going to have a theory about life's development, then we should use *all* the resources at our disposal.

These two conclusions return me to the skepticism of my opening sentences. Why bother? Why put forth a theory of development when no one can possibly devise a theory that describes everyone's life?

My answer is that we all do acquire imagery that guides our judgments about human life. Our only choice is between good imagery and poor imagery. More modestly stated, the choice is between inadequate imagery and less inadequate imagery.

I am deeply interested in the imagery that is presupposed by theories of development. I am concerned with finding imagery that allows people to resist a premature closure of what their lives mean. I take it that the specifically religious way of approaching development is to resist reductionism in theories about life. The great religious traditions probably cannot be said to have *theories* of human development, but they do insist that an answer must eventually be given, and they do have images and practices that embody a meaning of life as a whole.

According to religion, each person's development is unique, but one can learn something from past lives. Religion, with its centuries of experience, has at least as much right to the idea of development as do psychology and economics. I make the claim in Chapter 7 that a theory of human development has to include religious development. The claim may not be persuasive to everyone, but in any case religious development is an ancient idea and not just a contemporary fad.

Religious theory, as I have indicated, is not always prominent in religions. Religious theory comes second and is mainly a theory of resistance; that is, religions refuse to accept any construct of ideas as the final answer to life's question. My own procedure in writing this book is to try to push back the walls of current theories. My religious theorizing in Chapter 7 is nothing more than commentary on the best imagery I can find in religious traditions. My final chapter, which theorizes about development within religious education, is simply an effort to keep the educational imagination receptive to possibilities and resistant to bias.

PART ONE

A Survey of Developmentalists

1

Development and Its Theories

Contemporary writing is filled with references to development and theories of development. An educator cannot miss having some acquaintance with the issue of development. I have the impression, however, that treatments of developmental theory tend to be of two kinds. On one side there are casual references to Piaget, Erikson, Kohlberg, Fowler, et al., with the assumption that all these people say about the same thing. Handy charts often accompany such references so that at a glance the reader can find that Fowler stage 5 is equivalent to Piaget stage 4. On the other side, there are detailed expositions of a single theorist that go into every technical detail of the master's writings. In this case the reader may not have the background necessary to comprehend these complicated details. More important, what the reader may not find—but what he or she is really looking for—is some larger context in which to place the theory as a whole.

My aim in this book is to offer an alternative to those two kinds of writing. I intend to provide more detail than the first type does, but *more* in the sense of the *crucial* detail that enables the reader to make helpful distinctions. I will present fewer of the technical details than the second kind of writing does, aiming instead to suggest the basis for overall comprehension and intelligent criticism. It is my conviction that an attentiveness to the question of language and imagery is central to such an undertaking.

I will assume that the reader has some acquaintance with the main issues of this book. Nevertheless, when referring to major theorists I will give some synopsis of their work. I will also point the reader to more detailed books so that he or she can check on the accuracy of my summaries. The summaries are simply intended to help the reader locate where each theory fits. In short, my main interest in the first part of this book is providing a context for a responsible criticism of developmental theories. This criticism will lead into my own formulation of a theory in the second part of the book.

My specific perspective for the criticism of developmental theories is religious education. I am not aware that much has been written from that viewpoint. Of course, religious education books in the past as well as in the present have taken over theories of development and inserted them into the work of the religious educator. A religious educator must on occasion wonder if a given developmental theory is compatible with the theory and aims of religious education. My question in this book is: What theory of development would be most compatible with the meaning of religious education?

The book builds its case toward answering that question in Chapters 7, 8, and 9. The movement from one chapter to the next is intended to reflect the image of development that the book advocates: a constant circling back and an integrating of disparate elements. The writers referred to in Chapters 2 through 6 are not used as foils; I do not treat their work simply to try to show that they are wrong. On the contrary, I am looking for what can be learned from them.

As a religious educator I do not endorse any of those theories without some reservation. That stance extends even to the work of James Fowler (Chapter 6), who describes his theory as "faith development." The relation between that category and religious education development is a question much in need of exploration.

In some respects I am making a bold claim for a new theory, a theory that transcends previous theories. Every writer unavoidably makes a claim of that sort. After all, if the truth were adequately known, another book would not be needed. The implied arrogance in that stance is mitigated if a writer tries to learn from his or her colleagues, tries to make criticism pointed but gentle, and invites others to join in a project which at book's end is still sketchy. A modest attitude toward my own theorizing is especially demanded by the underdeveloped state of religious education itself.

The preceding sentence reveals the fact that my title has a double meaning. This book is about (1) the theory of development that is most appropriate to religious education and (2) the development of religious education. Not accidentally do those two topics meet in one and the same title. A precondition for the existence of religious education is an overall conception of what human life is and where it goes. Conversely, I wish to make the claim that a theory of development adequate to the mysteries of human life requires the contribution of religious education.

The reader may resist my neat two-way relation as merely a vicious circle. How can A (religious education) determine B (developmental theory) if B also determines A? My response is to replace the word *determine* with a word that connotes a give-and-take relationship: A influences B while in turn B influences A. Religious education and developmental theory are themselves at certain stages of development. What needs to be established is a healthy, reciprocal relationship so that each may profit from the other's criticism.

I have no choice but to grapple with both halves of the relationship. Such an approach may seem unduly messy compared to a picture in which one first establishes A and then moves on to handle B in relation to the fixed point A. In much of human life, though, and especially in anything religious, we do not have the luxury of having the world under our control. This unmanageability of key conditions is what makes human life both frustrating and interesting. As Chesterton put it, "The real trouble with this world of ours is not that it is an unreasonable world, nor even that it is a reasonable one. The commonest kind of trouble is that it is nearly reasonable, but not quite. Life is not an illogicality, yet it is a trap for logicians. It looks just a little more mathematical and regular than it is; its exactitude is obvious, but its inexactitude is hidden; its wildness lies in wait."[1]

. . .

In many places over the past decade I have put forward the thesis that religious education, both as an academic field and as a functioning profession, does not yet exist.[2] The word *yet* keeps the statement from sounding pessimistic. Actually, I am quite optimistic about the emergence of religious education in the late twentieth and early twenty-first centuries, provided there is a world at all. Either the world will face up to religious issues in educationally appropriate ways, or else the world is likely to tear itself apart. I do not think there is anything very peculiar in saying that religious education is coming to be in the twentieth century. Before the present century, religious education was not so urgently needed, and one might even say it was hardly possible.

Both the words *religious* and *education* as we use them today are largely the invention of the eighteenth and nineteenth centuries. It would be foolhardy to jump from that statement to the conclusion that we have nothing to learn about education, religion, and religious education from pre-eighteenth-century history. How an individual was initiated into the Christian mysteries during the fourth century may be important to a Christian church of the twentieth century. Nevertheless, the transformation of both the religious and the educational questions in modern times must be carefully attended to. That holds true even for a full appreciation of fourth-century practices.

The early twentieth century witnessed an ambitious attempt to create a field and a profession of religious education. In recent decades Protestant literature has tended to dismiss "the religious education movement" as one element in the naive liberalism of the early twentieth century. That the writers who advocated religious education in the early 1900s had their limitations and blind spots is evident to any reader of that material today. However, I think that what is just as obvious in the 1980s is the greater need for religious education and the great richness of its possibilities. The religious education movement was skewed by the predominance of U.S., white, male, liberal, Protestant Christians. That fact simply raises the question of what composition religious education should have.

At present the most visible thing that is related to religious education is the effort of particular religious groups to transmit their respective ways of life to the younger generation. These efforts have names like catechetics, Jewish education, or Christian education. If the term *religious education* is used at all, it is equated with one of those terms or some aspect of that work. (For example, in the Roman Catholic church, the term *religious education* tended to be used for the church's programs outside the Catholic school; despite changes in recent decades, that meaning has not disappeared.) I am distinguishing religious education here not only from the work of one group but also from a generic category that is simply wider than terms like *Jewish education* or *Christian education*. The existence of a concept called religious education challenges and transforms the Jewish way, the Protestant way, the Muslim way, or the Orthodox Christian way. Religious education is the name for the needed response in a radically and obviously pluralistic world. What can a child or an adult make of exhortations to follow "the way" when it is evident that there are many ways? At the same time it is obvious that those other people are not stupid, insincere, or irreligious. To state the issue in somewhat technical fashion: When a meaning system confronts another meaning system, then the meaning of *meaning system* changes. That is why religious education is a necessity of the twentieth century's pluralism: No religious group can relinquish its claim to "the way," and yet increasingly each group has to live with other people who are just as certain that they know "the way."

I think that churches and other religious groups are still at an early stage of accepting this new situation of diversity. There is still a hope that if they try a little harder or get more effective techniques, then the young will accept the way being offered. The further hope is that those so impressed in their youth will stay on that path for life despite today's seductive alternatives. Notice that with that set of assumptions, developmental theories can be attractive to the most conservative church people. After all, they are searching for a truly effective instrument with which to inculcate the saving truth.

Church educational endeavors are generally classified as either a minor branch of theology or else a separate field that theology guides. Sometimes this area is called religious education, although, as I have indicated, churches usually have another term. In contemporary Protestant denominations the term *Christian education* is most common. The content of the church's educational work is mainly specified by theology. Less obviously, the assumptions of the church and its theology strongly influence who is educated and how. The church declares, announces, proclaims with the purpose of inculcating, transmitting, and converting. There is a minimum age (five or six) below which efforts of this kind would be inefficient. There is a maximum age (late adolescence) beyond which this kind of educational effort is not likely to be successful.

The prominence of the developmental question in church literature can be easily appreciated by looking at the timetable just mentioned. In the space of a few years one must cover the work of generations. How does one match the Christian materials with the psychology of the child's learning? Anyone who can tell us which Bible stories will make sense to a seven-year-old and which stories require a twelve-year-old's capacity would be a great asset. A knowledge of the child's gradually unfolding abilities and interests can have revolutionary impact on a church world that until the middle of the twentieth century was dominated by "uniform lessons" and watered-down theology books as catechisms. I would not minimize the significance of this developmental revolution that has been occurring throughout the twentieth century. However, revolutions to be successful need to be carried through a complete turn, or else they stall with the new problems that emerge. Developmental theories raise other issues besides effective techniques for church education. They raise the questions of religious education as an enterprise distinct from the church's forming the young in the way and the truth.

The ages I specified above define the part of the young that the church education has been directed to. Children of an early age, as well as adults, are excluded. Churches are always trying to add "adult education" to their programs, but that is not really to get at the problem. The church and other religious organizations acted consistently in the past when they tried to hand on the best of the tradition to the next generation. In modern literate cultures that meant instructing literate children in the documents of the tradition; these documents, of course, were set in the midst of unwritten and nonverbal parts of the tradition and its practices. This ancient process still works to some degree, although we may be expending nearly all our energies in trying to shore up an inadequate model. A newly developed religious education becomes necessary even for the sake of preserving the best of the past.

A consistent pattern of religious education would require our moving from a content specified by Bible/theology, a method guided by announcing/converting, and a population of older children/adolescents. Not that any of these elements are bad or that the answer is to race toward what seems to be the opposites: from Bible to experience, from declaring to discussing, from children to adults. We have been down that road before with demands for that kind of relevancy. Despite their radical appearance, the calls for experience, discussion, and adult education can still be parochial if there is not an adequate context of religious education.

I come back then to my basic theme, the dialectical relation between the (emerging) meaning of religious education and the (not-yet-adequate) meaning of developmental theory. We need a meaning of development that can encompass the religious diversity of our day.

At the same time that meaning should suggest the forms and instruments that education can bring to the religious question. We need a meaning of religious education that will remind developmentalists not to settle prematurely on some plan for all human beings. The task of theorizing on development cannot be handled by adding a few adult stages to earlier developmental studies. The search must go deeper than that to the meaning of development itself. Does anyone know for sure what development means? More basic: How does one go about finding an answer to that question?

The Meaning of Development

I would like now to explore in a preliminary way the meaning of development. The whole book is a study of this idea and its intricacies, but it helps to step back and ask in the most direct way: What does it mean? I am not interested at this point in formulating a definition. The antecedent question is, What do people mean when they say the word *development*? This kind of approach to the question is favored in the twentieth century, with its acute awareness of the ambiguities of language. Before we can judge that a statement is true or false we have to know what the statement means. That meaning is not usually so obvious as common sense assumes.

The approach is not entirely new. Plato and Aristotle already did some of this kind of analysis, especially in the moral area. "What do men (and women) say that justice is?" Medieval philosophy was a continual exercise in linguistic distinctions. This concern has often been ridiculed, sometimes deservedly. At its best, however, this approach, far from losing us in esoteric technicalities, roots us in the concrete particularities of everyday life. To ask about the meaning of language is to refuse to try moving above speech to an abstract plane of ideas. An obliviousness to language often turns language into a coercive system of ideas.

When one investigates the meaning of a term, it becomes evident that the meaning spreads out beyond anyone's control. As a rule, the older and simpler the word, the more complex and unmanageable is its meaning. What does the word *love, freedom, goodness, hope,* or *truth* mean? Anyone has to look a little ridiculous who says "The real meaning of *love* is. . . ." Outside the realm of technical terms invented for a specific reason, words usually don't have true, correct, or accurate definitions. Words do have a range of meaning so that definition—a setting of limits to meaning—becomes mainly a question of finding imagery to convey the widest range of meaning or the most appropriate range of meaning.

For any term we could distinguish between the meaning that is obvious or dominant and meanings that are hidden, peripheral, or latent. Over centuries of usage what has been prominent in the meaning can become secondary, and vice versa.

Meaning does not die or entirely disappear; it is conveyed through language even when people are unaware of the historical roots of a term. Again, some words are used in very different contexts at the same time in history. Users in one context may never notice the usage in another context. I suspect, however, that there is nearly always some linking of meaning for the same word in two settings (for example, the use of intelligence in IQ tests and in military operations).

The predominant meaning of a term at any historical moment is governed not only by laws of etymology and logic but also by the power of those people and organizations who can shape language to their own advantage. As one adage states it: A language is a dialect that had an army and a navy. The U.S. government's use of *intelligence community* to describe its spying operations is a case in point. People who fuss over fine points of grammar and pronunciation can be oblivious to the political and economic struggles reflected in the use of language. When we use language we select from a range of meanings and then advocate a meaning that we prefer, usually a meaning that reflects our social standing or cultural class (for example, *professional, sophisticated, progressive*).

The way to get at this process, which for the most part occurs outside consciousness, is to become aware of fundamental metaphors that govern our speech. The question is almost never what is the "right" metaphor. One has to ask of language: Which metaphor least distorts the whole range of meaning? Which metaphor has the most fruitful social, political, institutional possibilities? Which metaphor gets closest to combining the universal and the concrete? I am interested in advocating a definition of *development* only after I have played with the imagery that the word calls up. Then, metaphorically speaking, I will advocate moving some meaning to center stage while trying to move other meaning(s) to the wings. The criteria for my choice can only emerge fully as I proceed, but as a start I would say: (1) My advocated meaning must not do violence to the etymology and history of the term, and (2) such meaning must be meaningful in the contemporary setting. What I am ultimately interested in is a meaning of *development* appropriate to religious education. However, I must first attend to what the word means in the whole range of contemporary usage.

Development is a very common term in the modern world. It seems to be one of those words like *growth, process, evolution,* and *progress* that define what *modern* means; that is, a stage advanced beyond ancient, primitive, or pre-modern. Moderns assume that people, organizations, and things develop and that the way to understand anybody or anything is to watch it develop. Our idea of development seems to originate with the rise of historical consciousness in the nineteenth century. Everything in the universe is assumed to un-fold, e-merge, or de-velop; that is, it starts at one stage, undergoes a systematic change, and arrives at a more complete stage.

I referred above to "our idea" of development, trying to avoid the myopia which assumes that development was discovered in the nineteenth and twentieth centuries. Ancient peoples were not unaware of change or process. Indeed, Greek philosophy and Indian religion can both be summed up as one long search for an answer to change, decay, and suffering. Curiously, some people refer to "process philosophy" of the twentieth century with the implication that previous philosophy was not about process. One would expect some stipulation about what kind of process is advocated today or specifically what modern philosophy has to say about process.

In listing modern words above I included *growth* and *progress*; in referring to ancient thought I cited the words *decay* and *suffering*. Perhaps that is where moderns and ancients differ in their theories of process, change, and development. We are inclined to think that ancient peoples were too timid in their approach to process, change, and development; we assume that we have discovered the positive meaning of those terms. Thus, a "process thinker" may preemptorily dismiss the "traditional" view for thinking of process as a mere in-between or something to be escaped from.

The modern view of change, process, and development has been decidedly optimistic. The very existence of the word *modern* is probably linked to a doctrine of progress. The ancient notions that things go downhill or in a circle have not been very attractive to the modern Western mind. Preeminently in the United States, progress has been our most important product. Progress is more easily defended at some technical level; it is a more difficult notion to sustain in ordinary human lives. The fact that progress is more an ideological doctrine than an incontestable fact has been surfacing during recent decades even in the United States of America. The questioning of progress returns us to the issue of what kind of development we have put our trust in. Is our image of development adequate to the movement of our lives?

The word *development* seems weighted on the side of movement *from* a given position. The etymological emphasis is on coming to birth or coming into existence: Something steps forth "out of its wrapper." Modern usage shifts the emphasis toward where we are going, incorporating a modern idea of progress without end. The etymological root, however, does not disappear. In photography, where the word is common, a picture is developed because the plate contains all the elements; the person developing the film brings to completion what is already there. Likewise, according to Erikson, developmental psychology presupposes a ground plan so that the study of the child can be conceived as an unfolding of what was fundamentally "given" from the start. [3]

When the assumption is stated that way it causes resistance. Surely development is not the mere uncovering of what has always been. The developing itself should be at least as important as the ground plan. Are not developmentalists looking for an image more like a painter trying creative mixes of color than a photographer running negatives through a developer? No doubt most modern developmental theories incline in that direction. But that inclination brings up a new problem. If the ground plan does not determine the stages and directions of development, what does? If the answer is not in the beginning, must it not be in the end? Aristotle and much of the medieval world thought so, but one of the words the modern world flees from is Aristotle's *telos,* the end toward which process moves. For Aristotle the "final cause" is last in execution but first in intention. This guiding idea was the religious or metaphysical speculation that modernity set out to avoid. [4] Can one find an image of development that avoids both a predetermined end point and a stifling biological determinism?

As I indicated in the Introduction, psychologists and economists are the ones who trade most heavily in the language of development. Psychologists probably assume that economists are borrowing a psychological term when they refer to developed, developing, or underdeveloped nations. One could make a case for that sequence: from embryology to psychology to studies of industrialization. Still, one could also argue that the whole of modern economics is based upon a notion of development; that is, we use the materials of nature and labor to move to a more desirable order. In this view the developmental psychologist is a latecomer to the modern economic scene, where development has been a central issue for several centuries.

The curious thing is that psychologists and economists seem hardly aware that *development* is a metaphor that transcends their own field of interest. Economists until recently barely probed their own use of the term. Some countries were declared the advanced or developed world while the rest of the world was assumed to need forming in the image of the developed. Note how Aristotle's *telos* easily slips back into the process. Economists may say that progress has no preordained end, but they nevertheless assume that progress means imitating the United States and western Europe. One need not explore the question very far to find that the criteria of development have been quantitative measurements. The development of nations meant the development of higher totals in ledger books. Little was indicated about quality or about what makes human life satisfying. The *New York Times* once dramatized this issue by pointing out that the best way most of us could contribute to the economy was to contract cancer; that added $175,000 (and rising each year) to the Gross National Product. The high technology of cancer treatment adds more dollars to the GNP than most individuals can contribute by worker productivity.

In recent years many people have objected to the assumption that the expansion of wealth is the measure of human progress.[5] However, effective criticism of economic systems has to include a refashioning of what development means at the personal level. Otherwise, development still means numbers. Small pockets of resistance use phrases like "small is beautiful" which still suggest that small and big are the main choices. But neither the book by that title, *Small Is Beautiful*, nor discourses to that effect convince most people that there is anything particularly beautiful about small size. What might be convincing to many people is an image of development that is concerned with form, proportion, and sharing. Those elements would involve not only psychological questions but philosophical, moral, and religious ones. Better to avoid those sticky questions and concentrate on increasing the flow of products. "Instead of 'Let my people go,' the modern Moses cries 'Let my people grow' so that they never have to learn about sharing and moderation."[6]

Psychologists seem to be oblivious of economic discussions about development. Of course one cannot expect a person to be constantly adverting to a usage outside his or her field. In this case, nonetheless, theorists of microcosmic development—the development of the individual or of structures within the individual—should not entirely forget the economic context. Otherwise, economic bias (as well as racial, ethnic, and sexual biases that crisscross the economic) works a devious influence on anyone's theory of "human development." Who developed the theories of the way people do or should develop? Did such authors have a vested interest in having the world move in the direction of their kind of people? I am referring not so much to outright fraud (though the history, for example, of IQ testing comes close to that) as to the limited and somewhat biased view that every author brings to this issue.

On the psychologist's side, the word *development* seemed to take a big leap into adulthood during the 1970s. That became evident at the time of the publication of Gail Sheehy's *Passages* in 1976.[7] Sheehy put into good journalistic summary the work that had been going on for a decade or more. The subtitle of *Passages* referring to "predictable crises" promised more than any book can deliver. In the text itself, though, Sheehy had the more modest attitude of "if this happens to you, don't be too surprised." Sheehy could not resolve all the methodological problems in the study of adults. What *Passages* did illuminate is the fact that "developmental psychology" has been for most of its history a part of child psychology. Lately, however, many people have been applying the term *development* to adults.

It is easy to miss the point here. The thing worth noticing is not the oft-mentioned difficulties of studying adult lives. Rather, it is the fact that developmental psychology was in the past able to sidestep the philosophic question which I am trying to surface here: the nature and direction of the change called development. Development was assumed to be the steps that a child went through on the way to becoming an adult. Since the author and the reader were adults, it could be assumed that everyone knows what an adult is. Thus *A Dictionary of Psychology* could say that development is "progressive change in an organism, continuously directed toward a certain end condition (e.g. the progressive change from embryo to the adult in any species)."[8] That works fine until we begin to doubt that the "end condition" or "the adult" is crystal clear in meaning.

The interest in adult development usually turns out to be either a trivial set of platitudes ("Adults change, too") or a reopening of the submerged question: What is development? But studies of the adult cannot be a superstructure on the developmental psychology that was the study of children. When adult as a fixed point is eliminated, then one cannot lay several stories of development upon a firm base of previous development theory. It is true that the closer one sticks to embryology, the easier it is to protect developmental systems of the past. In the other direction, the closer one gets to the development of the human as a whole, the more questionable become systems that are studies of childhood. For example, one of the most obvious facts about human beings is that they die. Developmental psychology in the past had little to say about that. Yet if one were going to write a theory of human development, death would have to occupy a central place. Freud seemed to move in that direction late in his life; however, this later work, which included a kind of death instinct, got a mixed reception. Perhaps it is simply not the province of psychologists to write the whole theory of human development.

Development in Religious Education

I should note at this point in a preliminary way that the modern history of religious education can be read as a struggle around the idea of development. Religious education development is not an invention of mine. There has long been a question whether development and religious education are compatible ideas. That question is at the forefront of two of the greatest writers in this area: Horace Bushnell, a forerunner of the religious education movement, and George Albert Coe, its greatest theorist.

Horace Bushnell is a central figure in the history of both public school education and Protestant church education. Much of today's discussion in church circles is still framed in the way Bushnell saw it over a century ago.[9] He was reacting against the evangelistic and revivalistic approach to religion that dominated the early decades of the nineteenth century. In that framework the child begins a sinner, and education is a preparation for conversion. Bushnell's alternative was that the child born into a Christian family is already Christian; education becomes a "nurturing" of what is already there. One can therefore find a kind of developmental theory in Bushnell: the presentation of doctrine only as the child is ready for it, and the calm, continual growth of the child into full Christian maturity.

George Albert Coe combined this religious view of Bushnell's with the educational psychology of the early twentieth century. Religious education, he thought, should be such as to make conversion unnecessary. The real necessity is to get out of the way of the child's unfolding or developing powers. "The central fact of the modern educational movement is a recognition of the child as a determining factor in the whole educational scheme. . . . Education is not to press the child into any prearranged mold, but to bring out his normal powers in their own natural order."[10]

At least in this quotation from early in his career, Coe reflects the naive hope of his educational contemporaries. They were discovering how to allow the child to come forth "out of the wrapper." The majority of Coe's religious brethren remained skeptical of this developmental idea. They did not see that this optimistic view of the child took sufficient, if any, account of the Christian doctrine of sin. To this day a large segment of the churches sees the choice as one between the conversion called for in the gospel and a theory of development derived from modern psychology and secular humanism. Faced with that choice, it is not just the right wing of the churches that votes for conversion. A book which is seemingly about "adult development" can say in reference to Jesus' preaching in Mark 1:15: "This change, at the heart of the Christian gospel, refers not to improvement or development but to a transformation of life."[11] Are the words *development* and *transformation* incompatible? Does conversion of life as a central category conflict with the meaning of development?

The conclusion I draw from this brief excursion is that Christian educators who are affirming the gospel ought to look carefully before rejecting the idea of development. On the other side, writers who advocate developmental theories risk failing as an earlier liberalism did, unless the idea of development is adequately thought out. Bushnell's formulation of the issue, nurture vs. conversion, still governs much of church writing. From an educational point of view the choice is clearly inadequate today. Neither Bushnell nor Coe provides a full-blown theory of development for the religious educator. Bushnell, however, in thinking that the child should be educated *in* conversion rather than *to* conversion, was on the right track. A theory of development within a social, political, institutional, and cosmic context might prove to be compatible with religious phenomena, including conversion.

Two Families of Development

On the current scene, two distinct schools or approaches have arisen from a psychological meaning of development. Two men stand in back of these approaches: Jean Piaget and Erik Erikson. The aims, methods, and results of these approaches are so dissimilar that some people wonder if the term *developmental theory* can apply to both approaches. Piagetians especially have the tendency to regard themselves as the true developmentalists and therefore the owners of words like *stage* and *structure.*

Writers often express the hope for a grand synthesis of Piaget and Erikson similar to the oft-expressed hope to combine Plato and Aristotle or Marx and Freud. No one boldly claims to have accomplished the synthesis, though many writers do suggest that they are moving toward that goal. By making corrections upon and additions to past theory they are approaching the point of including all of human development. Nearly anyone who speaks on the subject today intends to be inclusive, but the grand synthesis requires more than a statement that such levels as the social, affective, adult, and so on, are included. If imagery is not social, for example, from the beginning, one cannot add a social dimension to a theory. And as I noted earlier, adding adult stages to theories of child development will not work. Concerning a grand synthesis of the two main families I offer the following double observation: Anyone whose distinctive approach is Piagetian cannot incorporate Eriksonian material. And anyone who starts with an Eriksonian pattern can incorporate Piaget only in minor ways. Why this is true will, I hope, be clearer as I proceed.

Before I characterize the differences between these two approaches, an important agreement between Piaget and Erikson should be noted. Both are concerned with interaction: the relation between organism and environment. Both of them therefore test the limits of the literal meaning of development, that is, the unfolding of what is given from the beginning. The recognition that development is an idea embracing the personal and the nonpersonal tests the limits of psychology itself. It suggests that if *human development* is a legitimate term at all, it does not belong exclusively to psychologists. Instead of the psychologist peering into the individual psyche to uncover the laws of development, we have today a complex interdisciplinary task of tracking a movement whose laws depend in part on what is outside the organism. In freeing themselves from a determinism of beginnings, both Piaget and Erikson have to find a way to avoid a determinism of the end. In the final comments of this chapter I will come back to the way they do that.

In stressing now the differences between Piaget and Erikson, we might begin with a contrast that Lawrence Kohlberg makes. In looking for "an integrated theory of social and moral stages," Kohlberg says, we currently have two perspectives. While both are relational models, Piaget emphasizes the "world pole," and Erikson emphasizes the "self pole," which makes Erikson's a kind of existential psychology.[12] Kohlberg's contrast is attractively clear, but I do not find much merit in this description of differences. I do not imagine that Erikson with his constant reference to the social context would look kindly upon being classified as one who emphasizes self over world.

Piaget and Erikson have occasionally made brief and appreciative comments about each other's work. Piaget credits Erikson for having "introduced into Freudian psychoanalysis an important notion—the hypothesis that we continually assimilate the past to the present with a view to adaptations in the present."[13] Erikson recognizes that Piaget saw the desirability of having a comprehensive theory of development that could account for the personal unity of each stage through childhood and into adulthood; as a careful scientist, however, Piaget remained skeptical of arriving at such a theory.[14]

In a more extended comment on Piaget, Erikson sought to contrast their differences by saying that the Piagetian theory was born of the experimental tradition but his own from clinical experience.[15] According to Erikson, the experimenters take healthy people and put them through tests. From carefully controlled premises they draw limited conclusions about human nature. "But it is clear that their methodological modesty disguises the expectation that all their reliable data added together will eventually be equal to the total functioning of man." (Erikson excludes Piaget from this latter accusation.) The clinicians, Erikson continues, start with sick people and are forced into looking for the real core of personality and an ideal to guide human life. Here there is also a modest claim to be treating patients, but "we are sometimes sure that we could explain or even guide mankind if it would only consent to be our collective patient."[16]

Erikson emphasizes here that his own work emerges from concern with neurosis and pathology. I gather that as Erikson pursued his work he saw it as one of developing a theory of the healthy person more than of the sick. It seems to me necessary to describe the two families of developmental theory in a way that does not begin with sick versus healthy. I offer the following characterizations as introductory to the study of Piaget and Erikson.

The Eriksonian pattern is best described as a psycho-social approach to development. Its main interest is in social roles and self images as these change over a lifetime. Its method is one of clinical interviews that reconstruct a person's history. In Erikson's epigenetic cycles the person goes through predetermined cycles in which what is individually given intersects with social forms. The person makes his or her choices in response to the culture's established tasks.

The school of research that follows Piaget's lead is often called cognitive, though I prefer the name constructivist. Its major focus is how a person knows and how the mind structures experience. Its method is to pose problems or dilemmas to an individual and then to analyze the way someone constructs and formulates an answer. There is more interest in the how than the what (content) of responses. The assumption is that genetically given structures emerge in response to the environment. Although one cannot predict the chronological age for a stage's emergence, one can say for certain that the stages follow in an invariant sequence.

This compressed description of the two approaches may not adequately dramatize the great difference between them. However, the psycho-social approach is usually evident in its narrative style that refers to phases, ages, or seasons of the life cycle. Its strength is its comprehensive character, the possibility of talking about the whole life span. The constructivist method aims at something more typically scientific, using language that tries to measure exactly the operations of the mind. Its strength is the precise detail that its clear focus on mental operation provides.

. . .

Finally, I return to a major concern of this chapter, the images associated with the idea of development. My concern is what kinds of change are included as possibilities and what kinds of change are excluded by the assumed imagery. Some early twentieth-century writers assumed a correspondence between the given powers of the child and the mature workings of the adult. Psychology could then trace a straight line of development from point A to point B. Following laws that psychologists knew in part and some day would know in full, the child becomes an adult.

Both of these contemporary approaches—Piaget's and Erikson's—work from a quite complex set of assumptions that try to incorporate a wide range of possibilities. These two approaches try to avoid the arrogant claim of knowing what the perfected human being is. Erikson does that by offering a tension of opposites at every stage—even in the final stage. There is no end *point,* no final *object* although there are varying kinds and degrees of harmony that indicate successful development. Piaget, with very different tools but some philosophical similarity, describes a development that is guided by and aims toward equilibrium. That equilibrium is itself never static, and it allows an almost unlimited number of ways for achieving it. To avoid submitting the human being to a final object (health, wealth, power, reputation), Erikson borrows ideas like trust and integrity from philosophical and religious traditions. Piaget does not go that route but does translate the idea into mathematical notation.

John Peatling in his definition of *development* uses the intriguing mathematical term "stochastic process," a process that "inevitably involves a sequential probability from one state to a yet-next state."[17] The future is predictable only within laws of probability. One is all but certain of some patterns and directions; one is completely uncertain of what the final outcome will look like. The laws of psychology and of other sciences can never provide a description of the individual's human development. However, within a range of probability approaching 100% the sciences can predict some patterns of biological/psychological maturation.

For fending off some naive assumptions about development, the introduction of mathematical probabilities is useful. Mathematics can in this instance be a translation of a religious concern not to bow down to idols. As soon as the mathematically describable structures are placed into the context of personal life, though, the question of imagery arises. Curiously, the imagery to be assumed with the word *development* does not seem to interest Piaget, Erikson, and many of their followers. But for someone interested in religion and education, the question of imagery is unavoidably a central issue.

2

Psycho-Social Approach:
Erikson and Others

Using the distinction of Chapter 1 between the psycho-social and the constructivist approaches, I will look at the first in this chapter and the second in the chapter that follows. My aim in both chapters is to convey an overall sense of the relation of both approaches to development as this development might be conceived in religious education. This perspective requires me to summarize the main concerns of each theory while I try to highlight either points of conflict or intriguing suggestions for a religious educator.

I will touch first on the assumptions of Erik Erikson before looking at his description of ages. After looking at points in Erikson that refer to religion, I will mention some criticism of Erikson, especially by feminists. In the last part of the chapter I will look at other theorists who, inspired by Erikson's work, have been pursuing the study of adult stages of development.

As the term *psycho-social* indicates, the Eriksonian pattern tries to take account of both psychological and social data. The study of development is not only a matter of general interaction with environment but of specific kinds of interaction. Other people are not just pieces of one's environment; social environment is fundamentally different from physical environment. The individual "plays a role in society" which in turn helps to determine what and who the individual is. An element of unpredictability—indeed a massive amount of unpredictability—has to be admitted from the start. That means the rules and canons of experimental-mathematical science are not going to be observed.

A good deal of methodological modesty is called for in all the conclusions discussed in this chapter. Most of the authors referred to do in fact make a disclaimer to that effect even if they occasionally forget it. The disappointment in their failing to reach what can be called scientifically precise is balanced by a refreshing modesty in the tenor of the claims. Contrast that, for example, with the behaviorism early in this century: "Give me a dozen healthy infants, well formed, and my own specified world to bring them up in, and I'll guarantee to take anyone at random and train him to become any kind of specialist I might select."[1]

Psychoanalysis had already undermined this arrogant attitude of scientists who would play God. Freud unlocked the door to the unconscious and showed that we know little about the mysteries of the personality. However, every new discovery can be used as if it were a doctrine of final truth. Psychoanalysis often created a rigid new determinism in which the child's early development sealed her or his fate. Two psychologists, Alexander Thomas and Stella Chess, have been doing what Freud could not do: longitudinal studies of development from childhood to adulthood. They claim that psychoanalysis moves the immutability due to heredity over to an immutability due to infancy. They cite a response of Burton White to the question of early infancy's determinism: "To some extent I do believe that it is all over by 3." Thomas and Chess claim that White, like Freud before him, has no evidence on which to base that conclusion. Furthermore, Thomas and Chess offer their own counter-evidence. Life, they assert, is not simply the unfolding of infancy.[2]

Erik Erikson comes out of the Freudian tradition, but he has also tried to do a major overhaul of psychoanalysis. He has tried to incorporate the psychoanalytic categories into a socially oriented theory. He begins his charting of development with these two assumptions: (1) Human beings develop according to steps predetermined by the growing person's readiness, and (2) society is constituted to meet and to invite the succession of potentialities for interaction. Such a correlation between the organismic and the social is a big assumption, although one could argue that simply by trial and error or by survival of what fits them, individuals and society reach some kind of correlation. Such a correlation, it should be noted, does not determine whether there might be other powers of the individual that have not been or cannot be socialized.

Erikson is being consistent when he writes that "the chosen unit of observation must be the generation, not the individual."[3] He is interested in relationships, especially between the older and the younger generations. One can make sense of individual lives, he says, because they can be seen as repeating, embodying, and re-expressing the pattern of the generations. This image need not eliminate the notion of individual uniqueness. The more profound one's embodiment of one's people or era, the more unique is the individual. Erikson developed that idea in his studies of Luther and Gandhi.

The movement of the generations is presumably the reason for Erikson's use of the word *cycle*. I am surprised that people so easily refer to the "life cycle" today without reflecting on the peculiarity of the term. *Life span* and *life cycle* are now used interchangeably even though the imagery is not the same. Reflecting on the omnipresence of the term *life cycle* among psychologists and psychiatrists, Charles Kao writes: "How this Hindu-Buddhist notion of time and history crept into the Western mind is a worthy task for historians to undertake in their inquiries."[4]

Erikson talks about life cycle because of his concentration upon the generation. He interprets the individual's life from within that movement of the generations. The child who is on one side of the generational divide will eventually come around to the other side. In that restricted sense a cycle or at least a 180° movement is a meaningful image. Also the pattern of one generation "concluding itself in the next" is evident in the flow of the centuries.[5]

Erikson does make the jump to claiming that there is a cycle to individual life. This claim implies that as a person gets old he or she becomes like a child again. This doctrine is a common one in the history of religion: that old age is a preparation for rebirth as an infant. Erikson and others using the word *cycle* show little interest in those historical connotations of the word. Yet no question is more important to the study of adult development than the relation between the words *child* and *adult*. Is the image of cycle helpful to imagining this relation, or is it an obstacle to thinking?

Within the big cycles of generations and of individuals Erikson posits multiple small cycles of the individual's life. That is part of what Erikson wishes to convey through his word *epigenetic*, namely, that the characteristics at issue have a time of ascendant importance but are there at other times as well. The issues of childhood (trust, security) recur in adolescence and again at midlife. One cannot say it is the same question each time, but neither is it an entirely new question. Erikson can avoid a determinism based upon the beginning conditions by presenting each age as a new chance to resolve old problems, a new chance that is not separated from all the decisions that have previously occurred.

The best known formulation of Erikson's "eight ages of man" is his essay in *Childhood and Society* from the 1950s.[6] Over the years he has not made fundamental changes in that formulation. The description of the eight ages is somewhat sketchy, and Erikson's writing since then has not eliminated the sketchlike description of most of the ages. Here is the chart of Erikson's ages:

1. basic trust   vs.   basic mistrust
2. autonomy   vs.   shame
3. initiative   vs.   guilt
4. industry   vs.   inferiority
5. identity   vs.   role confusion
6. intimacy   vs.   isolation
7. generativity   vs.   stagnation
8. integrity   vs.   despair

I will not try to repeat here what Erikson has said on each of these eight. Rather, I will concentrate on what kind of chart we have here and then highlight a few points about it. Erikson has frequently pointed out that he does not have an achievement scale. He does not propose a description of qualities that should be preached to people who would strive to attain them. Two things seem to be implied here: (1) The first term in each pair is clearly the desirable one; however, it appears in personal life more by discovery or gift than by conscious acquisition; (2) the terms in the second column, instead of being bad qualities, are more like the minor characters in a play; they are bad only when they try to upstage the major characters. A conscious attempt to eliminate these qualities is unwise.

If my interpretation is correct, then Erikson has to bear some responsibility for misunderstandings that he complains about. His choice of terms in some cases throws all the weight to the first column instead of allowing some degree of ambiguity within each pair. Who could possibly want stagnation or despair or understand them as secondarily desirable? Or notice the difference between role diffusion (a plurality of personal characteristics that might be part of a modern individual's search for identity) and role confusion, which one cannot look kindly upon even as a subordinate element. In contrast, I think one could conceivably argue that mistrust, guilt, and shame are good things or necessary things to have in minor doses.

Erikson seems to be arguing the same case when he says that a "favorable ratio" of the first column of terms over the second is desirable. To use a sports metaphor, column one should win the game but not run up the score. Erikson maintains that it is the favorable ratio of column one over column two that produces the strengths corresponding to the needs of each age. Those eight strengths as described in *Insight and Responsibility* are: hope, will, purpose, competence, fidelity, love, care, and wisdom.[7] It is fairly easy to grasp the general meaning of these words, but what kind of list is it? Erikson was at first inclined to call them "virtues," and he has been averse to giving up the term entirely.[8] He acknowledged that virtue has moral connotations he did not intend. Their opposites, he says, are not vices but weaknesses or development that is inappropriate to needs. The salvaging of the word *virtue* will concern us in Chapter 5. It would seem to me that the strengths of character that Erikson wishes to describe could indeed be called virtues in the ancient sense of the term if not in its modern moralistic meaning. Virtue in the older tradition referred to dispositions facilitating good action rather than to trophies of the will. If Erikson's problem with the word *virtue* is its masculine etymological meaning ("manliness"), then that opens up a different discussion about development as a whole that I will come back to shortly.

The complicated chart of major and minor elements is Erikson's way of avoiding a determinism of a preordained end. In the language of the first chapter, development remains a stochastic process in which an observer's chances of prediction would increase with each epigenetic curve. The observer could get a rather high degree of probability about what will be involved the next time a crisis occurs. Predictability about how the person will resolve the next crisis would remain low. The individual moves along a path in which the tension of near opposites can never be resolved. The ratio of one term to the other has a nearly unlimited range of possibilities at the beginning of life. The range narrows as life matures, but the limits of the range are never known with certitude even by the individual in question, let alone by an observer.

Religious Implications

In this section I will comment on those aspects of Erikson's chart that seem to have religious implications. Erikson makes only occasional reference to religion, although that may be too often for some of his colleagues. In his scheme the dialectical tensions enable him to avoid the fixed *telos* or an ideology of progress. What keeps the contrasting pairs of each age in tension? Here is where Erikson seems to indicate a highly significant role for religion. "It is the world's religions which have striven to provide an all-inclusive world view for the containment of such human extremes as self-seeking vanity and self-abrogating humility, ruthless power seeking and loving surrender, a search for beliefs worth dying and killing for, and a wish to empathize and understand."[9]

More often Erikson seems to relegate religion to a smaller, helping role in each of his developmental ages. He places religion as an institution in the very first age along with the struggle of basic trust versus basic mistrust. At first glance that seems to imply that infants are religious and the rest of us are not. However, if one recalls that he is describing the relation between generations, then religion is at least as important for adult ages as it is for children. "The parental faith which supports the trust emerging in the newborn has throughout history sought its institutional safeguard (and, on occasion, found its greatest enemy) in organized religion."[10] He seems to require that parents have a religion or at least a quasi-religion, that is, "a vital faith [derived] from social action or scientific pursuit." While he criticizes those parents who are professedly religious but "in practice breathe mistrust both of life and man," he is even more critical of those who "are proud to be without religion but whose children cannot afford their being without it."[11]

The previous comments seem to refer to the relation between parent and child. The next generation up, the older adults, are also paired with the infant. The old play the role of grandparents, and beyond that, the old are the wise religious elders of the human community. The basic trust of the young child depends upon the integrity and the wisdom of the old. Erikson quotes Webster's dictionary, which defines trust as "the assured reliance on another's integrity." He notes wryly that the dictionary may be referring here to money, but he wishes to make the same connection between trust and integrity in the cycle of the generations. "Healthy children will not fear life if their elders have integrity enough not to fear death."[12]

Erikson is no doubt aware that his final age of integrity has moral and religious connotations. Etymologically, the word *integrity* is related to peace, health, wholeness, and holiness. If we are to realize such integration or integrity, we need a "post-narcissistic love of the human ego . . ., an experience which conveys some world order and spiritual sense."[13] Maintaining this integrity in the face of death is what Erikson calls wisdom, and for defining that strength he has to use the religious concept of "detached concern with life itself."[14] During the 1960s the term *disengagement* was used in psychological literature to describe the movement of old age; the concept was quickly discredited as negative and simplistic.[15] Erikson's "detachment," with its long religious and mystical history, provides a broader context that allows for some kinds of withdrawal, denial, and restriction. As always in Erikson, the latter age is prefigured earlier in life. Even when one is acquiring identity, the question in our technological age is what one "can afford and decide *not* to use, *not* to invent and *not* to exploit."[16] This concept has to play a central part in development as perceived by religious education.

The age that does not seem to fit the religious sentiment is generativity. That word seems to suggest activity directed outward without inwardness, mutuality, or a sense of limits. The choice of terms here is crucial because Erikson said that if he had not been writing from the standpoint of the child, generativity would be the center of his system.[17] As it is, he constantly goes back to generativity and warns against the tendency today toward selfishness and a lack of concern for the next generation.

Generativity has its most obvious expression in the procreation of children, and that is where Erikson lays stress. He has always acknowledged two other aspects of generativity: the productive and the creative.[18] These two aspects seem to be allowed as substitutes for the procreative, but it is this latter that he always returns to. If one does not have children, one must engage "in active pursuits which universally improve the condition of every child chosen to be born."[19]

Erikson is not the only one these days who is worried about the link between the generations. For the human race to continue, there has always been need of a bond between the unborn, the living, and the dead. In the past the human race could hardly imagine an uncoupling of one generation from the next. But the control of birth, the technological exploitation of resources, and the possibility of nuclear war have suddenly confronted the human race with a new question of whether and how the next generation will live. Erikson tries to broaden the meaning of generativity beyond giving birth to children. He wants to include "man's love for his works and ideas as well as for his children."[20] When describing care as the peculiar strength of this period, he says care is the "widening concern for what has been generated by love, necessity or accident."[21]

I think his word *care* here can be illuminating, especially when he plays with the variations *be careful, care for,* and *take care of.*[22] One can use the verb *to care* for all ages of human beings and for the nonpersonal world as well. I question whether the word *generativity* can be equally comprehensive. I suspect it may be too limited in both a political and a sexual context.

Erikson seldom tries to translate his system into political terms. That is certainly understandable; he makes no claim to be a political theorist. This fact, however, should remind us that the term *psychosocial*, while broad in meaning, is not equivalent to *human*. A theory of development, to the extent it claims to describe human life, has to be receptive to other disciplines. Erikson's stage of generativity would seem to be the time when an individual's attempts to control or to improve the world run up against the world's size, power, and intractability. According to Erikson, a man's generating of children, ideas, or products takes place not only in psychological and social contexts but in political, institutional, and ecological settings. The term *generativity* is not flexible or rich enough to describe the interplay of people, products, and ideas in the business, political, and technological worlds of today. Thus, a phenomenon such as the "male midlife crisis" is not particularly illuminated by Erikson's description of generativity. That topic needs situating in a context of politics, personal relationships, and a sense of mortality.

Feminist Criticism

The sexual limitations of the idea of generativity lead into a more general comment on the possible sexual bias of Erikson's "the eight ages of man." Before citing feminist criticism of Erikson I would note that he, more than most of his colleagues, was aware of this issue when he set out his descriptions. Ironically, his attempt to state differences between men and women made him more vulnerable to criticism than were many writers who simply ignored the question. What I mean is strikingly illustrated when he refers to the quality of generativity and the corresponding virtue of care: "Here I emphatically include woman, when I speak of man. For woman's preparation for care is anchored more decisively in her body, which is, as it were, the morphological model of care, at once protective abode and fountain of food."[23]

What Erikson has done here is to give over the aggressive meaning of this stage to what has been the male role (procreate, produce, create). Women are then brought in to provide restraint and defend the body. One could do worse, although feminist writers today are saying that we must do better. Erikson is surely not one of the great culprits here; at least he was trying. As I have indicated, the concept of generativity may hinder him from progress toward sexually inclusive language.

Erikson does wish to bring out that children are not just generated but must be cared for. The long-held belief still residual in our language was that men did the generating. The verb *to father* still means to impregnate, while *to mother* means to nurture the child in infancy. The recent attempt to invent the verb *to parent* may succeed in creating a context in which fathering and mothering might be reimagined. The new verb unfortunately could also just abstract from reality and create an obfuscation. A new literature on fatherhood has emerged over the last decade.[24] It needs to be linked with feminist writing so as to create a context of mutuality in child care. Furthermore, as one of these writers on fatherhood suggests, we need a verb *to child*; that is, a more perceptive study of children reveals that "there are a variety of ways to child one's parents."[25] This point is thoroughly compatible with Erikson's concern to study mutual relationships in the generational cycle.

Where Erikson is less helpful, and where feminist criticism is needed, is in the meaning he sees in work. Erikson, like most modern writers, tends to equate work with production. Thus he can speak of generating products as well as children. What the modern world calls economy is built around the idea of producing things and exchanging them in the marketplace. Modernity has meant an increase in the products available, especially as human labor was replaced by efficient machinery. Few people would deny the progress inherent in the expansion of material goods and the reduction of physically laborious toil. Nonetheless, some serious flaws have become evident, and various reformers have tried to correct them. Karl Marx, the most famous of these critics of the workplace, began with an analysis of the "fetishism of commodity." He sought to liberate workers from oppression, but Marxism has proved to be no panacea.

One thing insufficiently appreciated in both capitalism and Marxism is the realm of what gets classified as "woman's work." Certain daily tasks must be performed if life is to go on. "Woman's work is never done." *Care* is an appropriate term to summarize them: care for the child, the sick and the aged; care for plants, animals, food, clothing; care for arranging, beautifying, cleaning the home. This kind of work issues in no finished product or at least not in a product that remains as a monument to future generations. Yet an argument could plausibly be made that this kind of work is the most important work in the world. Amazingly, our standard ways of speaking still exclude this work from the very meaning of work.

Erikson, I repeat, is not especially at fault here. His use of the word *care* offers resistance to the culture's bias concerning work. But if we wish to have a developmental theory in the future that appreciates what both men and women do in this world, Erikson's choice of generativity as the central category of adulthood must be seriously questioned. We are just at the beginning of a revolution that will tap the possibilities of women for work outside the home and will reground men in forms of work that are not classified as production. Any educational model that misses this point today is sadly inadequate. Religious education development is especially concerned with work in relation to vocation or calling.[26]

Probably each of Erikson's ages as well as the sequence of ages needs examination from a feminist perspective. For Erikson, the movement after the first age of trust seems to be one of separation and of standing on one's own. Initiative, for example, is described in male terms, with the concomitant fear of the age being "castration complex."[27] Erikson makes a point these days that he switched from a term like "phallic stage" to "infantile sexuality."[28] That does not entirely meet the criticism that the movement of childhood years is toward an identity of separateness. After noting that the "identity crisis" really describes only men, Jean Baker Miller asks if it is a sign of immaturity for children to wish not to leave a world where people do care.[29]

Erikson in some ways invited the criticism he has received from feminist writers. With a somewhat paternalistic tone he wrote in the 1960s: "What [women] have not begun to earn, partially because they have not cared to ask for it, is the *equal right to be effectively unique*, and to use hard-won rights in the service of what they uniquely represent in human evolution."[30] Erikson is commenting here on the issue of women becoming either the same as men or uniquely themselves. The peculiar word *unique* is not sufficiently clarified in Erikson's use of it. He does say that "each, to be really unique, depends on a mutuality with an equally unique partner."[31] Here is the basis of a rich philosophical vision of the person that could be helpful to feminism. But Erikson's unfortunate choice of terms in the above quotation does not encourage a uniqueness of mutuality.[32]

Erikson's epigenetic principle and his tension of polar opposites should be flexible enough to respond to feminist criticism. The relational categories that women are demanding should fit into Erikson's patterns if he were willing to rename many of his categories. However, I do not think he sees the need for revision. In a recent interview he says, "It has been said that my life-cycle theory does not fit women, that in men identity comes first and then intimacy, but in women intimacy first and then identity. There is, of course, a lot to be said for that, especially in the light of a traditional system in which the woman's very name is going to depend on the man she is going to marry."[33] I find that statement a strange misconception of what the criticism has been about, as if a switch of ages 5 and 6, a reversal of intimacy and generativity, is what women are asking for.

What I find most dismaying in the same interview is that Erikson has not seriously addressed the question of what image his developmental theory assumes. He praises his wife Joan's weaving for providing a visual form for his theory. The weavings show the presence of each quality in each stage, dominant in one and subdued in the others. What I called the minor characters and what Erikson here calls the dystole is also woven into the fabric. Joan Erikson comments that perhaps the top and bottom of each weaving should be tied together; the result would be a cylinder rather than a flat weaving.

Erik Erikson responds that "maybe something like the helix would be the best overall configuration for showing the generational cycle."[34] After this one passing reference to a helix or spiral image, he passes on to another topic. In the final three chapters of this book I will try to show the importance of this question and what the guiding imagery should be. Erikson has helped to make popular the term *life cycle*, a strange term that surely raises a question of imagery. Is development to be imagined as a cylinder, a helix, or what? The implicit or explicit answer to that question will determine the value of much of the research on adult development.

Following Erikson: Adult Development

In the remainder of this chapter I would like to indicate the current interest in adult development, much of it inspired by Erikson's ages of man. In the preceding paragraphs I have noted that Erikson's ambiguities leave him open to feminist criticism. For much of the literature in this field there is little ambiguity: The writing is relentlessly sexist. That is one major indication that we do not yet have a literature of adult development or human development. We have studies of a select part of the culture, generally the part that represents the dominant ideal of the culture. One cannot hope for a quick cure to this problem. The study of generations takes generations to accomplish. We have no way to go back and correct the sample of longitudinal studies begun in the 1920s or 1940s. Nonetheless, many male writers seem oblivious to the question itself. They would of course admit that women should be included in sampling, but they seem unaware of the possible male bias in our meanings of growth, development, and adulthood.

As I pointed out in the preceding chapter, the study of adult development cannot be merely an addition of some stages to the older developmental psychology. The developmental psychology (of children) had a consistent framework when it assumed there was a fixed point of "being an adult" in relation to which everything could be measured. If one really admits adult development, then one must reconceptualize the development of children, and it is not obvious how to go about such a process of reconceptualization without a fixed point. Despite all the apparent interest in adult development, we are still at the beginning stage of asking what adulthood (and thereby childhood) means. The sexist tenor of much of the writing is symptomatic of the fact that the meaning of adulthood is being taken for granted even while much of the human race is beginning to question the meanings of growth, development, and progress.

Erikson is better than most writers in playing with the notion of adulthood. He recognizes that while *child* and *adult* are chronological categories that are mutually exclusive, *childlike* and *adultlike* refer to qualities that can interplay at every stage of life. He gets to the heart of the issue when he writes: "If the cycle, in many ways, turns back on its own beginnings, so that the very old become again like children, the question is whether the return is to a childlikeness seasoned with wisdom—or to a finite childishness."[35] With that distinction of *childish* and *childlike,* one has the instrument to reflect on the relation between adult and child.

Unfortunately, when Erikson sets up a chart of normality a few pages later, that distinction is nowhere nearly so clear. One now is supposed to be not a childlike adult but an "adult adult"; a straight line of psychological maturing accompanies a straight line of chronological growth. The meanings of *childish* and *childlike* are conflated. The elements of playfulness and paradox are all but eliminated in that growth line. Becoming adult means getting to the top while integrating all the lower stages into one's personality. This ideal seems so obvious that most men writing on adult development have assumed the ideal without questioning it. Instead, they spend their energies dividing up the adult years into proper segments while not asking what "being adult" means.

I will comment on some of the best-known works simply to locate them in relation to issues raised in this chapter. Then I will come back to one of them, *Seasons of a Man's Life,* for a more extended comment. Daniel Levinson, et al., *The Seasons of a Man's Life* and George Vaillant, *Adaptation to Life,* are studies with all-male samples. Levinson's study in the 1970s is all male by choice; Vaillant's use of a male sample was necessitated by his using data that go back to the 1940s origin of the study.[36] *Adaptation to Life* shows what happens to upper-class men of power and wealth. The metaphor of adaptation seems to be fruitful for describing the kinds of struggle they endure (e.g., living up to the expectations engendered by wealth and power, getting out from under the shadow of domineering parents). What this study has to teach the rest of us about adult stages is unclear, at least until it can be set in comparison to other studies of other groups. The Harvard graduates who make up the study are not a representative sample even of white men in the country.

The Levinson team's study makes several conscious assumptions to protect the validity of its modest data. It did not have the benefit of longitudinal data collected over a forty- or fifty-year period. Long personal interviews had to substitute for that kind of data. The study was designed so that the sample included different socio-economic strata of contemporary society. Although the number studied in each group is very small (ten), at least the effort made was in the right direction. The choice to make it a study of men is legitimate, particularly because a comparable study of women was indicated for future publication. Perhaps only from a number of studies of men and studies of women will better questions and more inclusive imagery emerge. Then we can confidently proceed to studies of human development.

What perhaps is most significant in studies like those of Vaillant and Levinson is the sense of limit that emerges in men's lives. Men run up against limits and experience them as unexpected, unhealthy, or unjust. Women almost certainly have a different sense of limits from very early in life. The adult male's peculiar confrontation with a sense of limits may suggest inadequacies in our meaning of development that indicate the direction in which the imagery of development should change. Levinson's imagery of "seasons" is an attempt at new imagery. I will comment on it after looking at a few other studies.

Roger Gould's *Transformations* and Bernard Boelen's *Personal Maturity* are examples of books that operate with extraordinary blindspots concerning development and adulthood.[37] Gould had published an interesting article based upon one study conducted in a hospital.[38] The book that followed was apparently intended as popular theory. It has few references to anyone's research, an exhortatory style, and a string of anecdotes. The text sets off down a trail defined by "childhood consciousness vs. adult consciousness." A word like *demonic* is regularly associated with childhood, while "a rational, adult view of reality" is held out as the ideal. If all goes well we reach the ideal by about age fifty. The final chapter is a consideration of "individual growth and its effects on social issues."[39] This brief conclusion serves only as reminder that the book is worked out in categories that are asocial and apolitical. Not accidentally, the book is consistently sexist in language and condescending in its few references to women.

While Gould's study comes out of psychoanalytic tradition, Bernard Boelen's *Personal Maturity* is rooted in existentialist philosophy. However, they share a good deal in their assumption of life's progress toward the free and rational (male) adult. Boelen has an elaborate scheme of ten stages through which the man must move toward adulthood. "Man is not born mature. He has to pass through various stages, not in the sense of leaving them behind, but successively integrates them into ever higher levels of maturity."[40] All the integrating is in service to moving in one direction: to the top.

A peculiarity in Boelen's detailed set of stages is that, like Gould's, the whole thing seems to end by about age fifty. That is, the language of both men is ageist as well as sexist. What does a person become *after* she or he is an adult? The answer implied by the use of the word *adult* is: One becomes old. The dominant ideal of adulthood in our culture, which the books by Boelen and Gould exemplify, is the rational, independent, productive, efficient man. Old people do not fit comfortably into that ideal. In fact, older people keep slipping off the end of adulthood.

For all the apparent enthusiasm and optimism in theories of "adult growth," there is an unstated sadness and despair in much of this writing. Books like those by Gould and Boelen describe a moment at the pinnacle followed by a precipitous decline beyond adulthood. For readers who are skeptical of the point I am making here, I suggest they examine case by case the use of the word *adult* in studies of adult development. I think they will find that its most common meaning is to designate a stage of life in between adolescence and an unnamed territory after adulthood. I return to Erikson's question of what life moves toward: an adulthood in which rationality and independence are situated within a childlike attitude, or else a childishness after one is no longer certified as an adult.

Of studies that at least have the flexibility and ambiguity of Erikson, Bernice Neugarten's work over the years (which I will refer to in later chapters) and Marjorie Lowenthal, et al., *Four Stages of Life*, are representative.[41] Lowenthal is clearly concerned with making comparisons across generations and between men and women. The book does not claim to have solved the problem of method, but it is filled with revealing passages. There are illuminating comparisons between middle-aged men and middle-aged women as well as between middle-aged men and "pre-retirement" men. Lowenthal says there has been a lag in attitudinal change. "The present and projected life-styles of these young people of both sexes were family-centered and male dominant."[42] That was the case, the author says, despite the fact that we are entering an era when people will have twenty to thirty years of post-parenting life.

Four Stages of Life has two things about it that are particularly refreshing: (1) its assumption that adulthood does not end just beyond age forty or fifty, and (2) its assumption and its evidence that men and women are in some ways different and in some ways very much the same. Both assumptions, it might be thought, are common sense, but I have already pointed out that the first is not commonly assumed. The second assumption is still trying to get a hearing. Studies in the past assumed that men and women are the same; therefore, we need only study men, and they happen to be available. In reaction, there has been a strong tendency to say that men and women are different. What needs exploration is the possibility, if not the likelihood, that such things as "identity crisis" occur in both men and women but at different times and in different forms. On this point Lowenthal notes that "women of all ages felt that they had already gone through the most troubled time of their lives, while the majority of men felt that the worst was yet to come."[43]

The picture of middle-aged men in *Four Stages of Life* is particularly grim, darker than in Vaillant or Levinson. Yet the added context of the other generations and the other sex provides more intelligibility and possibly more hope. These middle-aged men are not just struggling with some individual time line; they are caught in the middle of several kinds of forces. They often feel that they are on the receiving end of all the cultural movements. The young, the old, women, and blacks seem to have only one common enemy: middle-aged white men. Yet most of the latter do not recognize themselves as a class of oppressors. Instead, they are often confused by the attack upon their ideals. The hopeful element in *Four Stages of Life* is the presence of alternatives, especially among the men of the older generation. Some men may be discovering a little later in life "a sharp increase in goals of ease and contentment, in comparison with the middle-aged."[44] We cannot get an accurate picture of human development until we see where men go after the age of fifty in relation to women, children, work, and the universe.[45]

I return to some final comments on Levinson's "seasons perspective." *Seasons of a Man's Life* attracted the most attention in the late-1970s burst of writing on the subject. Levinson, with acknowledged debt to Erikson, tries to take account of internal psychological factors and external social factors. The focus is on individual life structure in contrast to Erikson's focus on ego or personality. The structure develops according to *viability,* the degree to which one can function successfully in the society, and *suitability,* the degree to which the life structure allows a man to live out his most cherished dreams.

Levinson speaks of periods of life rather than stages. He readily uses chronological age and social tasks for describing these periods. Levinson picks out the thirties and forties for his major concern while assuming some larger theory of development from Erikson, Jung, Neugarten, or others. Levinson does not speculate much on this bigger picture. Anyone has a right to pick a restricted area for research; I suspect, however, that one cannot avoid assimilating the culture's assumptions about development unless one consciously resists them.

In Levinson's framework a man is first a novice in the adult world. He has a dream of success and, if fortunate, a mentor.[46] In his thirties he is concerned with "becoming one's own man," which includes both independence from society and attention by society.[47] In his forties the polarities of his life become evident and cry out for attention: young/old, destructive/creative, masculine/feminine, attachment/separateness.[48]

Levinson verifies earlier studies on the sense of mortality that becomes strong in middle-aged men. He coins the helpful neologism *de-illusioned* to describe what happens to them.[49] (*Disillusionment* is too strong and too negative a term to describe the shift that occurs in men of each group.) When the sense of limitation surfaces, especially in relation to one's own mortality, then the old games are no longer worth playing. What new illusions, games, and rituals are appropriate for men past middle age is not clear, he says. That will have to be found in political, religious, and philosophical research as well as in psychology.

The metaphor of seasons simply sidesteps for the moment the question of where it all goes. Perhaps Levinson believes that this metaphor avoids the dominant image of an arrow of time. To some extent that is true, but *seasons* is not a full-blown alternative. What it allows Levinson to do is to make judgments about appropriateness. Each of the seasons of the year has an appropriate form, so we can confidently say of snow in summer that it shouldn't be. Analogously, Levinson can say that having a mentor at age forty-five is wrong (i.e., inappropriate) and that being de-illusioned at twenty-five is incorrect developmentally. The metaphor of seasons saves our judgments of good and bad from being moralistic.

Eventually, though, one must use *good* and *bad* in ways that transcend the metaphor of seasons. We do make judgments about how the "seasons" of our life go together and for what purpose. In its primary meaning the word *seasons* is related to climate, weather, and environment. In this meaning we can avoid questions of how seasonal change fits in with massive changes in the earth's atmosphere. Nearly all the answers involve magnitudes that are irrelevant to our historical lives. But in regard to the development of a person's life the questions cannot be forever sidestepped with the single metaphor of seasons.

Assuming that something else is intended than the repetition of a four-segment circle, where do the seasons go, what if anything do they add up to, and how do the shifts in the middle of life fit some image of life as a whole? I quoted Charles Kao at the beginning of this chapter as he asked how a Hindu-Buddhist idea of life cycle became so widely accepted by psychologists today. Kao goes on to say: "Even the Hindu-Buddhists want to be emancipated from the cycle of rebirth (*samsara*) for *nirvana*. Life is not just a cycle."[50] The images of life cycle and seasons may be useful tools for psychologists, but such language should not be mistaken for an adequate description of human development.

3

Constructivist Approach: Piaget

To pick up and read one of Jean Piaget's sixty books is to enter a world very different from the one described in the literature of life-span development. While many of the books that use a psycho-social approach are popular and even faddish, the literature by and about Piaget is daunting and sometimes impenetrable. Piaget called his area of study genetic epistemology, that is, concern with the growth of structures of knowing as these are traced from their origin in the biological organism.

In this chapter I can only touch upon a few key issues in Piaget's constructivist approach. For the many details of Piaget's system I refer the reader to one of the many summaries or commentaries that now exist.[1] My main interests are: (1) the assumptions that underlie Piaget's theory of development, (2) the imagery that runs thoughout the system, and (3) the critical questions that have been raised, especially from the standpoint of education.

Lest the point be obscured in any criticisms that follow, the first thing to be said of Piaget is that he may well rank among the great geniuses of the twentieth century. Since his life spanned the first eight decades of this century, the next two decades and more will be needed to make an adequate assessment of his work. Besides having passionately loyal disciples, he also has harsh critics who disdain the content and method of his research. The existence of this latter group, of course, does not disprove his genius.

Most of his critics would probably grant that whatever the weaknesses of his system, Piaget did transform the terms of the debate in some long-standing controversies. Modern philosophy has struggled with the conflict of empiricist and rationalist positions; these systems had speculated on whether knowledge originates from pure sensation or from the mind. This dichotomy found expression in the biological sciences as the nature-versus-nurture debate. The question was whether the qualities and traits of the organism are given through an hereditary process or whether they mainly depend on environment and upbringing.

The philosophical controversy reached a culmination with Immanuel Kant's system, in which the mind plays an active role by imposing categories on perceptual data. Kant recognized that ideas such as space, time, and causality are not perceived by the senses but instead are in some way given by the mind. Kant constructed a system of categories on speculative grounds, although he was influenced by the Newtonian science of his time regarding the fixed nature of space and time. During the past century and a half, changes in mathematics and science have undermined the Kantian categories. At the same time these very changes have given support to the Kantian principle of knowledge as a mental construct.

The greatness of Jean Piaget's work is that it provides experimental data to validate Kant's principle. The issue could not be resolved by simply declaring that the mind contributes forms to knowledge. Piaget sought to trace in painstaking detail how these forms are constructed and when they appear in an individual's life. Lacking any clear method to accomplish this project, Piaget had to invent his own, often relying on instinct and intuition, and often concentrating on his own children. He left himself open to criticism about method, and many scientists attack him on those grounds. Nevertheless, many people who criticize Piaget today would have to admit that he opened the way to their own line of study.

What I am proposing is that Piaget accomplished something almost unheard of: a step of progress in philosophy. Piaget does not offer a solution; undoubtedly empiricists and rationalists will continue their argument. The influence of Piaget will probably last, however, and the argument will be more refined because of Piaget's contribution. A special irony attends this conclusion because Piaget did not at all wish to be a philosopher. Perhaps the most accurate thing we can say is that despite his attitude toward philosophers and despite the limitations of his own philosophy, Piaget made a lasting contribution to the history of philosophy.

For documenting this last statement I turn to his revealing auto-biographical essay "An Account of and an Analysis of Disenchant-ment" in the book *Insights and Illusions of Philosophy*.[2] If one wishes to get at the assumptions of Piaget and some possible reasons for those assumptions, this essay is crucial. The title of the book is misleading, but the essay's title is indicative of the book's thesis: The story of philosophy is almost all disillusionment and very little insight. The young Jean Piaget's journey is away from the seductive illusions of philosophy to the secure knowledge of experimental science.

Toward the beginning of that essay, in a rare reference to religion, Piaget writes: "I was brought up in the Protestant faith by a believing mother, whereas my father was a nonbeliever, and I was therefore already acutely aware of the conflict of science and religion."[3] The formula is redolent of the late nineteenth and early twentieth cen-turies: Protestant faith in which the mother believed and the father didn't; little more need be said. One chose either religion and its ancient formulas or science with its unceasing illuminations. When the young Swiss student arrived at the French school he found what seemed to be a way out of the science-versus-religion debate: phi-losophy. He took to that study with passionate hopes: "I would devote my life to philosophy whose central aim I saw as the reconciliation between science on the one hand and religious values on the other."[4]

As with many adolescents before and after him, Piaget's intoxi-cation with the grand sweep of philosophy did not survive exposure to a teacher who "got me to appreciate rational values" and thereby woke him from his philosophical dreams. The struggle then became to secure a truly scientific psychology over against a faculty of phi-losophy that still thought of psychology as under its control. For Piaget, philosophy with its claim to superior knowledge is the chief obstacle to scientific work in psychology.

In the introduction to *Insights and Illusions of Philosophy* Piaget says that the book's "thesis is simple, and in some circles mundane: viz., that philosophy, as its name implies, is a 'wisdom,' which man as a rational being finds essential for coordinating his different activ-ities, but is not knowledge properly so called, possessing safeguards and methods of verification characteristic of what is usually called 'knowledge.'"[5] His position may be simple and mundane, but it rep-resents a devastating attack upon what most philosophers have meant by wisdom, and it is a very narrow definition of what is meant by knowledge. Piaget tries to unseat philosophy's claim to a separate realm of superior truth by retaining the separateness while evacuating the claim to any truth at all.

Philosophy is thus given a "heuristic function": It "raises problems but does not solve them."[6] Only experiment and deduction have the function of "cognitive verification which is alone constitutive of truth." Piaget objected to being called a positivist. Positivism, he says, is wrong in dismissing questions about the meaning of life. What can be said about the meaning of life is a matter of hypothesis "without (present) meaning from the cognitive point of view," but the problem "forces itself on us in the form of 'engagement.'"[7]

Whether such a position should be called positivism is, I think, debatable. Piaget did not believe in a theoretical unity of science, as most positivists do, so that for them all special sciences become a part of physics. More important, however, the separation of two realms, science and wisdom, with only the former counting as knowledge, does seem to be a variation on a simpler positivism that declared religion and metaphysics to be meaningless and ethics merely emotive. Piaget notes that wisdom actually should be in the plural: "There can be several wisdoms while there exists only one truth."[8] Few philosophers would deny the second part of that statement, but unstated in that formula is the assumption that an experimental method of science reaches that one truth.

The philosophy that Piaget always refers to is the phenomenology and existentialism of France. He does not give much evidence of acquaintance with philosophical schools in Germany, England, or the United States. He also seems unaware that the philosophy implied in his own separation of knowledge and wisdom is, if not positivism, then a kind of phenomenology or existentialism. If one allows for "engagement" with the meaning of life through a realm other than rational knowledge, the result is something like the existentialism that Piaget roundly attacked. Phenomenology with its claim to intuit essences, and existentialism with its glorification of freedom, were not born of a superiority complex. They were defenses against the hegemony of scientific method; their irrational tendencies are the other side of Piaget's view of science.

I think it is ironic that Piaget could write in the 1960s: "One may therefore hope that the links between philosophy and science will be renewed when the phenomenological and existentialist fashion in philosophy will have waned."[9] Most of that fashion had long since passed and with it the simple opposition between wisdom and knowledge. Piaget was aware that his formulation of the issue within the French university of the 1920s was a parochial one. Forty years later, however, he had still offered no alternative formulation, and there is surprisingly little criticism today directed at this uncorrected naiveté of the 1920s.

Related to that assumption of the 1920s are Piaget's brief reflection on social bias and his passing references to the social dimensions of his theory. As part of his attack on the illusions of philosophy he singles out the danger of individual bias: "We must adopt systematically a method of cooperation as in science, where truth is only achieved as a result of verification carried out by many co-workers in the field of facts and that of deduction."[10] This sentiment of Piaget's is simply the idealistic hope which the experimental/mathematical sciences had bequeathed to the modern world. The eighteenth and nineteenth centuries passionately believed in it, and the ideal has in part proved to be true. Modern science did dispel not only darkness but a great deal of prejudice. The activity of pursuing the facts remains a great ideal of the modern era.

The main enemy of science's objectivity, according to Piaget, is that "the self, believing itself free, is unconsciously affected by the suggestions or the pressures of the social group."[11] Indeed, that will always be a problem, but thinkers in the early twentieth century seemed to lack imagination about sources of bias and distortions of objectivity. Much of their thinking was cast in the framework of individual and social group; the individual's relation to the group was properly rational or else distorted by pressure. One reads little about political power, economic interest, or institutional frameworks—for example, the vested interests of university professors and scientists.

Do certain parts of the world have a stake in maintaining the picture of science's neutrality as a means to national, racial, and economic control? Piaget's grand ideal of a pure science in touch with the one truth is understandable in the context of the 1920s, but serious questions have arisen since that time.

One does not have to turn away cynically from the words *science, objectivity,* and *unbiased.* Indeed, what is needed is to turn to the words themselves. If one does not attend to the language being used, then one abandons the political realm for an area of life that is supposedly apolitical. Piaget is strikingly unconcerned with language as a political reality, a way of being in this world with one's fellow human beings. A psychologist, it is true, does not have to be a politician or a political scientist. Nonetheless, even to ask a child questions requires a sensitivity to the ambiguities of language and the relation between language and its context.

The question of language also involves the choice of one's governing metaphors. Even the most technical fields with their self-consistent jargons are connected to the fund of ordinary language through one or several metaphors (for example, the market of economics). When the imagery and language are not reflected upon, then unintended meanings creep into the discussion, and elaborate definitions have to be created to keep out ordinary meaning (consider psychology's use of "the ego"). An accompanying danger is that the choice of image excludes important meanings without ever discussing them (the market in economics excludes things which may be of great value but are not for sale: much in family life, art, or religion). Arthur Eddington compared the choice of an image to the use of a fishing net. Every net excludes some fish as too big and others as too small. One has to gauge the net to serve one's fishing purposes.

In this regard one of Piaget's chief decisions (or assumptions) is to see everything through the metaphor of *action*.[12] Is that word and image sufficiently comprehensive to bear the whole theory of development? One way to answer that question is to consider what the opposite is. *Passion? Inactivity? Receptiveness?* If the opposite is also important, then the word and image may be too restrictive. Likewise, one might try alternative imagery that incorporates the proposed image. Piaget seems to have chosen *action* because he was fighting against a world conceived as static objects; he was resisting a naive empiricism which assumes the world is a collection of objects waiting to be looked upon and measured. For Piaget, *to look* is already an action, a way of transforming the relation between organism and environment.

A more inclusive image and term might be *interaction,* that is, the give-and-take between the human being and the surrounding world. The word *action* weights the discussion on the side of the individual human agent. Perhaps necessarily, the psychologist or genetic epistemologist studies the initiatives of the human being. Although the environment is a kind of partner, its structures are not given the same weight as the person. For Piaget an action is a human operation starting with elementary forms of pulling and pushing, progressing to intellectual forms of joining and putting in order. The roots of intellectual action are never entirely separated from the body. The connotations of the word *action* keep us in touch with the kind of thing a bodily agent does for its survival from the first moment of existence.

Some Key Categories

An image and term that is central to Piaget's whole outlook is *equilibrium.* He views the organism as a self-regulating system that always achieves a balance of forces. When Piaget began his work the word *cybernetics* had not yet been coined. Cybernetics is the study of self-regulating systems, whether alive or not. As cybernetics evolved in recent decades, Piaget saw the field as validating and filling out his basic concepts. Piaget defined equilibrium within a context of cybernetics as "a series of active compensations on the part of the subject in response to external disturbances and an adjustment that is both retroactive (loop systems or feedback) and anticipatory, constituting a permanent system of compensations."[13]

Piaget's system can thus be viewed as a grand mathematical equation in which the game is to increase the complexity on both sides of the equal sign. The equilibrating of the human organism has an elegance about its factors: They move toward mobility and stability at the same time. At their most perfected, the operations of the human mind preserve the integrity of both the epistemological structure and the environment. The mind at its most formal level performs operations that are always reversible: What is put together in mathematical thinking can always be taken apart, a trait not always found in the lower operations of the physical world.

Piaget always said of his work that it began in biology and ended in epistemology. Psychogenesis is an integral part of embryogenesis.[14] Insofar as he studies the mind as an aspect of the organism, he defines knowledge so that it is always biologically useful. "Our knowledge stems neither from sensation nor from perception alone but from the entire action, of which perception merely constitutes the function of signalization. The characteristic of intelligence is not to contemplate but to 'transform' and its mechanism is essentially operatory."[15] Since knowledge and intelligence are defined logically within his system, then the definitions cannot be refuted. One should note, however, that in his definitions Piaget contrasts action with contemplation and expressly says the latter does not describe human intelligence. Small wonder that philosophy and religion cannot—by definitions—achieve intellectual knowledge. We can know an object, according to Piaget, only by acting on it and transforming it, either by modifying it to explore its nature (physical knowledge) or by enriching the object with characteristics and new relationships (logico-mathematical knowledge). The imagery of the logico-mathematical realm softens the aggressive-sounding nature of words such as *action*, *operation*, and *transformation*. It remains true, nevertheless, that the human individual does the acting and the environment is the reactor.

The concept of equilibrium is designed to deal with the sticky issue of final causes. As I pointed out in Chapter 1, finality is a concept that modern science from its beginning tried to eliminate. But finality keeps sneaking back in the form of a plan given at the beginning of a process or in the claim of someone to know where the process ends. Piaget claims to know that the end is equilibrium, but in his system equilibrium is also the process. At any moment the equilibrium is "based on a succession of increasing sequential probabilities such that each stage becomes the most probable, after the occurrence of the preceding one without being it from the start."[16] Thus a scientific concept of *telonomy* (a movement whose course can be charted) has replaced the metaphysical idea of finality.

This description of an interactive process as a set of probabilities is an ingenious way around the philosophical/religious question of why. It avoids the dilemma of nurture versus nature, replacing it with formulas of what is more likely and what is less likely as the particular organism lives in a particular environment. Of course one might speculate that the presence of human beings in the environment throws measures of probability into an impossibly complex situation. Piaget says that "the intervention of social factors" does not alter the idea of psychogenesis toward equilibrium. The computations of cybernetics are supposed to be a way of handling the mass of information that "social intervention" represents.

If this kind of movement in and toward equilibrium extends to all of human life there seems to be a danger of an exhausting activism.

While the human organism is limited and is perhaps in the long run a self-correcting mechanism, this account leaves out the apparently infinite desires of the human being and its capacity for self-destruction in the short run. Piaget's view is not so neutral or free of value judgments as a set of formulas might suggest. He has to assume that a baby has an inborn need to use and to improve psychological structures. Competence and curiosity move human development in the direction of more complex structure.[17] On the scale of a bigger cultural pattern this inherent drive leads to evolutionary progress. Piaget ends *Psychology of the Child* by referring to children who face "endlessly recurring problems and who sometimes arrive at solutions that are slightly better than those of previous generations."[18]

However modestly stated be that claim, it is still a contention of evolutionary progress. This progress is the inevitable result of *opening* (an increase in the possibilities acquired by the organism in the course of evolution) and *integration* ("making the developmental process more and more autonomous in relation to the environment").[19]

Like Erikson, though not so frequently, Piaget uses the word epigenetic. Piaget sees later development as already initially present in more primitive forms. For example, the adolescent's fully developed notion of causality is already discernible in the infant's magical views of reality. As one would expect with this cycling back to reach new complexity in the equilibrium, infancy represents a kind of trial run in the entire cycle. For the first level of life (up to eighteen months or two years) Piaget describes six stages that are later to be played out in a more sophisticated and elaborate pattern.

Where Piaget is strikingly different from Erikson is his nearly exclusive preoccupation with (1) structures of knowing and (2) childhood. Erikson and those inspired by him look for wide-ranging cycles such as midlife recapitulating adolescence or old age profoundly connected to childhood. Piaget, in 1955, poked fun at the idea that anyone had discovered principles governing the unity of personality at different stages of life. He offered himself as a case in point: "multiple, divisé, contradictoire." He could force himself to be serious, he said, but sometimes he was childish or adolescent.[20] With that kind of damper he seemed to declare useless all attempts to describe development in adult life. Despite an occasional reference to adulthood ("At all ages of life . . . development lasts until senility"), Piaget has little to offer beyond structures completed in adolescence. The constructing done with those structures continues, especially in areas of technology and science, but in Piagetian terms the individual's developmental process is complete.[21]

The split between the individual psyche of childhood and the social forms of adulthood is related to another split, what Piaget calls cognitive and affective. "When behavior is studied in its cognitive aspect, we are concerned with its structures; when behavior is studied in its affective aspect, we are concerned with its energetics. While these two aspects cannot be reduced to a single aspect they are nevertheless inseparable and complementary."[22] Piaget intends here to speak of one reality (behavior) that has two "aspects." Unfortunately, his language of "cognitive" and "affective" was doomed from the beginning to lead to two "domains" and to educational discussions of cognitve aims and affective aims as if two such separate things existed.

Piaget's use of the word *structures* as the meaning of *cognitive* is not an obvious use of language, but he is the one doing the defining. *Energetics* is not a common word for the meaning of *affective*, though one can intuit some of the meaning he intends. He regularly associates the affective and the social: Other people help to energize behavior. Thus, under *cognitive* and *affective* we have the individual and transindividual aspects of behavior. Sometimes *affective* and *interpersonal* are practically interchangeable terms.[23] Having made action the primary metaphor, Piaget cannot avoid making the cognitive (the individual's behavior under the aspect of structure) the main category. Then the affective (the individual's behavior as energized in an interpersonal context) is declared to be parallel, complementary, and inseparable. What it cannot be is equal in importance. If one starts from the social, one can find individualistic aspects within the social. If one starts from the individual, then the social can emerge only as the multiplication of individuals. Piaget assumes that the two categories of individual and social (*social* refers to several individuals) include all human structures. The belief was shared by many people in Piaget's time; it still surfaces when reformers try to add affective aims to cognitive or when reformers assume that having reached social reality, everything has been taken into account. In Piaget's scheme, the political, economic, religious, and institutional are effectively banished in a linguistic universe comprised only of the cognitive and affective.[24]

These previous choices of language lead to a final, important category of Piaget's: decentration. This somewhat strange word that Piaget coined means to move from the center or to distance one's thinking from a centeredness on the self. From his point of view it is a straightforward term which captures the movement in his developmental theory. "All valid knowledge presupposes a decentration. The whole of the history of science is made up of decentrations."[25] To get a more valid view of things, Piaget claims, one must abstract from personal limitations and see the world from a higher plane. The infant does not know there is an "other" at all. The child at succeeding stages becomes ever more capable of taking the viewpoint of others; fully developed, an individual can engage in abstract thinking without interference from his or her bodily or emotional limits.

A difficulty that Piaget encountered with the term *decentration* arose in his assumption that since the infant is not decentered it is "egocentric." He complained that people misunderstood the word *egocentric* as a moral term whereas he meant it as a technical and descriptive term. His inability to sever the word from a moral meaning is symptomatic of a basic problem with the image of decentering.

The trouble with talking about a small child's egocentricity is that he or she has not yet developed a sense of personal centeredness. Piaget's calling the nondifferentiation of subject and object *egocentric* is thoroughly misleading. He implies that the child must move away from its centeredness. However, the ability to take the view of another person, far from requiring the elimination of a personal center, strongly depends upon the development of centeredness.

Piaget's word *decenter* refers only to a place away from which movement occurs. If the entire process is referred to by the word *decentration,* then one can only conclude that the movement is from centeredness to uncenteredness. Piaget's language implies that the obstacle to reaching the truth is the personal center itself. Although for Piaget taking the view of another is a test of cognitive ability, the place of truth is not between persons but above persons. That is, one person's view is not centered or recentered by another person's view, as would be the case in a communal, social, or political meaning of the truth. The second person is merely a means by which the first person reaches a higher level of abstraction.

In a harsh judgment on this imagery, M. Merleau-Ponty said that Piaget takes the viewpoint of God.[26] Piaget hotly rejected the accusation, but the location of his knowledge does seem to be above any human center and beyond the limits of bodiliness. Decentration is an image which confirms that Piaget's interest is the "cognitive" structure of the individual. As I will later show, however, the great religious interest in centeredness indicates religion's concern with the personal, communal, and aesthetic.

Piaget's Levels of Development

I turn now to the different levels within Piaget's system of development. Without recounting all the details of his experiments, or of the experiments of his critics, I would like to mention some of the main themes that arise in the discussion of these levels. Piaget speaks of three levels of development, the second having what amounts to two distinct parts. Ages are approximate and are never the main focus of the system.

(I) Sensori-motor: until 18 months/2 years
(IIA) Pre-operational: 2 to 7/8 years
(IIB) Concrete operational: 7/8 to 11/12 years
(III) Formal operational: 11/12 to 14/15 years

Within the first level Piaget describes six stages which are the whole system in preview. Within the other levels and even with reference to specific skills he also refers to stages that constitute a cycle of growth.

(I) *Sensori-motor.* One of Piaget's great insights was that to understand how the mind works, one must trace its development from infancy. This is similar, of course, to Freud's theory of an infantile world. Piaget began by asking questions of children and then decided he had to study the physical behavior of infants to get his answers. He worked out an ingenious set of experiments that investigate how an infant step by step grasps spatial and temporal sequences, causality, and the permanent character of objects. Given the inherent difficulty of studying these phenomena, though, neither Piaget nor anyone else is likely to produce definitive evidence on what infants think. Experiments trying to disprove some of Piaget's claims are very often variations on Piaget's own experiments.

One image that Piaget used for the infant's inner life is that of a film running slowly.[27] The child's mental life, he said, is almost a succession of still photos rather than a movie. Since the organism has not developed and integrated all of its powers, the data have to be brought forth one piece at a time. Thus, when an object is removed from view, the infant, having neither the reasoning power nor the memory of past experience, cannot conclude that the object still exists. The child gradually discovers how to coordinate incoming information because it wishes to succeed, that is, to satisfy its innate needs and interests. In discussing the child's sixth and last stage of the sensori-motor level, Piaget can already speak of "systematic intelligence" and of acts "controlled from within by the consciousness of relationships [thus marking] the beginning of deduction."[28]

Despite Piaget's impressive description of the small child, the bulk of Piaget's evidence seems to bring out the poverty of the infant's inner life. The necessity of a step-by-step construction of the world means that an infant of a few weeks or a few months is not prepared to enter human exchanges. Parents of infants tend to think otherwise. And much recent research supports the parents' impression that the infant's responding person-to-person is not an illusion. John Bowlby's studies of "attachment" during more than three decades have been one major focus.[29] Bowlby concentrated on the bond between mother and infant, but over the years the discussion by others has broadened to include: (1) the infant's bonding with other adults besides the mother, (2) differences in the mother's bonding with boy and girl infants, and (3) characteristics and permanency of maternal deprivation.[30]

John Bowlby has come under attack for narrowing attention to the single bond with the mother. Bowlby and his critics do agree on one thing: that the infant's experience is more varied and more personally oriented than Piaget supposed. One study, for example, claims to show that infants three to eight days old make a specific response to voices and voice-like sounds; another study shows that a three-second delay in response to a six-month-old child can obstruct learning.[31] These and similar studies have not disconfirmed Piaget; still, even researchers sympathetic to Piaget have chipped away at his evidence. One recent study of Piaget concludes: "There is increasing evidence that the newborn baby's perceptual system is already (innately) equipped to *discover* various environmental features which according to Piaget have to be gradually *constructed* by way of the baby's instrumental activities. Such features include invariants such as object-permanence, depth and other (nonmetric) spatial relations."[32]

(IIA) Piaget describes the changes needed at the level of the *preoperational* (2 to 7/8) before coherent reversible systems of thought are possible. At this age the child must: (1) develop a way of representing what has been absorbed at the level of physical action, (2) decenter the self within a larger and more complex world than the infant is aware of, and (3) communicate in language with other people who share this world. The chief mark of the pre-operational phase is the absence of notions of conservation. The child cannot juggle two pieces of information so as to see that one of them cancels or balances out the other. Thus we have Piaget's well-known experiment of pouring liquid from a short and wide container into a tall and narrow one. The child of four or five is likely to say that there is more liquid in the tall container. Notions of the conservation of substance, weight, and volume come at different ages within the operational phase.[33]

In the transition from representation in (bodily) action to representation in thought, Piaget gives an important role to "symbolic play." Children's play is obviously not a new discovery; however, the twentieth century has been rediscovering the significance of play, not as a diversion but as a necessary part of life. Piaget's system of equilibrium includes adaptation to reality and assimilation of reality. The child adapts itself to the external world by the process of imitation. In assimilation the child is taking the world into itself but at this early age lacks the language to express the experience. Symbolic play transforms reality according to the needs of the self. Free of coercion, the child creates symbols—and the child plays—with what it cannot otherwise manage.[34] Thus, the child may express anger or frustration at a toy animal; at other times the child may withdraw into a secret hiding place.

Piaget's reflections on play are enlightening, and they certainly fit within his system. Indeed, the explanation fits so well that play, in our view, can quickly be reduced to a mechanism for getting over a deficiency of language. For Piaget, play seems to be nothing less and nothing more than a necessary stage on the way to reversibility.

Once the adult has attained the objectivity that characterizes knowledge, then play is left behind with the things of a child. Suppose, in contrast, that play is a human manner of dealing with personal involvement in ways that discursive speech cannot match.[35] This question cannot be settled by studying the play of four- and five-year-olds. The issue concerns the relation of speech to the non-linguistic context of speech. Before pursuing this issue in regard to the concrete operational child, there is one more related point to be made about the pre-operational level.

I have referred to play as being a complement to *discursive* speech. By that I mean to suggest that speech itself can be used playfully, as can be seen in the work of poets and storytellers. Religion is, among other things, a playfulness both with language and with non-verbal rituals. The young child is a poet, a mythmaker, and a ritualist.[36] Piaget's location of play opens up possibilities, but his assumption that language follows mental structures prematurely limits what language can do for the young child. Piaget has little to say of storytelling and fairy tales at the age when the child's imagination can take flight to other parts of the world and to other worlds. One Piagetian commentator describes the child of concrete operations as "sober book-keeper, organizer of the real, distruster of the elusive, subtle, hypothetical."[37] That is true, but the pre-operational child delights in wild fancy and plays not only with what she or he has "constructed" but with what she or he hears.

What I point to here as my final comment on the pre-operational and as leading into the concrete operational is the place of language itself. Young children have a great interest in storytelling and an amazing ability to understand the plot even while misunderstanding many of the words. Their questions are seldom directed to the meaning of the words in isolation. They are more interested in the intentions and motives of characters in the story. The great fairy tales passed down over the centuries seem to be a secret language among children through which adults reveal what is really going on without knowing they are doing so. In later chapters I will come back to the profound sense of good and evil that young children can have. The Piagetian scheme, if not eliminating this perception, certainly does not highlight it. Even what Piaget is interested in studying—mental operations—may be distorted by a literalistic approach to the pre-operational child's use of language.[38]

(IIB) *Concrete operational.* This term refers to solving problems related directly to objects and not to verbally stated hypotheses. Concrete operations proceed through step-by-step reasoning because the child cannot yet handle generalized combinations. For example, arranging a series of things according to size is first done by a kind of trial and error until the series comes out right. Children have trouble with prepositions (e.g., *above* and *under*), especially with recognizing that A can be above B while under C. Transitive and reciprocal relations require similar insight. For example, there is always a moment of dumbfounded excitement when the child discovers that her father has a father or that her mother is someone's (Grandma's) child. Or the discovery that my brother has a brother who is myself requires an abstraction and a logic that wasn't there before. When the child discovers that if A is smaller than B and B is smaller than C then A is necessarily smaller than C, then seriation of things according to size becomes a simple matter.

Piaget tries to show that the concrete-operational child can recognize logic at work but that the child is not prepared to think in the purely logical terms that open up new combinations and possibilities. A concrete-operational child cannot grasp formulas such as "if p, then q; not q, therefore, not p" but can recognize that sequence in concrete forms (if it rains, the street is wet; the street is not wet; therefore it is not raining). That is the reason, as math teachers know, why arithmetic but not algebra can be taught in elementary school. Arithmetic procedures can be referred to concrete objects ("if I add two apples and three apples . . ."), whereas algebra is a second-level abstraction, a bending back of thought upon thinking.

The evolution from physical action to abstract hypothesis may be more varied than Piaget suggests. Much of the recent criticism of his work concerns his views on the use of language among concrete-operational children. Piaget's own use of language is reducible to algebraic form: One instructs children to perform X with reference to Y. Language is a more or less efficient instrument for getting at mental structures. There is a peculiar paradox here: Language is declared to be separable from and consequent upon mental structures; then the researcher uses language to discover those structures: The researcher says "Choose which beaker has more liquid." Even could it be proved, which it cannot, that mental structures precede and determine language, that would not solve the researcher's dilemma in using language. In human interactions beyond infancy, access to these mental structures is mainly through language. Two routes of criticism have developed concerning Piaget's experiments. The first sees these experiments as too tangled in human speech. Its reform effort is in the direction of reducing language to its most unambiguous forms. It would make the instructions extemely simple and would devise nonverbal replies where possible: The researcher may ask for a push of a button rather than words; answers may be simplified to yes/no rather than consisting of a description of events.[39]

The second route of criticism and reform is, interestingly enough, in the opposite direction. Its approach is to frame the questions in ways sensitive to a larger context of meaning. It gets the child to respond in ways that make human sense to a child. Here the rich ambiguity of language is prized, and the qualities that the child brings (e.g., interest in purpose and motivation) are included rather than eliminated from the research. For example, in Piaget's well-known experiment on class inclusion, that is, the relation of sets and subsets of things, the child is shown seven red flowers and three white flowers. The child on being asked "Are there more white flowers or flowers?" is likely to answer incorrectly. Piaget concludes that the child cannot handle the logic of class inclusion. Other researchers have suggested that to a child (and indeed to adults in most situations) the question doesn't make any human sense. The child's real problem is: Why is this adult asking me that dumb question? The child's response in this situation is dictated by the dynamics of the setting and by the apparent motives of the questioner in asking a senseless question.

Piaget has a second study on taking the perspective of another. A child is asked whether plane A can be seen from point X. In a variation on that experiment the child is asked whether a policeman could see a child who was hiding. The responses improved because a child can make sense of that question being asked by relating it to intention, guilt, and punishment.[40] To put this issue in cybernetic terms, one has to ask dozens of questions about what information the subject is using, when it appears, how it is obtained, what it is used for, who is with the subject, what level of trust there is, etc. The criticism of Piaget's algebraic descriptions is not merely that the method fails to arrive at the answer but that it actually takes him in the wrong direction from the answers.

Of these two approaches to criticizing Piaget's use of language, the first may be of some value in some kinds of research, the second is an important consideration for educators. There is a danger of underestimating children's capacities at the age of concrete operations. The child who cannot do the kind of abstract work that elementary schools demand may be classified as a "slow learner" or even as incapable of learning. The caution that current research adds to Piagetian conclusions is that adults may credit children with knowing less than they really do. As David Elkind says, the slow learner is usually learning something other than what we intend; and slow learners are quick to learn that they are classified as slow learners.[41]

(III) *Formal Operational.* The coming of formal operations (11/12 to 14/15) marks "the metaphysical age par excellence."[42] At this time the child is able to handle hypotheses and to reason about propositions outside present observations. There is a disconnecting of thought and object whch makes possible a separation of form and content in propositions. The youngster is now able to combine the two kinds of reversibility discovered earlier: inversion ($+ A - A = 0$) and reciprocity or symmetry (if $A \leq B$ and $B \leq A$, then $A = B$). The youngster when given a problem of combinations and permutations can explain the possibilities rather than just find the answer. Proceeding from the possible to the real is "the most distinctive property of formal thought."[43]

With the arrival of formal operations—what for Piaget is intelligence without qualification—the young adolescent is able to construct an ideal world. Unlimited alternatives are rather suddenly available to a mind previously limited to the world at hand. Adolescents have more ideas than they can handle and are unprepared to make choices among alternatives. "Consequently, young adolescents often appear stupid because they are, in fact, too bright."[44]

Understandably, perhaps, the young adolescent hides the mental confusion with harsh criticism, moody rebellion, and endless debating. He or she can be contemptuous of the adult world for having compromised, for not living up to the highest ideals. At the same time the youngster desperately needs adult guidance in trying to maneuver the tricky waters of adolescence. Pressing adults on why something must be done is part of the process of grappling with indecisiveness. The fact that the young rebel against figures of authority is no proof that they want a world without authority.

Piaget's analysis of formal operations is less criticized than his description of earlier levels.[45] He sometimes seems to overestimate the logical capacities of adolescents (and adults), whereas he may underestimate younger children. In the former case the evidence that the capacity is there justifies saying people have the capacity whether or not they regularly use it. But the absence of evidence for certain kinds of thinking in the younger child does not prove that she or he lacks the capacities; it may simply be that Piagetian experiments fail to reveal the capacity.

What Piaget sets out to describe has in fact reached its completion in adolescence (though he says that in some cultures that may not be true).[46] No new mental systems emerge after adolescence. That conclusion puts a severe strain on any transfer of his meaning of development to moral or religious development in adults. Piaget's system has little to offer outside its restricted area: the capacity of children to abstract and to reason. Piaget did write a treatise on "the moral judgment of the child," a book I will examine at the beginning of the next chapter. The restrictions built into his approach to morality should be obvious enough. In trying to draw implications for religion one has to be even more cautious. Piaget does have some useful directions for teachers of the young concerning what children can grasp. But for filling out the meaning of religious development we will have to draw from sources other than Piaget.

4

Moral Reasoning: Piaget to Kohlberg

As described in the previous chapter, Jean Piaget's interest was the steps by which a child comes to make abstract judgments. These judgments can be studied as structures of logical reasoning. An aspect of this reasoning power is what Piaget calls moral judgments, those judgments pertaining to the ordering of society. For Piaget, *moral* is almost another name for *social/affective*. That is, the social context of cognition has laws to protect the individual. As the child develops it comes to see the necessity and value of these rules governing social harmony.

At the beginning of *The Moral Judgment of the Child*, Piaget defines morality this way: "All morality consists in a system of rules, and the essence of all morality is to be sought for in the respect which the individual acquires for these rules."[1] This definition is remarkably narrow in its meaning of morality, putting all its weight upon rules and an individual's confrontation with rules. Within this context moral development is by definition an individual's reasoning about a system of rules.

Piaget is here following Immanuel Kant, the dominant figure in modern Western philosophy's search for a foundation to ethics. Alasdair McIntyre is probably not exaggerating when he writes, "For many who have never heard of philosophy, let alone Kant, morality is roughly what Kant said it was."[2] Kant's conception of morality fixes one in the dilemma of (1) wishing to be autonomous, (2) needing to do one's duty. Kant's solution is that duty "presents itself as obedience to a law that is universally binding on all rational beings. . . . I become aware of it as a set of precepts which in prescribing to myself I can consistently will should be obeyed by all rational beings."[3] We have to obey the law, but it is not opposed to our autonomy because we create the law. There is a perfect rational correspondence: What is truly good for me is good for everyone else and vice versa.

With this optimistic assumption ethics can be established as a field independent of religious sanctions. The whole of morality is declared to be a matter of rational calculation; if everyone could just see that it is in his or her best interest to be reasonable, then we would have social harmony. Interestingly, this principle is compatible with both a conservative code of morality and a liberal outlook. When Piaget wrote his book in the 1920s, his moral views represented a fairly conservative order. Piaget harshly criticized Emil Durkheim for basing morality on "authority." Durkheim wishes, said Piaget, to transmit the mores of the past through the schoolmaster as society's priest. Piaget's own moral code seems to differ little from Durkheim's, but according to Piaget the child would reach the respect for rules by exercising his or her own autonomous reasoning.[4]

The whole scheme of Piaget's moral development is very simple: movement from thinking that rules are external to understanding that they are intrinsic to our own good. Piaget refers to "two moralities" rather than to two stages of morality. The first morality he calls heteronomous, meaning that rules are external, sacred, and unchangeable. A second morality, called autonomous, grows up parallel to the first, conflicts with, and finally replaces the first. The second morality is one of cooperation, intention, and solidarity. The child eventually comes to see that laws are a matter of mutual consent and so at times they can and should be changed for the good running of society.

Piaget acknowledges that very young children operate by rules but do not reflect upon them. By his definition of morality Piaget has to say that the child up to five or six years of age is at a pre-moral level. The child does not yet obey his or her father as a representation of society/law (on this point Piaget differs from Kant) but only as a physically superior being. I think Piaget is inaccurately portrayed as saying that children start with an automatic respect for authority. Rather, he holds that the child begins by having to accept subordination to adult commands and only gradually comes to respect persons in authority as embodying law.[5] Where Piaget does seem to be in error is in assuming that children progressively divest themselves of a rigid attachment to rules. He seems to think that children are ready

in pre-adolescence to use rules flexibly for purposes of social cooperation.[6]

Piaget's response to that criticism might be that he is describing
what can be and should be. In practice, he would say, adults often
reinforce the "moral realism" of the first morality and thus retard
the arrival of autonomy.[7] If Piaget's theory is accurate, the main job
of adults is to get out of the way. In addition, adults should see to it
that a child has opportunities for cooperating with other children.
Through discussing rules of play among themselves children can come
to see the importance of intention and the need for compromise and
flexibility. The child's own intention interacts with the original intent
of the law. Children should come to see what democracy means: "an
attitude toward law as a product of the collective will, and not as
something emanating from a transcendent will."[8]

Piaget's concept of equilibrium functions here as a social category,
although as usual his chief concern is the individual's operations.
Equilibrium of organism and environment functions through the rar-
ified operations of the logico-mathematical level; at least that is where
the child's morality must eventually arrive when society and self are
in perfect balance. At the heteronomous level morality still has a
material bias. For example, the size of the discrepancy between a
falsehood and the objective truth determines the seriousness of the
moral failure; also, breaking three of mother's dishes is worse than
breaking one. Later, the child appreciates the role of intention. What
makes a false statement a lie is the intent to deceive; intentionally
breaking one dish is a moral fault; accidentally breaking three dishes
is not. What finally counts is the ability to take the viewpoint of every
individual in the social system. Then the lawmaker, which each of us
is, will deal fairly with each individual. Social harmony will reign as
soon as we are all reasonable, disinterested, and objective.

Kohlberg's Assumptions

Lawrence Kohlberg is a social psychologist who, inspired by Piaget's
work on morality, constructed his own scheme in the 1950s. Kohlberg
has been more successful than he could have imagined when he
began, his name now almost synonymous with the words *moral development.* Over the past decade, however, he has suffered a backlash

from people unhappy with his hegemony over the entire area. Given the division of the field into Kohlbergians and anti-Kohlbergians, I will treat Kohlberg's system in this chapter and will then turn in the next chapter to critics and their alternatives.

A chief concern of Kohlberg's has always been education. He saw moral education as caught between two inadequate positions: (1) indoctrination, which gives over morality to the objective realm of rules, and (2) values clarification, which does not escape subjectivism. What is today called indoctrination has a long history; it assumes that individuals must be told what the truth is and have limits imposed on their questioning. In the 1960s and 1970s, values clarification came into prominence as a reaction to indoctrination. Since it assumed there was no objective morality, values clarification consisted almost entirely of techniques for stimulating awareness. As a "school of thought" it was so lacking in substance it could hardly avoid being more than a passing vogue. However, other forms of moral subjectivism had preceded values clarification and no doubt will recur after the interest in techniques for clarifying values has passed.

Piaget's definition of morality quoted above ("a system of rules" and "respect which the individual acquires for these rules") bridges these two positions: At least it indicates that indoctrination and values clarification have only half the problem in view. An adequate moral education would have to transcend the dichotomy of subjective and objective moralities; it would have to reconceptualize the problem as one of interaction. Then a process of personal clarification might be useful as part of the human quest for an adequate morality.

Kohlberg offers his own system as this third way: a stimulation of the "natural" development of the child's own moral judgment. Does such development of the reasoning power escape subjectivism? In popular summaries Kohlberg is often grouped with values clarification, a kinship he opposes. To the extent, however, that he rejects concern with behavior and moral content he is ineluctably driven toward subjectivism. I think it may be admissible to be only indirectly concerned with external behavior, but Kohlberg went further: "It must be stressed that it is the over-concern with the conforming *behavior* characteristic of traditional approaches to moral education that lies behind most of the mistakes of educators in the moral realm."[9] Note that Kohlberg underlines the noun *behavior*, not the qualifier *conforming.* He is not saying that teachers should allow more flexibility in the range of behavior but that their concern should not be behavior.

I think that here and throughout his writings Kohlberg is not as Piagetian as he is assumed to be.[10] Piaget's intended equilibrium was always social: the organism in its environment, the individual cooperating with other individuals. Kohlberg takes the "cognitive" concern out of an interpersonal realm and pushes it through the roof. Kohlberg's first two levels have some congruence with Piaget's two moralities. Kohlberg's third level (the postconventional) is often charted parallel to Piaget's formal operations, but it has little connection to Piaget's moralities. The equilibrium in Kohlberg is located within the judgment itself; morality is reasoning about conflicting claims. Morality always has to concern dilemmas because the equilibration takes place in discourse. Piaget's meaning of morality (rules and respect for rules) plays little part in Kohlberg's theory. One can call reasoning about dilemmas "social," but note how far we have traveled from the meaning of social as interactions of people in society.

The image of equilibrium obscures the difference between Piaget and Kohlberg. Piaget at least wishes to be concerned with the social, while Kohlberg wishes to leave behind the social (persons in interaction) for a philosophical ideal. There may be a value in his describing ideals that transcend society, but he would do better to drop the apparatus of equilibrium. Kohlberg could use categories like mind, imagination, passion, will, or whatever seems to contribute to moral ideals. Instead, Kohlberg quotes Piaget as saying that "the rule of justice is a sort of immanent condition of social relationships or a law governing their equilibrium."[11] Kohlberg says he agrees essentially with the conception of justice as "an interactional emergent." But he takes justice as something emerging from and then emerging beyond the social. What he retains is the image of equilibrium, not as social but in purest logico-mathematical form, justice as an abstract calculation.

Kohlberg can therefore seem to agree with Piaget that morality is a matter of justice; but whereas Piaget was talking about an "immanent condition of social relationships," Kohlberg is talking about a mathematical principle of equality. "There is only one principled basis for resolving claims: justice or equality. Treat every man's claim impartially regardless of the man."[12] Kohlberg seems not to have the slightest doubt that that's what justice means and that justice means only that. He disparages any attempt to complement justice with a pattern of virtues. Know what justice is, and everything else will follow.

With the premise that the end point of moral development is justice and that justice is equality, Kohlberg seems to fall into that finalism that Piaget, Erikson, and others try carefully to avoid. For all of Kohlberg's talk of equilibrium there is no tension of opposites, there is no set of complexities describable only in terms of mathematical probabilities. At the end is a single mathematical formula, easily articulable in the adage: Treat every man's claim impartially. The equilibrium is a mere tension of conflict within a hypothetical problem (that is, within the mind of whoever is thinking about the problem), not the relation of child/adult, organism/environment, person/community. That being the case, it is unnecessary to study young children, social behavior, or nonverbal rituals. A moral development scheme can be constructed from verbal responses to hypothetical dilemmas.

Despite the claim that he is investigating not content but structure or form, Kohlberg's finalism has a definite content: justice defined as equality. That principle also translates into the obligation to respect the rights of another person. The furthest Kohlberg can go in divorcing the form and the content of morality is to end with no content *except* the right of persons to be respected and to receive impartial treatment. Although it is highly abstract, this principle represents a definite content in his moral system.[13]

Kohlberg sometimes admits that he is representing the view of modern democratic liberalism. Does he thereby admit a bias in this universal theory? Not at all. If one supposes that history is moving along the same stages as the individual, then the correlation in morality between individuals of principled thinking and modern Western democracies is confirming evidence of the theory rather than evidence of cultural bias. Kohlberg subscribes to this parallel movement under the heading of what he calls the "liberal faith": "Under the right conditions basic changes in both individuals and societies tend to be in a forward direction in a series of steps or stages moving toward greater justice in terms of equity or recognition of universal human rights."[14] In the end, therefore, Kohlberg is willing to sacrifice his Kantian formalism for a liberal ideology of progress toward human rights. When Kohlberg confronts the implication of Kant's absolute that one may never lie, he disagrees with Kant: "The case is always higher than the principle."[15]

With that admission Kohlberg undermines one of the two reasons for his popularity. The first of these reasons is that he promised a way out of the liberal-versus-conservative controversy. Politically and educationally the culture faces an impasse of conservatives defending a fixed code and liberals advocating an evolving morality. To the conservatives Kohlberg could be heard to say that there is a fixed natural system of morality (the form), while to the liberals he could seem to be defending a process of constant evolution (in content). Anyone who is popular on both sides of the divide is vulnerable to a backlash when the other side of the system becomes visible.

In some of his writings Kohlberg admits the liberal bias in the content, thereby drawing the ire of conservatives. But he has also acknowledged that liberal systems do not work for the whole population. Toward the end of the 1970s he was willing to appropriate the word *indoctrination,* thereby shocking his liberal supporters.[16] Kohlberg says that in a world where children lie and steal, not many people are going to arrive at his universal morality through reasoning to it. Most of the population will have to accept the higher morality on faith or be indoctrinated into it.

A second major reason for Kohlberg's popularity and the expectations he raised in the public schools is his claim to offer moral education completely separate from religion. From its mid-nineteenth-century beginnings, the public school has been nearly obsessed with educating children morally and yet avoiding the "divisiveness" of religion.[17] The concern with morals has been a constant one, and it remains to the present day. Gallup polls in recent years indicate that seventy to eighty per cent of the public favors moral instruction in the schools.[18] Kohlberg agrees: "We believe that the public school should engage in moral education and that the basis for such education should be universal principles of justice, not particular religious and personal values."[19] The opposition in this statement is neatly put: principles of justice = universal, religion = particular. Kohlberg has always been puzzled or shocked by people who could not "distinguish the sector of morality called 'natural law' from the sector based on religious creed or revelation."[20]

A widespread assumption has morality derived from religion so that the origin, content, and effectiveness of morality are religious issues. Kohlberg reacts directly against this position, arguing for "the recognition in some degree of the autonomy of morality and moral discourse."[21] But he fails to explore the phrase "in some degree." Instead he takes the badly conceived dependence of morality upon religion and turns it upside down: "Our hypothesis, then, is almost the direct opposite of divine command theory." Instead of religion being allowed to have *its autonomy in some degree,* it is made into a function of morality. "The main function of religion is not to supply moral prescriptions but to support moral judgment and action as purposeful human activities."[22] Reversals of dependency relationships are never entirely secure. Although Kohlberg makes religion (in the form of "a faith") subsequent to moral steps, there remains a final ironic twist by which the moral stages "require" religion (a faith). I return to that irony below in Kohlberg's suggestion of a seventh stage.

What Kohlberg does not investigate is the possibility that religion and morality could have a mutually beneficial relation. Religion claims universality as much as does morality, but in its own forms. Morality may overrule religion when religion is irrational and destructive. In return, religion can contribute to morality by shaping vision, providing stories, and directing desires. Kohlberg says he finds a person's religion has no significant effect on morality, a finding that says more about the limits of Kohlbergian dilemmas than about the nature of religion. Several thousand years of history have been affected by Jewish and Christian beliefs that morality is intimately related to religion. One does not end that relation with a declaration of divorce. Kohlberg's total separation of morality and religion obscures what is present in people's lives. The public school that intends to educate morally has to accept this complexity and the resulting problem of method. Religion, for better or for worse, influences nearly all moral issues. The public school cannot *separate* morality and religion; it can *distinguish* moral and religious aspects of various issues as it proceeds through historical and other analyses.

Kohlberg's Stages

From the time of his 1958 dissertation, Kohlberg has had essentially the same three-level, six-stage theory of moral reasoning.[23] There have been refinements in the description of the stages and some attempts at addition (see reference below to stage 4½). In recent years he seems to have abandoned stage 6 only to come back to it as the essential element in defining the system. His fundamental claim is that he has simply taken over Piaget's constructivist psychology and elaborated moral stages consistent with Piaget. As I have pointed out, however, Piaget's moral stages are quite simple and are hardly the basis for Kohlberg's stages. In making a correlation to Piaget's reasoning ability Kohlberg has to use formal operations as corresponding to the top half of his system. Thus, what Piaget contributes to Kohlberg's stages 4, 5, and 6 is merely that a person is capable of thinking abstractly about various things, including morality.

Kohlberg's three levels (preconventional, conventional, postconventional), each divided into two stages, look this way:

1. Obedience and punishment orientation. Egoistic deference to superior power.
2. Naively egoistic orientation. Right action is what instrumentally satisfies the self's needs and occasionally the needs of others.
3. Good boy, nice girl orientation. Orientation to approval and to pleasing and helping others.
4. Authority and social order orientation. Orientation to doing duty and showing respect for authority.
5. Contractual legalistic orientation. Duty defined in terms of contract; general avoidance of violating the rights of others.
6. Conscience or principle orientation. Orientation to principles of choice involving appeal to logical universality and consistency.[24]

What characterizes the movement from stage 1 to stage 6 is an increase in the power to differentiate (e.g., to see that life is important, independently of factual properties of the life in question), along with an increase in universality (e.g., in stage 1 there are important persons; in stage 3 all family members are important; in stage 6 all persons are important). With the finer distinctions made along the way, we approach the prescriptivity of stage 6. That is, everyone above stage 1 knows that life is a higher value than property, but until we get to stage 6 there remain instrumental tinges to the valuing of life (he is important to my family, or she is important to the nation). Only at the top is the sacredness of life affirmed without qualification.

"Stages form an order of increasingly differentiated and integrated structures to fulfill a common function [that is, judgment concerning moral dilemmas]. Accordingly, higher stages displace (or rather, reintegrate) the structures found at lower stages."[25] The reintegration means that the higher-stage person understands the lower and could act that way but will prefer the highest stage available to him or her.

Kohlberg has constructed an intricate and intriguing system of supposedly invariant stages and universal application. With other developmentalists he warns against using his system as an achievement scale whereby the classifier, having declared someone a stage 2 or a stage 4, has passed final judgment. Kohlberg cannot be held responsible for every misunderstanding and overstatement of his system.[26] However, he does have a responsibility to name his system accurately. If he calls his description "moral development," then he should not be surprised that people conclude that a stage 5 person is better than a stage 2 person. If he would always refer to "stages of moral reasoning," then people would not infer that what is in question is a person's moral life, moral goodness, and moral maturity.

With reference to both the affective realm and action Kohlberg makes the same argument: "I am only studying X and I make no scientific claims to know Y. However, it just so happens that Y follows the pattern of X." Thus, a disclaimer on the modesty of one's method still leads to sweepingly comprehensive conclusions; stages of moral reasoning slip over into stages of moral development. In regard to "affect" Kohlberg asserts with Piaget that it has a common structural base with cognition. Therefore, if one studies cognition one finds out about stages of affective growth, too.[27] As I pointed out in the previous chapter, cognitive and affective may have the same structure— by Piaget's definitions of those peculiar terms. But that doesn't tell us much of anything about the relation of thinking and feeling—for example, about what happens to our thinking when we are emotionally involved in the dilemma.

With reference to action Kohlberg claims a convergence of thinking and behavior rather than parallelism. At the highest stage cognition and action are inseparable. At the lower stages there can be opinion or conventional belief which does not lead to virtuous activity. Citing Plato as his authority, Kohlberg says: "True knowledge of principles of justice does entail virtuous action."[28] I think that unless one works through a system of interconnection throughout the stages, then the declaration that knowing the truth equals doing the truth comes close to being a tautology. What does knowing the truth mean? Doing the truth. What is doing the truth? Knowing the truth. Plato had a pattern of virtues that prepare for a final simplicity. Kohlberg's system heads toward an algebraic formula that may have no connection with virtuous behavior. If Kohlberg means that everyone who can grasp the principle of justice (respect every person's rights) also practices the principle, that flies in the face of all human experience. If he means that people who act unjustly do not *really* understand the principle of justice, then it is unclear what his whole system reveals and what if anything is meant by saying that true knowledge and action are identical in stage 6.

Kohlberg contends that each individual goes through these stages without jumping over any of them. The individual is able to understand only the next stage up from wherever he or she is. The capacity to think in these different ways is organically based, though not tied to chronological measuring. A child of six years is presumably incapable of being a stage 5 or 6. A person eighteen years old is presumably not lacking in what is biologically needed to be a stage 5. Over the years, however, Kohlberg has acknowledged the importance of social environment and institutional setting. He would now say that if a youngster has not reached stage 4 by the time of leaving secondary school, he or she is not likely to get there later.[29]

Although the child's capacity to go through these stages is not given in experience, both the existence and the rate of progress depend on experience. The adult's modest but crucial job is to provide occasions for discussions in which role-taking occurs. If a stage 3 discusses a moral dilemma with a stage 4, then there is an opportunity for the stage 3 to understand stage 4 and progress toward it. Of course the teacher ought to provide a model of judgment more advanced than the student's. Furthermore, over the years Kohlberg has increasingly emphasized that the whole environment must embody justice if the child is to have a model for thinking justly. If a school, orphanage, or home has blatantly unjust rules, the child is blocked not only from principled thinking but even from conventional morality.[30]

Kohlberg's system moves toward a single principle of justice. Although he often uses the word *principle* in the plural, it refers either to various formulations of *the* principle of justice ("treat every man impartially," "respect every man's rights") or to concerns that finally turn out to be not principles. A concern like welfare is "meta-ethically" an important principle, but it is not the principle of moral choice. That is, for Kohlberg welfare or benevolence or love is one of the pre-conditions for experiencing moral conflict but not a mechanism for its resolution. Love is a stage 3 label rather than a guide to action, which is what "all thoughtful men" define a principle to be.[31]

Justice as the principle of decision-making is sometimes called a virtue by Kohlberg.[32] That usage of the word *virtue* is somewhat surprising, because he regularly uses the word in a disparaging way: "Virtue and vices are labels by which people award praise or blame others."[33] Or in the phrase he finds difficult to resist, he refers to "the bag of virtues approach." With this phrase he characterizes most past moral education and thereby dismisses it. He seems to have in mind something like the image of Ben Franklin checking off in his diary how many virtues he had practiced that day.

In the next chapter I raise the question of a morality of virtue rooted in the rich soil of a tradition Kohlberg gives no evidence of being familiar with. For him morality is reducible to judgment or decision; at the highest level the decision is a simple, rational one. At the lower levels prudence or respect for authority can be guides, but the "man of conscience" needs no guide or virtue except justice.

The "man of conscience" who is ready to sacrifice all for the principle of justice is the end toward which Kohlberg's system moves. By the same token it is the one element inexplicable within the system itself. When a stage 3 begins to ask "Why should I act this way?" the answer comes over the horizon: stage 4. If a stage 4 person looks for a reason to obey the law, the answer is the social contract theory of stage 5. Every rung on the ladder hangs from the rung above. Everything flows smoothly until one gets to stage 6 and asks: Why be moral? Why treat every man's claim impartially? Why respect the rights of every individual? To those crucial questions Kohlberg's system has no answer at all.

Kohlberg and Religion

At this point religion comes back into the picture. I said earlier that Kohlberg banishes religion's control of morality by declaring that religion *follows* morality rather than the other way around. I noted, however, that the simple reversal of a leader/follower relation does not free the symbiotic pair to explore a more mutually beneficial relation. In Kohlberg's system, religion, as "a faith," returns with a vengeance. It subverts the entire process that leads toward respect of each person. The religion that comes back to envelop Kohlberg's system is a mysticism of the kind in which persons disappear altogether.

Kohlberg contrasts his position here to that of Kant and Dewey, both of whom resisted stepping above the moral into the mystical. Kohlberg appropriately names this mystical realm stage 7. The movement into it, according to Kohlberg, begins with "despair," but then as the "oneness of being" is disclosed, we identify ourselves with the infinite perspective. The essential thing at this level "is the sense of being a part of the whole of life and the adoption of a cosmic *as opposed to* a universal humanistic stage 6 perspective" (my italics).[34] The final resolution of Kohlberg's system is an all-embracing cosmic unity in which the humanistic stage is an obstacle that has to be transcended. Everything is sacrificed at the altar of an undifferentiated unity.

Kohlberg is driven by his own logic into this kind of unity. His stages move away from a tension of opposites; they ascend above physical, social, political, and institutional equilibria. When Kohlberg's calculative principle of equality is transcended, the only thing higher is simple unity. Beyond the situation of each subject perceiving the same principle is the principle itself without the multiplicity of subjects. Perfect harmony is finally achieved when there is no longer a subjective-objective dichotomy.

Kohlberg's concern is to find an experience that is "nondualistic." While that term can describe what all the great religions move toward, it can be interpreted in fundamentally different ways. If *nondualistic* referred simply to numerical unity, then the word *nondualistic* would be unnecessary. Philosophers often miss the religious paradox of this term in both Eastern and Western religions.[35] One can move toward eliminating the difference between subject and object either by trying to eliminate human subjectivity or else by creating deeper human communion. The second way can sound destructive of the human ego because it includes the stripping away of a superficial self; however, the result is the revelation of a deeper self. This second movement toward nondualism is in the opposite direction from Kohlbergian stages toward the highest perspective. Because Kohlberg assumes that nondualism is a simple notion, he utterly misunderstands a religious thinker like Teilhard de Chardin, whom he cites for support.

In his long essay on stage 7 mysticism, Kohlberg looks to thinkers of the past and present. He refers to Marcus Aurelius and Spinoza; then he names Whitehead, Bergson, and Teilhard de Chardin of the twentieth century. In this latter group Teilhard is the only person cited in detail. He is described as someone who constructed a scientific system by reason alone and then placed faith in a revelation of God above the structure. Although it is possible to read certain passages of Teilhard that way, the whole context of his life and writings invalidates such an overall reading. Interestingly, Kohlberg relies mainly on the *Divine Milieu,* where—starting with the title— Teilhard is particularly clear about his milieu and his assumptions.

Kohlberg states that Teilhard's scientific theory leads to an hypothesis of the existence of God. According to Kohlberg, Teilhard's decision to accept or reject the hypothesis is rationally based on a determination of how well it accounts for the totality of experience. "Christian faith serves to complete his system and to make explicit and clear what has been suggested but vague. The Christian revelation confirms his psychological faith and provides it with new depth and inspiration."[36] Hence for Teilhard there is a thorough separation between reason and faith, science and religion. God is necessary at the top to complete the system.

Kohlberg seems to have missed the preface to the *Divine Milieu,* in which Teilhard writes: "The subject under consideration is actual, concrete, 'supernaturalized' man—but seen in the realm of conscious psychology only. So there was no need to distinguish explicitly between natural and supernatural, between divine influence and human operation. But although the technical terms are absent, the thing is everywhere taken for granted. Not only as a theoretically admitted reality, the notion of grace impregnates the whole atmosphere of my book."[37] This assumption of the divine as infinitely near and dispersed everywhere creates imagery which is fundamentally opposed to a mystical stage above reason. In Teilhard's "developmental theory," movement is toward communion at the center: "God reveals himself everywhere, beneath our groping efforts, as a *universal milieu,* only because he is the *ultimate point* upon which all realities converge. Each element of the world, whatever it may be, only exists *hic et nunc,* in the manner of a cone whose generatrices meet in God who draws them together."[38]

When religion is located above ordinary experience (and faith is imagined as above reason) then God can be sought only by leaving the world below. Unwittingly, this movement ends in a pantheism or in an undifferentiated unity. An absolute above experience devalues the experience of arriving at the absolute. The paradoxical way to avoid pantheism is to explore imagery that at first appears close to pantheism: the divine at the center of things. One does not look above things for God; "the light of heaven becomes perceptible and attainable to him in the crystalline transparency of beings."[39] In this imagery God does not eliminate the differences among creatures but "pushes to its furthest possible limit the differentiation among the creatures he concentrates within himself."[40] The last stage, says Teilhard, is not a grand cosmic unity where all differences are ploughed under. "The essential aspiration of all mysticism [is] *to be united* (that is to become the other) *while remaining oneself.*"[41]

Problems and Symptoms

We can note in this final section some of the problems that have arisen with Kohlberg's six stages. These problems have led to criticism of his system and to calls for an alternative, the topic I will pursue in the next chapter.

A first problem is that the system is oriented toward the two highest stages but only a small minority gets there. That fact does not invalidate the system, but it raises doubts whether the movement up through Kohlberg's stages has been accurately described for all people. Those who reach principled reasoning were at one time said to be five to ten per cent of the population. The hope was that by using new teaching techniques and by changing environments, the latent capacities of a larger percentage would be revealed. Kohlberg seemed undisturbed by the correlation of his stage advancement with I.Q., middle-class upbringing, and college education.[42] The absence of principled reasoning in "preliteral villages or tribal communities" was for Kohlberg, as I have noted, evidence not of his system's cultural bias but of the fact that individuals and societies advance together. Kohlberg's apparent bias against women is more difficult to dismiss, and I will pay special attention to that question in the next chapter.

During the 1970s Kohlberg's optimism seemed gradually to fade. Although he had proclaimed in the 1960s that he had cross-cultural evidence for the universal validity of his stages, the application of the system seemed curiously at the mercy of shifting political winds. At the end of the 1960s he perceived a quest for justice moving across the land. He seemed to expect a great many people to be on the way to stage 6: "Our longitudinal studies indicate that all our middle class stage 2 college students grow out of it to become principled adults."[43]

In a 1976 talk, however, he said that "further research by my colleagues and myself . . . dictated a retrenchment from stage 6 Platonic idealism to stage 5 rational liberalism. . . . Empirical research between 1968 and 1976 did not confirm my theoretical statements about a sixth and highest stage."[44] By the end of the decade Kohlberg was even less optimistic; he wrote: "The present paper represents a further retrenchment to stage 4 goals as the ends of civic education."[45]

This "retrenchment" can be taken as simply a realistic admission that the original projection was too optimistic. However, at what point does one admit that the system is not being reformed but abandoned? Has Kohlberg slowly withdrawn back to Piaget's conception of morality (rules and respect for rules) while he still talks of principled judgment, postconventional morality, man of conscience, etc., as if these categories were still central to the scheme? Having disparaged stages 3 and 4 as being merely conventional, he now has to back into a defense of stages 3 and 4 as the best that are salvageable. Surely our society would have a better chance of defending Kohlberg's stages 3 and 4 if instead of being disdainfully labeled conventional they were described in wholly positive terms. Kohlberg's stages 3 and 4 represent nothing less than interpersonal love and a respect for social order.

A six-stage theory in which the desirable upper two have been all but abandoned inevitably starts doubts about whether people are progressing from stage 1 to stage 4. If the researcher himself does not view stage 4 as highly desirable, then he probably will think students need prodding to make them act that way. Here is where Kohlberg introduces what to his followers was a shocking term: indoctrination. One can no longer trust that the majority of students will progress to stage 4 by discussions of dilemmas and by role-playing. Kohlberg introduces other methods whose aim, frankly stated, is to indoctrinate children with liberal, democratic values: "Our cluster approach is not merely socratic and developmental, it is indoctrinative."[46]

His philosophy of civic education is, he admits, conventional, but he claims that the educational approach is unconventional and new. This new approach refers mainly to governance of a small school community by direct democracy. Such experience of a small community with democratic rules will, Kohlberg hopes, solidify the student as a stage-4 citizen while intimating the stage 5 he or she cannot grasp until later in life. I think that the introduction of some self-government and democratic experience into schools is surely praiseworthy. No doubt it can be part of the answer to real life's problems.[47]

I have two reservations about Kohlberg's proposal: (1) The use of the pretentious term *just community* for this modest step in school governance promises more than it can deliver. What could and should be promised to students is a reduction in injustice, some respect for their personal dignity, and the beginning of cooperation in school. (2) Related to this inflated claim is the admission that the real intention is indoctrination. Kohlberg is a latecomer to the small-group techniques that have been studied and used extensively for more than three decades. There is ample evidence that small-group experience can be helpful to personal development; one should expect nothing less and nothing more than that. If someone intends to teach an agenda of civic education through small groups, then group experience is no longer community but something closer to manipulation by managerial technique.

Another anomaly in Kolhberg's system can be seen either as a small problem that refines the theory or as a symptom of big trouble. Kohlberg had identified some students as stage 4 who then changed, but not to stage 5; they seemed to regress to stage 2. The theory did not allow that pattern, and Kohlberg's explanation was to invent stage 4½: Some of the hedonism of stage 2 reemerges, but structurally the students are still at stage 4.[48] Kohlberg decided that on the one side he had overestimated high-school students in assuming that they had reached stage 4 and were ready for transition to stage 5. On the other side he maintained that after the apparent reversal in stage 4½ they prove they are stage 4 or higher.

Kohlberg's discussion of stage 4½ raises a fundamental question about the imagery assumed by his theory. He presumes to know where development is headed (viz., the principle of justice), and he has no room for circling back. The system points relentlessly upward, not even possessing the circular movements within stages that Piaget retains. A straight line is little problem if one is interested only in the capacity to make abstract judgments, but Kohlberg obviously wishes to say something more. His casual pronouncement that the cognitive and affective are rooted in the same structure and develop along parallel lines obscures the question of how judgment is related to personal maturity. His discovery of stage 4½ should at least cast doubt on his assumption that if one studies the "cognitive," then everything else falls into place. Within the confines of Kohlberg's system there is no room to explore imagery and language for describing moral development that does not travel in a straight line. The next chapter offers an alternative discription of morality.

Conclusion

Two conclusions can be drawn here, the first in appreciation of Kohlberg and the second leading beyond him.

1. The discussion of moral dilemmas and the development of perspective through role-taking are worthwhile activities in elementary, junior high, and secondary schools. Ethics courses in the university can also make fruitful use of these techniques. However, two distinctions must not be overlooked: School and education are not equivalent, and moral reasoning and moral development are not equivalent. Keeping those two distinctions in mind, the school teacher can proceed to do the main work of the school: instructing students to develop the life of the mind. Students are also educated in other ways through family, church, sports, and so on. The school teacher's main instrument is the text, written and oral, by which the teacher instructs. The word *instruction* carries the connotation of definite content and directive method, but instruction is very different from indoctrination. To be effective the instruction needs an environment that at least is not aesthetically repulsive or institutionally repressive. Kohlberg's personal involvement in high school governance and in the workings of other institutions for young people is an admirable

dedication, and it can no doubt enrich our understanding of needed reforms.

2. Kohlberg has little to offer concerning Piaget's sensori-motor and pre-operational child. He has the effect of reinforcing Piaget's dismissal of morality at that age. I think a large part of common sense, educational practice, and religious history would be much more hesitant to declare the years up to six "pre-moral." If our moral system has nothing to say about younger children, then we may have to examine the adequacy of our system.

Something similar can be said of adults. The rational capacity to be morally principled has apparently arrived for most people by age 18, but only a tiny minority seems to get there. What does Kohlberg have to offer as explanation and solution? Only that adults need the kind of social experience that will bring out their latent powers. That does not say much about the precarious journey and never-fully-realized integrity that every adult must contend with. For that we need other moral categories.

5

An Alternative Approach
to Moral Development

The theory of moral development described in the preceding chapter assumes that the word *morality* is easily definable. For Piaget, morality consists of rules and the individual's respect for rules. Kohlberg simplifies that definition further: Morality is obedience to a single rule of justice understood as equality. Development is therefore seen as movement to that point where the mind can perceive "that each individual should be treated impartially." With such impartiality, the individual doing the judging and all other individuals will be better off. Morality is preeminently a matter of *reasonableness.*

Suppose, though, that one does not begin with such a meaning for morality. What then becomes of moral development? At the least it involves a more complex image than Kohlberg offers. William Bennett and Edwin Delattre, two critics of Kohlberg, write: "Morality is concerned with doing good, with sacrifice, altruism, love, courage, honor and compassion, and with fidelity and large-mindedness regarding one's station, commitments, family, friends, colleagues and society in general."[1] Although they offer no neat and manageable definition in that statement, they do remind us of elements that have been part of moral discourse in the past, elements that should be examined rather than banished by definition.

What I propose to do in this chapter is indicate an alternative way of imagining, conceptualizing, and articulating morality. Kohlberg's name has dominated the discussion of moral development and moral education for the past two decades, but not everyone has been persuaded that his theory holds all the answers. Criticism grew up both from within Kohlberg's theory and from starting points very different from Kohlberg's. The first kind of criticism recognizes biases inherent in Kohlberg's assumptions or method. The second kind of criticism offers a different philosophical foundation. This latter philosophical approach often overlaps with religious concerns, or at least it does not promptly segregate religion as Kohlberg does.

These criticisms do not constitute a single school, so it is difficult to name *the* alternative to Kohlberg. Nonetheless, it might be helpful to make a preliminary contrast of two approaches to morality. Craig Dykstra, at the beginning of *Vision and Character: A Christian Educator's Alternative to Kohlberg*, names the two approaches: judicial ethics and visional ethics.[2] I would have no argument with the first choice, judicial. What Dykstra means by *judicial* and what he opposes as inadequate is justice conceived as a rule and morality as a judgment about that rule. The second word, *visional*, is part of the alternative but does not sufficiently describe the issues at stake. After all, Kohlberg ends with a kind of vision of unity to which justice leads. At the start of inquiry I would avoid trying to find a single word. Instead, I refer to virtue/care/character/community as the interlocking categories of an alternative approach to moral development.

Of the criticism that took its starting point within Kohlberg's camp, the work of Carol Gilligan is probably the most interesting contribution. What started Gilligan on her way was suspicion of sexual bias in Kohlberg's work. He had begun his study in the 1950s with seventy-two young men; his moral dilemmas featured men as the key players; the movement from stage 3 to stage 4 could reflect the difference between a traditional feminine role and a masculine one. Women, generally speaking, scored lower on Kohlberg's scale. Gilligan's question was whether women are in fact less developed morally, or whether the theory as a whole is biased against women. She suspected that women might be speaking "in a different voice" which registered poorly in male-oriented systems.[3]

Gilligan was not the first to suggest such a difference. Sigmund Freud, for example, had written: "I cannot evade the notion . . . that for women the level of what is ethically normal is different from what it is in men. Their super-ego is never so impersonal, so independent of the emotional origins as we require it to be in men."[4] Many contemporary feminists would agree with those sentiments provided that "impersonal" and "independent of emotional origins" are not assumed to be qualities of moral improvement. Indeed, some feminists are inclined to turn the categories upside down and declare Freud's super-ego men to be the retardees. *Ms.* magazine's interview with Carol Gilligan carried the headline: *Are Women More Moral Than Men?*[5] That kind of reversal can actually be a throwback to the nineteenth century, when it was assumed that women were more moral than men. John Stuart Mill in *On the Subjection of Women* wrote that this supposed moral advantage for women was "an empty compliment, which must provoke a bitter smile from every woman of spirit."[6]

I do not see Gilligan trying to prove women are better than men or even offering a theory of women's development. She is trying to correct the male bias in what purports to be a theory of human development. She pays her respects to Kohlberg's theory. She has co-authored an article with him, and she remains a colleague after having parted intellectual ways with him.[7] In her writing she retains some of Kohlberg's apparatus, especially the language of precon-ventional, conventional and postconventional. She sometimes refers to her ethic as one of responsibility, although that word is more the moral question than the answer. For her, the category that may best fill out the meaning of responsibility is care: a concern to maintain relationships, anticipate consequences, and avoid violence.

Kohlberg has on occasion said he agrees with Gilligan's criticism of sex bias in his theory.[8] That is, he admits that stages 3 and 4 were so constructed that women generally scored toward stage 3 and men toward stage 4. From the available evidence, however, Kohlberg does not seem to understand or to acknowledge that Gilligan has called into question his theory's fundamental assumptions. In his book *The Philosophy of Moral Development,* Kohlberg dispatches Gilligan with the single sentence: "Shawver and Gilligan have not worked out an alternative account of a highest moral stage but have, rather, pointed to alternative attitudes in the development of higher stages of ethical orientation."[9] Kohlberg is probably correct in saying that neither Carol Gilligan nor David Shawver has "an alternative account of a highest stage." That is because their attack is more fundamental: They are questioning the idea that there is a highest stage.

Gilligan's alternative may not always be clear, because she has retained some of Kohlberg's language. Nonetheless, I think what she has found is that moral development is not toward higher and highest.

Development as she comes to describe it is a circling back to reappropriate in more profoundly human ways the connection and care from which we all begin. One can hardly deny that Kohlberg's stage 4 is higher than stage 3, his stage 6 higher than stage 5. To move through his stages is by definition to achieve a higher position, a more generalized and abstract point of view. The question is whether a higher morality is necessarily a better morality. This distinction is difficult to make because in the moral notions assumed today the only way to go is up. Success is above and failure is below. A genuine alternative to Kohlberg is not "an alternative account of a highest moral stage" but an ethic of virtue/care/character/community in which movement is not simply from lower to higher.

Gilligan developed her theory on the basis of a study of women who were considering abortion. Their moral judgment was not directed toward a hypothetical problem of someone else's but to a painfully real problem of their own. The criticism is often made that Kohlberg measures only how people think. In one sense, however, that is the most that any researcher can do. Still, there may be several kinds of thinking. The use of the word *cognitive* today regularly obscures this fact. When one objects to the narrowness of the word *cognitive*, the response of the cognitivist is to say that the affective can be added. The solution only compounds the problem. The trouble with Kohlberg's cognitive is that it does not measure what people think when they are actually involved in a moral problem. Instead of dealing with that kind of thinking, which of its nature includes feelings, he deals with one kind of thinking—the kind that can be dissociated from personal feelings.

Gilligan's choice of abortion is particularly appropriate. One can hardly imagine an issue closer to bodily life, emotional reaction, and political conflict. Someone might argue that in fact the issue is so volatile that the data on it ten years from now may be very different. Gilligan would admit that she needs more data over a longer period to construct a theory with a claim to universal validity. But for the present she has opened a new way of talking about development, a way that reconnects morality to the concerns in the Bennett/Delattre description of morality referred to at the beginning of this chapter.

Gilligan contrasts herself and Kohlberg by saying that his is a morality of rights and hers is a morality of responsibility.[10] As I said above, however, the idea of responsibility is used by almost all ethicists and moralists. In itself it indicates only that we are respondents or answerers. Kohlberg does have a kind of responsibility to the rights of others and to the principle of justice. Gilligan's real difference from Kohlberg lies in her answers to the questions of *to whom, with what,* and *for what purpose* we are responsible. Gilligan's theory supposes that we respond *to* the interdependence of persons among themselves and with nature. We respond *with* a moral self that includes thinking, feeling, choosing, acting. We respond *for* the purpose of caring for others and not doing violence to them or to nature.

Gilligan finds three levels or stages in the women she reports on. She also tries to describe transitions from stage 1 to stage 2 and from stage 2 to stage 3. At a first level the women have a tenuous concept of self. A moral question for these women can be an issue of survival for their image of self. The relevant question for the woman is how to get rid of the problem and to hurt herself the least. Caught as she is in what is experienced as the culture's conflict between femininity and adulthood, no choice will be a good one. Our society expects that a good woman will obey whatever is demanded of her by the significant powers in her life. The "bad woman" tries to get rid of the commitments that are perpetuating the self-deception, that one really has a self. *Selfishness* is the word we use for morally immature people, although they may not have enough of a self to be self-centered.[11]

In the transition to the second level, the woman's self-concept includes doing the right thing by society's standards. For example, to be a mother requires assuming parental responsibility for the care of the child. To care responsibly for another person, one must of course be able to care for oneself. Gilligan quotes one young woman: "So I see myself as becoming more mature in ways of making decisions and taking care of myself, doing something for myself. I think it is going to help me in other ways, if I have other decisions to make put upon me, which would take some responsibility. And I would know that I could make them."[12]

Gilligan characterizes this second level of morality as one of goodness defined by self-sacrifice. "The woman at this point validates her claim to social membership through the adoption of societal values. Consensual judgment about goodness becomes the overriding concern as survival is now seen to depend on acceptance by others."[13]

The trouble here is that the woman now gets caught in society's traditional image of women, which conflicts with this emerging self. Gilligan describes a strange, backward reciprocity in which the woman feels responsible for the actions of everyone—except herself. A morality of care is still submerged here in a psychology of dependence. Everyone involved may feel manipulated: the woman who is sacrificing herself, and those for whom she sacrifices.

In the transition from stage 2 to stage 3, Gilligan says, there is a shift from goodness to truth as the criterion for judgment.[14] Gilligan's choice of terms here is at best a clumsy way of saying that the woman gets a truer picture of goodness. She makes an inward acknowledgment of the self and accepts responsibility for decisions. She painfully faces the abortion issue as one which cannot be resolved by living up to the conventional picture of a feminine self and moral self-sacrifice. She may be accused of selfishness as she tries to expand her moral sensibilities to include her own feelings of wholeness. The moral principle she discovers is: Care for everyone—including yourself.

Whereas Gilligan draws some correlation between her second level and Kohlberg's, her postconventional is in fundamental disagreement with Kolhberg's stages 5 and 6. On Kohlberg's scale, women fail to progress because they remain concerned with the particulars of the dilemma: who is doing it, with what intention, with what consequences. In Gilligan's scheme these questions are not transcended in the name of a higher value, such as goodness or justice. "The women's judgments pointed toward an identification of the violence inherent in the dilemma itself, which is seen to compromise the justice of any of its possible resolutions. This construction of the dilemma leads the women to recast the moral judgment from a consideration of the good to a choice between evils."[15] They experience the dilemma as so painfully real that they can experience neither choice as the good choice; the question is which of the choices is the lesser evil.

Gilligan describes this most developed morality as one of principled nonviolence. Here we have no intellectual softness. Instead, the person is acutely aware that we live in a violent world in which there are no uncontaminated decisions. The most responsible person grasps that fact and yet is not paralyzed by it. The person has a passion for nonviolence and makes the decision to take a step toward greater care. I think Gilligan has a brilliant insight here, one which connects the two separate meanings of development discussed in Chapter 1: the psychological and the economic/political. The person who acts on principled nonviolence is never isolated from economic, political, military, ecological frameworks. An attitude of principled nonviolence also has the effect of connecting moral decisions with religious history, where the notion of nonviolence has its most obvious examples.

I think Gilligan would be acting prematurely if she were to draw a firm line between men and women in regard to moral development. What she has really discovered is the inadequacy of that judicial ethics which has dominated Western philosophy in recent centuries. She refers to *The Merchant of Venice,* Solomon's judgment between the two women, and Abraham's readiness to sacrifice his son. These examples suggest to her that men have long been on the side of a stern principle of justice uncomplemented by the strains of mercy and care. That picture may be generally true, but the evidence is insufficient to construct a universal theory in which men and women have always been and must always be in radical moral contrast. Gilligan's passing references to Solomon and Abraham need to be pursued so we can better understand the relation of justice and mercy in the Hebrew Bible.[16] The moral notions of the Christian New Testament might also help to clarify an ethic that I will subsequently call virtue/care/character/community.

Religious Imagery and Moral Development

I turn at this point to other criticisms of Kohlberg that are not averse to drawing upon religious imagery and language. In doing so I do not wish to jump from moral philosophy to theological ethics. Rather, by studying the imagery of development I am trying to avoid getting locked within psychology, theology, or any other discipline. At issue in this section is the inadequacy of a theory of moral development as development if it is unaware of or hostile to religious imagery and language.

Many writers who are interested in the Christian life, religious journey, spiritual formation, and allied topics, are opposed to Kohlberg's theory of moral development. From that starting point we can go in one of two directions: (1) resist Kohlberg's takeover of the term *moral development,* or (2) abandon the term *development* and insist that the real issue is journey, pilgrimage, growth, and so on. Although I can see the logic of choosing the second, my choice is the first. I think the word *development* is an important and unavoidable term in the twentieth century. There are good reasons for resisting the Kohlberg meaning of development—reasons based upon the very meaning of development itself as understood by Erikson, Piaget, and other contemporary writers. I also think that the usual approach of religious education must be to resist the reduction of meaning for terms that might help our educational and religious undertakings.

For illustrating the tendency to abandon the word *development*, I cite two fine and thoughtful books: *A Community of Character* by Stanley Hauerwas and *Vision and Character* by Craig Dykstra.[17] Both writers say that *development* and *moral development* could be acceptable terms, but they also seem to grant that the terms are locked into the meaning that Kohlberg gives them. Both writers think that the word *growth,* although not perfect, is preferable to *development.*

Stanley Hauerwas says at one point: "I hope to show how the concepts of virtue and character help account for the kind of moral development required of those who have undertaken to live faithful to the Christian story."[18] In his summary, therefore, he says that "Christians have always been concerned with moral development, but . . . the kind of moral growth they wish to promote is not equivalent with current theories of moral development."[19]

The two quotations above seem clear enough, but earlier in the chapter Hauerwas is more negative about the word *development*: "To be holy or perfect suggests more radical transformation and continued growth in the Christian life than can be captured by the idea of development."[20] It seems here that *development* is incapable of including: (1) radical transformation, or (2) continued growth. More forcefully, Hauerwas says of radical transformation: "The Christian moral life is finally not one of '*development*' but of conversion." I gather that the italicizing of *development* here suggests "current meaning of *development.*" Nevertheless, development and conversion are here pitted against each other.

Craig Dykstra's concerns are similar. In summarizing a section on transformation, he writes: "Though the dynamics of the imagination are fundamental to human development, normal growth through imaginal transformation is not itself developmental in the sense that one moves progressively through higher stages."[21] The word *development* seems here to connote higher stages which Dykstra sees in conflict with his description of transformation. Like Hauerwas he also sees development in conflict with continued growth: "Developmental theory sets out a path in advance and implies that all persons who are growing morally are following that path. Developmental theory knows where that path begins and where it ends. To grow morally is to get on track and stay there until the end is reached and growth stops."[22]

It is ironic that Hauerwas and Dykstra think that development cannot be combined with continued growth. Such growth (or progress) is exactly the reason for the existence of developmental theories—in opposition to what seemed to be the closed systems of Christian moral philosophy. As I indicated in Chapter 1, theories of development arose as the modern world tried to remove final causes. Both the psycho-social theories of Chapter 2 and the constructivism of Chapter 3 described processes that are a tension of opposites. There is no object, end point, or preestablished form in a developmental theory that is true to its intention. Carol Gilligan's principled nonviolence reestablishes the process in moral development. If Kohlberg's system collapses the tension and offers a principle at the end, then the accurate criticism is that his theory is not one of moral development. If the religious life is one of continued growth, progress, or journey, then that fact should remind developmentalists what their original calling is.

In addition to continued growth, the other common concern of Hauerwas and Dykstra—the centrality of conversion or transformation—is intimately related to the first concern. The reason why development is continued growth or progress is that it is continual conversion. If forward movement is also a circling back, if outward movement is also an interior deepening, then the movement is not imagined as progress toward an object at the end. The religious meaning of conversion could be made more intelligible by being placed in a developmental framework. In turn, we should test out any theory of human development by asking whether it can include the religious phenomena of conversion to a better life and disintegration to a worse life. Kohlberg fails on this count, not because he has a theory of moral development but because his moral categories are so narrow that they cannot include the con-verting or circular movement that is necessary for any developmental theory.

Moral theory that makes allowance for religious impulse has to recognize images of conversion, repentance, change of heart, and similar imagery. From the standpoint of any of the major religions, moral development cannot proceed simply by insight, perspective, and a more general understanding of moral situations. Kohlberg states his choice by saying that "morally mature men are governed by the principles of justice rather than a set of rules."[23] As far as religion is concerned, *neither* rules nor principles are adequate for handling the moral conflicts of interest. Mature men and women are governed by a discipline of life within a community that shapes our character through vision, stories, rituals, and innumerable gifts.

Carol Gilligan in exploring an ethic of care gets close to the religious concern. The women experience terrible conflicts as they try to affirm their own lives and the lives of people they care for. In the midst of their struggles, what can quite suddenly become apparent is that life—each day's life—is a gift. Human beings are never secure, because the abyss of non-being can open to them at any moment. They can try to avoid the void by grasping at possessions, seeking power over other people, or wandering into self-distractions.[24] Or they can in the experience of life's limitations come up against the reality of life itself. The most mature of Gilligan's women can accept life as a mysterious gift and accordingly try to make their decisions life-affirming. People who get that far are acutely aware of the limits of human beings and aware of how they feel caught in their own failures.

I have admitted that the point at issue in this section is a tactical question of whether to fight for the word *development* or relinquish it to a dominant recent usage. My position is that religious-minded people have a right to share in the word *development* as well as in more specifically religious terms such as *pilgrimage* or *sanctification*. We need some terms to bridge the gap between religious and non-religious areas. One can use *growth* or *progress* as an alternative to *development*. But the etymology of both these words, and the imagery associated with them, make them at least as problematic as the word *development*. As I have tried to suggest, developmental theory to be true to itself is in quest of religious language. And while it is certainly possible to speak of "religious growth," the strange paradoxes of religious language become evident in the context of human development.

Virtue and Care

Throughout most of Western history, the response of the person to the exigencies of the moral situation was described in the language of an ethic of virtue. I think that *virtue* including *care* will lead us back to *character* in *community*. As we have seen, Kohlberg ridicules the word *virtue*, and Erikson after a brief fling played down the word. Nevertheless, reflection on the virtues and on the virtuous person offers the genuine alternative to Kohlberg's judgment and principle. Is morality a series of reasonable judgments, as Kolhberg says, or is it the formation of good character?

In Greek philosophy and in most of Christian history, morality is not reducible to acts or decisions. Rather, morally good decisions flow from the person of morally good character. However, the classical picture did not entirely avoid a circular understanding of the relation between virtuous activity and virtuous persons. An honest person practices the virtue of honesty, and in turn honest actions bring about the development of honest persons. A radical reconstruction of the lists of virtues may be necessary, but a fundamental insight of Plato, Aristotle, and Aquinas remains: We become virtuous beings by participating in the life, story, and vision of moral communities.

Virtue comes from the Latin translation of a Greek word meaning "strength" or "excellence." The virtuous person is someone whose strengths are integrated. Since the human being is capable of unlimited desires, the power to act needs to be directed, because to choose any object is to prevent oneself from choosing others. Virtue is a disposition to choose easily without having to reinvent one's purpose or sense of direction each time. It is an "assured capacity to call up practiced understanding."[25] One acquires virtue by a repetition that includes understanding. In Latin, virtue was a *habitus*; the connotations of the English *habit* are not very helpful here. *Habit* often connotes mindlessness or compulsion. But *virtue* is a word that should imply effortlessness and a degree of delight. We enjoy the challenge of using skills that have been trained and perfected. When virtue has become "second nature" to us, then we can relax, trust our impulses, and take joy in living.

Aristotle had a list of virtues that suited his own place and time. He also had his own theory of equilibrium or tension of opposites: Virtue is a golden mean between vicious extremes. Christian philosophers took over the main virtues of Plato, Aristotle, and other schools such as Stoicism. Christianity set the virtues in a context of unique persons, creativity, and historical process. Morality was now understood as the response of a person to the creator God. The preeminent Christian virtues became the "theological" virtues of faith, hope, and love. These virtues, however, find their expression in the "cardinal" moral virtues that the Greeks had described: prudence, justice, courage, and temperance.

I think we could use in our day a restatement of these virtues or the virtuous life. The need is for a person to respond faithfully and care-fully to what is present at any moment.[26] The unity of our lives is not reached by a principle but is more in the nature of a novel with a major plot and several sub-plots: The main direction of the story line can be perceived although the choice from among possibilities is never certain. What those choices are depends upon getting ourselves into situations, interpreting what the situations mean (including very often the willingness to wait for the meaning to appear), and putting a discipline of small actions into our lives.[27]

Two of the cardinal virtues, courage and temperance, concern the discipline of emotion in everyday life. In the modern world the former would still be praised, at least sometimes, but the latter would arouse little enthusiasm. The two are nonetheless related, being restrictions of some bodily tendencies for the sake of a more complete integration. Courage requires a commitment to important causes in the face of danger and despite the tendency to flee. Temperance requires a commitment to bodily pleasure despite a tendency either to abandon bodiliness or to seek pleasure indiscriminately.[28] The need for commitment to bodily pleasure may seem strange in our day, but we are still afflicted with angelism, a flight to rationalistic philosophies instead of accepting ourselves as creatures of the earth. Under temperance Aquinas could write: "If one knowingly abstained from wine to the point of oppressing nature seriously, he would not be free of guilt."[29] If temperance had always been defined as a commitment to pleasures that help integrate life, it might today have a different reputation. It would certainly not be identified with joylessness and priggishness. On the whole, Jewish tradition kept a much better balance than Christianity on the place of pleasure. Thus the Talmud says: "A man will have to give account in the judgment day of every good thing which he might have enjoyed and did not."[30]

In this ethical system, courage and temperance are necessary satellites to the other two cardinal virtues: justice and prudence. Justice set within a complex of virtues has content different from Kohlberg's, and it judges by criteria different from Kohlberg's formalism, with its sole content of impartiality. Kohlberg writes: "Justice is both a sociological and psychological concept. A just solution of the social conflict is a better equilibrated resolution of a conflict. By definition, justice is a recognition of conflicting claims in light of principles and procedures that appear fair to the parties involved in the conflict."[31] An ethic of virtues does not accept this reductionistic definition of justice. Hebrew and Christian traditions conceive of justice as religious in character, more specifically as a divine attribute. God's justice is another name for creative love; the creature's justice is to respond to the gift of life in consort with other creatures. Justice situated in the midst of human life and in light of a religious vision takes on more meaning. The formula "to each his [her] own" is then interpreted with new depth of understanding. Justice cannot be settled by a single principle of equality.

Justice means recognizing the other as *other*, that is, as another participant in life's journey. The Kantian formula of treating the other person as end, not means, does not go far enough. A choice between means and end is still tied to an instrumental way of thinking: either an instrument on the way or the goal itself. In a religious view the creature as a recipient of life is not the end, but that does not imply that it is a means or instrument. Another person is an invitation to respond within a community of mutual love. And even where love is not yet possible, justice is still required. Justice requires that we listen to the other person to discover what "to each his [her] own" involves in each situation. Intention, motive, special circumstances, behaviors, long-range implications can all come into play. As Michael Walzer points out, the formula of "to each according to his [her] needs" may be fine for basic medical care but it does not address political power, fame, leisure time, rare books and sailboats."[33] We need for justice's sake the care-ful thinking that was called prudence so that the community can devise further guidelines for the distribution of goods.

One may doubt that the richer meanings of prudence can be restored. To most people today prudence probably denotes a cautious, sometimes overly restrictive, way of deciding things. In Kohlberg's system it is one of those preliminary concerns that is shucked off when we get to the true principle, justice.[34] But in an ethic of virtue/care/character/community, prudence holds a central place as regulator of all the virtues.[35] Prudence, I would stress, means careful knowing. The theory of moral development that calls itself cognitive identifies any competitor as non-cognitive, affective, or emotivist.[36] Those alternatives indicate the bankruptcy of the tradition calling itself cognitive. An ethic of virtue/care/character/community is intellectual in content and demands that one use the best knowledge available. However, its interplay of thinking, feeling, and choosing means that its knowledge is not reducible to a rationalistic system: The knowledge is not entirely separable from personal intentions and historical situations.

The feminist and ecological movements are aspects of a growing realization that we need new moral ground to stand upon. We cannot leave the body beneath us as we take the "higher" view. We cannot forget that we share the earth's blessings with the animal and vegetable world. Carol Gilligan's description of maturity as principled non-violence could be a help to rethinking prudence. Far from being minimalist calculation, prudence requires that one listen to the rhythms of the body and of nature so that when one acts it is the self that moves and not merely the will. The real caution of prudence is: Do violence to no one, including yourself. Or as a medieval prayer puts it: Beyond a wholesome discipline, be gentle with yourself.

In responding to the needs of others we need to perceive that each woman and each man is a unique historical and bodily creature. Our moral thinking moves by deepening understanding and by analogizing. We seldom deduce conclusions from principles. Rather we move from a few persons, activities, and events that we grasp and are grasped by to more remote situations that are similar. We know that killing innocent people is wrong. A clear case of self-defense is easily moved to. We find it more difficult, though, to move to abortion or warfare. Moral thinking of this kind is inseparable from imagination and from contemplation.[37] Anything that expands or deepens imagination contributes to moral education, a role I am suggesting can be played by religion.

Character and Community

We cannot attain a virtuous character by aggressively acquiring the virtues, one after the other. Character results from how we respond, with a self that has been given each of us, to the social setting and physical environment in which we live. Morality is unavoidably response, but the question is, response to what? We are not sole masters of our moral fate; we depend on other people and other things for our moral development. Kohlberg and many before him have tried to reduce that dependence so that teachers and social environment are merely conditions and not causes of moral growth. However, in Kohlberg's view the natural unfolding sometimes stalls, and that leads him back to indoctrination. In Gilligan's view, compassion for one's fellow creature is central to moral growth. The responding is not to a belief in individual rights but to one's image of self, to needs of other people, and to an overall sense of wholeness.[38]

One value of Jewish, Christian, and other religious traditions is that they enrich the narrative, imagery, and scope of the community to which we respond. The community of which we are part has great events in its past, a wide scope of joys and sorrows in the present, and more people than we first assume. The modern supposition that religion just adds more rules or gives us motivation to obey reason's rules is a travesty of a living religion. The crucial role of religion in moral development is to provide a community narrative of what people we are part of and to provide exemplars of a moral/religious life we can learn from. Religion gives a sense of adventure to the moral enterprise and thereby sustains the necessary discipline for the moral life—a discipline as necessary as long, arduous practice is for a musician, athlete, or scientist.

One of the marks of a community is the story its people hold in common, a story expressed in symbols, codes of behavior, styles of humor, modes of dress and address, ways of sharing sorrow, and the like. The "quest for community" in this country does not get very far when it consists merely of a group of individuals getting together for emotional warmth or economic efficiency. In the good days such community life is pleasant and desirable, but when the bad days come, as they must, there is not enough of a common story to sustain the group. That is why for a community, in contrast to a group, task force or committee, some religious or quasi-religious bond is needed.[39]

Far from decreasing in importance today, the story/community basis of moral development has become more urgently needed. The diversity of experience and the multiple roles we play are problems now faced by everyone, not by just a few sophisticated thinkers. The religious community can provide a stable basis for the development of personal consistency without denying the wild diversity in the world; the Jewish Sabbath, for example, provides a calm and consistent rhythm no matter what the clamor and the diversity of the other six days. Spokespersons of a tradition may see their role as emphasizing unity, but unity cannot be stressed to the point of uniformity. "Traditions, when vital, embody continuities of conflict."[40] That is one reason why doctrinal systems cannot replace the narrative form of a religious group's self-understanding. Each individual can identify with different elements of the story at different times of his or her life. No heretical denials are involved in such identification. The story is there as something transcending us as individuals and within which I can discover myself.

An ethic of virtue/care/character/community does not choose the individual over the social or the particular over the universal. To accept life in a community is implicitly an affirmation of life itself. It is a recognition that this people that I call my people is an embodiment of the universal human community. Vital communities give us a sense of limits that provide a protective circle around our fragile selves. The most active communities are often a response to destructive forces that need to be resisted. Albert Camus defined religion as a protest against the universal death sentence. Every religious community is a protest against or resistance to some force of death or destruction.[41]

The communal and religious view of morality does not begin by asking which choice is good and which is bad. Rather, it asks how we can resist forces of destruction which we did not cause but which are in some way part of us. By opposing specific evils we let flow the forces of life. Those forces, too, are not of our making nor directly under our control, but they are to be received with gratitude. Religious commands have a content that forbids what destroys life (don't murder, don't steal). Such commands are both a particular and a universal way to affirm life. The prescription "do good to as many people as possible" is a generalization that leads into mathematical calculations. But the principle "do violence to no one, including yourself" is a practical and universal guide.

The mature person is deeply rooted in a community, and he or she experiences that community as an embodiment of the universal human community yet to be achieved. The very limitations of a community's existence create a tension with the greater world outside the community; the bond with a few human beings conveys the sense of what a human bond is. The sharing with those in the community who are less fortunate makes the mature person realize his or her kinship with all the less fortunate people in the world.

One of the cases Kohlberg cites for stage 6 morality is Martin Luther King, Jr. No doubt King had the "cognitive" power Kohlberg ascribes to him, but that says very little about the wellsprings of his life or even about the nature of his thinking. Surely the driving powers of his life are found in his black experience and biblical religion. Like other great religious leaders, he had a sense of history, a sense of drama and symbol, and a commitment to what he called the beloved community. The quest for that community involved a resistance to evil and a call for repentance. King's basic principle—an asymmetric reaction to violence as a step toward reconciliation with one's enemies—produced a moral discourse very different from Kohlberg's. [42]

Religion always entails some resistance to forces that gravitate toward idolatry. Anything that people can lay down their life for is capable of being idolized: for example, sex, money, ideology, the multinational corporation. In our day the nation-state easily becomes an idol, for it commands total obedience. Especially in its power to wage modern warfare, the nation is a potential threat to every religious group. When the nation confuses itself with dream or myth (as in the United States' relationship to the dream named America) then religious groups must be willing to oppose specific policies. [43]

The point is not to be anti-patriotic; the ethic here described considers patriotism a virtue. It also believes, however, that the citizen can properly love her or his country only if the country is not an idol and is not confused with a utopian dream. Tempered and effective criticism is possible from within a community that has its own story, that is, a community whose story is not confined by the boundaries of the nation-state. Resistance to the nation-state on specific issues need not be solely in the name of rights but can be based on the principle that the nation's justice lies under the judgment of God.[44]

Teaching and Discipleship

The ethic of virtue/care/character/community is communicated mainly through inspiration and imitation. Specific skills and detailed knowledge are eventually needed, but they probably cannot be taught unless trust and care are an integral part of the community's life. We become moral people because we share in the life of a moral community. At the beginning we absorb the attitudes and behaviors that make good character possible. Gradually we become agents of our destiny, although our activity is always a response to people and things around us.

Many religious traditions initiate their members into discipleship by educating them in the attitudes and behaviors expected of them. If this teaching element of a religion is lost, then the process goes bad. When the communal context of religious teaching is obscured, then "making disciples" means that a powerful figure attracts blind followers. The guru as authoritarian leader poses a terrible threat in our day. Still, this education in discipleship, this training of novices on the path of wisdom, is essential to religious life. We need to create and maintain the kinds of community where each member of the group can be teacher to the rest. At any moment an individual can step into the center and play the role of the teacher on particular issues. The old can teach the young, and vice versa. The academically skilled need to teach the less knowledgeable while being ready to learn from them. If the community itself is the guru, then the problem of authoritarianism is largely eliminated.[45] We are disciples of "a way," one formed in part by trial and error through centuries of practice. Religious groups often look for guidance from their founders (Jesus, Mohammed, Gautama). The founder may say "follow me" but also points beyond his or her individual self to the true way of the universe.

The holy person is a demonstration of morality, transforming the conventional morality. Great religious reformers both simplify existing codes and apply the moral ideals more broadly. The moral system can never be the same again once it has been transformed by the living image of the saintly individual.

When Immanuel Kant was laying the foundations for the judicial ethic that has dominated recent times, he wrote: "Even the Holy One of the Gospels must first be compared with our ideal of moral perfection before we can recognize him as such." Basil Mitchell rightly comments that this description flies in the face of common sense: "It is absurd to suppose that [Peter,] the fisherman of Galilee . . . had compared Jesus with his ideal of moral perfection (just as it was before any encounter took place) and had satisfied himself that he had, so to speak, achieved the required standard."[46] Rather, Peter, like other people, presumably had a beginning notion of goodness and moral maturity. Jesus of Nazareth confirmed some of Peter's notions while presenting a puzzle and challenge on other counts. After a long period of learning and with some lapses along the way, Peter's moral sense, including the courage to die for his convictions, attained maturity.

Conclusions

I ended the last chapter with the conclusion that Kohlberg's judicial ethics has almost nothing to offer concerning the young child and the adult. The contrasting ethic described above would be especially attentive to the formation of the young child. The child up to five or six years is not pre-moral. Some of the most important aspects of moral development and moral education occur in infancy with the care the child receives and in childhood with games, stories, image formation, and language. The child of five or six can be an intensely moral being, awake to the struggle of great forces of good and evil. I will comment in Chapter 8 on the educational experiences that contribute to the moral education of the child.

Robert Coles has long been a critic of moral systems that are biased against the unlettered, the poor, and the child. He recounts the example of a six-year-old black girl named Ruby.[47] In 1960 she had to pass through a screaming mob to get into school. The child said she didn't blame them, that she prayed for them and felt sorry for them. Most of the adults assumed she was pretending and thought that eventually she would crack. The fact is, she did not; at six years of age she already knew about reconciliation and bearing ills patiently. How? Part of the explanation is the wisdom of generations passed on to her by her mother, who would say: "It's just part of what happens to us, to our kind of folks. What you have to do is the best you can. What else can you do—with the police against you, most of the time, and the laws against you?"

I would suspect that Ruby also morally inspired her mother. Each member of a community including the young, can be teacher to the rest. From as early as a few months of age each boy and girl "childs" its parents in a unique way. When the child is very small the parent may have a momentary illusion of omnipotence. As the child grows up, and by adolescence if not earlier, the parent is aware of how finite a creature a human being is. The moral adult is acutely aware of limitations and is not paralyzed by the insight. The moral adult is ready to learn from anyone and anything, knowing that moral development must continue or moral atrophy will occur.

The matter of continuance or atrophy needs special highlighting in contrasting the two ethics. In the judicial ethic the moral stage, once attained, is forever secure. (Kohlberg, as I noted, was nevertheless forced by the data to admit that temporary regression sometimes occurs.) Religious traditions are fundamentally different from Kohlberg on this point. "Count no one holy until dead" is a sentiment found in various religions. Individual virtues do not suddenly disappear, these religions hold, but the integrity of the virtues in a person of character can erode. Hence the person of many virtues is capable of great evil. Courage, for example, can be combined with an unjust life. [48]

The character of life as gift and the need to live *in* conversion make the practice of moral goodness a constant but never frenzied activity. The activity includes attention to the evil within ourselves and in the world. We must calmly but relentlessly say no to the terrible power to withhold ourselves from the source of our lives, the One whom religious people address as God. The question of the moral development of adults is not an issue that can be tacked onto a Piagetian scheme of childhood powers. Moral development begins before birth and does not finish until the individual gives up the spirit.

6

Faith Development: Fowler

During the past decade in church circles a new name was often added to the series of Erikson, Piaget, and Kohlberg. James Fowler emerged as the proponent of a theory supported by empirical research and called faith development. A number of his essays appeared in the 1970s, followed by his major work, *Stages of Faith*, in 1981. No large body of criticism of his work yet exists, although his work has given rise to a number of doctoral dissertations and has been enthusiastically received by many religious educators.[1] In this chapter I will look first at some of the issues behind Fowler's theory, second at the stages he describes, and third at the meaning of faith he adopts. On each of these points I will offer some criticism.

I am deeply interested in the kind of project Fowler has undertaken. What is his intention in constructing a theory called faith development? Do we really need another developmental theory, and how does his differ from previous ones? I think it is clear that Fowler is concerned with the lack of attention to people's spiritual, religious, or faith journeys in today's secular world, including the world of educational institutions. Psychology in its behavioristic and constructivist wings has had an inborn bias against religious issues. Although I will express some disagreements with Fowler, I share his concern that we need to explore a "logic of conviction" not reducible to the logic of rational certainty.[2]

In choosing the term *faith development*, Fowler attempts to use a category that will build two kinds of bridges: (1) a bridge between the secular world and the world of religious traditions and (2) bridges between the many religious traditions that use a word corresponding to *faith*. I do not see much evidence that either kind of bridge has been successfully built by faith development, although it may be too early to judge. Also, we cannot expect one person to do more than give us a start. Nevertheless, I do have a suspicion that Fowler's use of *faith* cannot build those bridges. My criticism in the last part of the chapter is a suggestion for using the word *faith* in a way that might open more fruitful conversations.

How does Fowler's theory of faith development differ from the theories previously described? An interesting place to begin is with a comment by Lawrence Kohlberg. Fowler's name is inevitably linked with that of Kohlberg, and since a 1974 article, Kohlberg has acknowledged Fowler's work as a possible complement to his own. In *The Philosophy of Moral Development* Kohlberg writes: "Fowler's broad definition of faith, which does not distinguish it from moral judgment, leads to confusions."[3] Kohlberg associates Fowler with Jane Loevinger's theory of ego development. Kohlberg then proposes that within a unity called "ethical development" we can distinguish moral judgment and religious judgment. While most people use the terms *ethical* and *moral* with no clear distinction of meaning, Kohlberg here offers an intriguing possibility. Using *ethical development* to mean both moral and religious development might create the context for a dialogue between morality and religion. However, he disregards his own suggestion and proceeds to use *ethical* and *moral* as practically synonymous.

What Kohlberg does here is quite clear. He acknowledges that there may be more to the development of ethical life than is covered by his own theory. Religious judgment might be something to study for those who are interested in that kind of thing. But in the end Kohlberg is certain that what can be scientifically described and what counts as universal is moral judgment. Yet as I pointed out in Chapter 4, Kohlberg is attracted to a mystical unity above reason, but that stage is practically inarticulable.

James Fowler's perception of his own work is on a different track from where Kohlberg locates it. Fowler does not confuse faith and moral judgment; rather, he tries to establish the context of moral judgment. Fowler's project requires an alternative epistemology, that is, a meaning of knowledge different from Kohlberg's meaning. Kohlberg has allowed that Fowler's theory may be an interesting appendix to his own, but I wonder if Kohlberg has ever considered that Fowler's theory subsumes his own moral reasoning as one narrow form of knowing.

Fowler's criticism of Kohlberg is always restrained and gracious. After criticizing Piaget for his narrow basis of moral judgment, Fowler writes: "My contention is that Kohlberg's theory already begins a fruitful (if largely unacknowledged) expansion of the notion of cognition in a way that we must further broaden (and deepen) in a structural-developmental approach to faith."[4] The gentle form of the criticism here may obscure how radical the criticism is. Fowler could have said that he is offering a different description of knowing, commitment, and development. The progress he attributes to Kohlberg (incorporation of Robert Selman's work on perspective-taking and acknowledgment of certain social experiences by which one passes beyond stage 4) is surely not an abandonment of a Piagetian-style rationalism.

Fowler began developing his theory in the early 1970s. As a counselor at Interpreter's House in North Carolina, he listened to people's stories of journey or pilgrimage. He used Erik Erikson as his guide to begin thinking about a developmental scheme for this material. He then went to Harvard, where Erikson was still teaching his course on the human life cycle. Fowler also made the acquaintance of Lawrence Kohlberg, who was establishing a center for moral education at Harvard. Through Kohlberg, Fowler came to understand the Piagetian approach to development and saw new possibilities for constructing a stage theory. From 1973 to the present he has continued to work and rework his description of faith stages.

I claimed in the first chapter that one must choose between Piaget and Erikson as the major force in one's theory of development. Fowler has wished to avoid that choice and instead to bridge the two traditions. Most people would probably see a preponderance of Piaget (and Kohlberg) in the stages of Fowler. Fowler uses the word *stage* in the technical sense of Piagetian tradition, that is, "an integrated set of operational structures that constitute the thought processes of a person at a given time."[5]

Fowler admits that the explicit forms and language are Piagetian in origin. He also says, however, that "Erikson's influence on me has been more pervasive and subtle."[6] Fowler's relationship to the two traditions has been consistent since early in his work. One critic of Fowler charges that he has been eliminating the Eriksonian influence (and thereby the concern for the affective).[7] The same writer attributes to Kohlberg an *increasing* attention to the affective. Kohlberg, as we have seen, refers to something like Erikson's affective and social concerns, but he has no way to incorporate the material. Fowler is at least as concerned as is Kohlberg with the adult, the social, and the affective, but he too has trouble with where to put Erikson once Piaget has established the framework.

A fundamental question is whether Piagetian-style theory is appropriate if one wishes to describe a journey of faith. What the meaning of *stage* in this context requires is a separation of the how and the what; that is, structure in Piagetian terms has little reference to content. Fowler would probably agree that something is gained and something is lost by this separation. On the positive side, the structure of faith can conceivably be studied in the life of any person, whether Jew, Buddhist, Christian, or atheist. The danger in such a generalized meaning is that the particular "content" by which, say, a Protestant or a Jew lives is obscured, at least temporarily. Like Kohlberg, but with more candor, Fowler has to bring back the content somewhere in the theory. In the last stage—and what he has called a lure throughout the preceding stages—Fowler has the image of kingdom of God as a definite content.

Fowler tries to heal the split between the how and the what of thinking. However, he has this problem only because he has accepted Piaget's separation of structure and content. I think that at some point Fowler may wish to reconsider his decision to go that route. For the limited area of children's abstract thinking, Piaget's distinction of structure and content is useful. For the area of Fowler's concerns, though, the split between how and what may get in the way.

The separation of structure and content in religion is, I suspect, only possible in modern, Western Christianity. Of course, all theorizing upon religion moves from the vitality of a religious life toward a system of ideas. The question here is whether a theory of structure and content as separable elements can mean anything religiously. Fowler is caught, like everyone else, in the limitations of language and imagery. All imagery fails, some very quickly. The powerfully sustaining images of religious life are those that do not fail so quickly that we have to start a patching operation with material from conflicting sources. Much of Fowler's effort is directed against the limitations of the image of stages in Piagetian terms.

Let me take one crucial illustration. In Piagetian stages the child progresses by decentration, that is, by taking a point of view more and more removed from an egocentric viewpoint. Kohlberg follows that premise, making his moral stages depend on a higher and higher perspective. The centering of the world in one's ego disappears, but into what? From what center does the advanced-stage mind view the world? Piaget moves toward a more and more complicated mathematical equation. Kohlberg, not illogically, ends in a mystical unity where the person disappears.

James Fowler has always seen the movement of faith as a more complex pattern than one toward higher abstraction. As is true for his religious mentors (e.g., Paul Tillich), Fowler sees depth, interiority, and centeredness as positive images. While a person decenters his or her vision in an expanding world (ceasing to be egotistical and narcissistic in a moral sense), the individual is more deeply centered in personal agency, courage, responsibility, and other virtues. Religiously, the movement is not to abandon a personal center but to discover a deeper center, one closer to our ultimate integrity.

Fowler has sometimes tried two cones inverted in each other to indicate the twofold change.[9]

There is a double movement of giving up one's superficial center with its narrow outlook (one of the cones is expanding) while accepting a profound center to life (the other cone is narrowing). The book jacket of *Stages of Faith* has a picture of multiplying colors flowing upward. The picture is supposed to convey an alternative to going up the steps of a ladder. I doubt that many people will see a significant difference. The diagrams on pages 275, 289, and 290, with expanding circles spiraling after one another, come closer to his intention of illustrating the image of center.

A question always asked about any theory of development is whether one's intention is descriptive or prescriptive. There is probably something wrong with that question. Anyone claiming that it is meant only to be descriptive is difficult to believe. True, one can write a theory of criminality without advocating crime. However, anyone describing human development is probably making a contribution, however small, to the pattern's being accepted as "normal." Fowler is forthright in admitting that "it has become clear that we are trying to do both descriptive and normative work."[10] One should note the qualification that "the stage theory provides a formally descriptive and normative model."[11] One stage structurally or formally considered can be judged better than another. The *structure* of stage 5 is better than that of stage 3, but that does not mean that a stage-5 *person* is better than a stage 3.

Because Fowler offers his theory as a "normative model" he expects that it can be directly useful for education. In *Life Maps* he writes that the stages "should help clarify the aims of education and religious socialization."[12] In *Stages of Faith* he elaborates upon that ambitious hope: "Education and nurture should aim at the full realization of the potential strength of faith at each stage and at keeping the reworking of faith that comes with stage changes current with the parallel transitional work in psychosocial eras."[13] Fowler warns that the stages are not "goals toward which to hurry people." I take it that they *are* goals and that what is wrong is the hurrying. But we should do what is possible to get people to advance across the stages as soon as they are ready.

Fowler refers to each stage as having an integrity of its own; therefore a person can live a rich life at any of the stages. Despite that, however, he is distressed at the willingness of people to settle down at the early or middle stages. He says, for example, that most religious institutions are stage 3, which means that individuals are not challenged to become stage 4. His rhetoric becomes harsh in describing television preachers who have mastered the art of preaching at stage 3, "offering a tacit version of Christian theology that centers in vicarious interpersonal warmth and meaning. . . . They constitute a parody of authentic Christianity and an abomination against biblical faith."[14]

This judgment on the basis of "authentic Christianity" and "biblical faith" may seem out of place in the midst of describing his stages. However, Fowler freely admits, at least when he describes stage 6, that he has had authentic Christianity and biblical faith in view all along the way. Fowler surely knows that to have a "normative endpoint" in a developmental scheme is a problem. I wonder, however, if like Kohlberg he underestimates the size and nature of the problem.

As I indicated in the first three chapters, developmental theories arose as a way of avoiding determinisms of both the beginning and the end. Piaget and Erikson in different ways create a tension of opposites so that their systems have no endpoints. They both recognize the paradox: To know the end of development is to subvert the notion of development because then the process of developing is merely an unfinished case of the developed and is therefore not very important. Fowler expresses surprise that "whenever I speak on stages of faith and try to describe the structural features and styles of each stage, it is always stage 6 that people are most interested in."[15] Naturally, if people find out where it all leads, then everything else becomes preliminary material which is reducible to steps on the way to the end.

What can Fowler do to avoid this plight? He needs imagery that resists being turned into a final solution to life's problems, imagery that keeps turning the question of an end back into the process itself. No single phrase or picture will be sufficient to avoid the danger; or, at least, even the best phrase or image will tend to turn into the object at the end. The mystical strand in each of the religions is a never-ending protest against turning heaven or even God into the end of life. Development requires the description of a kind of process that is definite but never-ending. I suspect that each religious tradition has such imagery but that it is nearly impossible to grasp it from the outside. In *Life Maps* Fowler refers to an "ecological metaphor" of ultimate environment which "if translated into Jewish or Christian terms would be called 'Kingdom of God' or as Teilhard de Chardin expresses it, 'the Divine Milieu.'"[16] Kingdom of God and Divine Milieu strike me as very different images, but perhaps the two images here are meant to be complementary rather than equivalent. In any case, Teilhard de Chardin does not appear in *Stages of Faith,* and all the weight rests on the Kingdom of God. I will discuss this image under stage 6. My point for the moment is that religious images have to guide and transform each stage of life; they are not simply "content" for describing the end of life's journey.

Fowler's Stages

Having raised some questions about constructivist theory and the image of the theory's movement, I turn now to the stages themselves. Fowler begins with a preparatory stage of undifferentiated faith. Here there is no identifiable structure. "Though really a pre-stage and largely inaccessible to empirical research of the kind we pursue, the quality of mutuality and the strength of trust, autonomy, hope and courage (or their opposites) developed in this phase underlie (or threaten to undermine) all that comes later in faith development."[17] The flavor of this description is clearly Eriksonian, and I have expressed my doubt about integrating this description with the stage descriptions that follow, at least stages 1 to 4. Fowler, in contrast to Kohlberg, is admitting with this pre-stage the limitations of his six stages.

If Fowler ever moves away from Piagetian stages, I imagine he will extend this description of undifferentiated faith beyond the three pages in *Stages of Faith*. I think he will also make more explicit connections between this pre-stage and what he calls stages 5 and 6. This infant stage is not constructed from direct interview data, but apparently stage 6 isn't either. We can today reconstruct some of the inner life of infants through psychoanalytic and other techniques. More important, if the question is not the *structure* of faith but some other meaning of faith—along with the meaning of hope, love, revelation, grace, and other religious categories—there might be more to say about the infant's development.

The first four of Fowler's stages are:

1. Intuitive-Projective (2 to 6/7 years)
2. Mythic-Literal (6/7 to 11/12 years)
3. Synthetic-Conventional (11/12 to 17/18 or later)
4. Individuating-Reflexive (young adulthood or later)

The first thing most people notice about Fowler's stages is that their names are not easy to remember. Fowler wants to force people to read what he has written under those imposing categories. He does not wish to be turned into a chart of catchy tags like Kohlberg's "good boy/nice girl" or "I'll scratch your back, you scratch mine." I will respect that wish by not substituting some phrase or sentence for his own description. His descriptions and interview data for each of the stages can be found in *Life Maps*, pp. 42-101, and *Stages of*

Faith, pp. 122-213. Here I would like to suggest some interpretive questions and make a few comments.

Each of the stages is a unified whole which Fowler can correlate not only with a form of logic but with a level of role-taking, a conception of authority, and a way of understanding symbols. What accompanies the idea of stable unities at each stage is that the movements between stages—transitions—become traumatic shake-ups. An individual is pressed toward transition when new experiences (e.g., leaving home) bring on new perspectives or when authority figures no longer supply a satisfactory answer. Fowler does not wish to equate stage change with the well-known phenomenon of religious conversion. He prefers to keep conversion for describing a shift in content (centers of value, images of power, master stories). He then constructs a complicated pattern of six possibilities for the relation of stage change and conversion. The Piagetian separation of structure and content introduces the need for this complicated answer which does not seem to throw any great light on the meaning of conversion.

Fowler's early stages correspond with Piaget's. By stage 3 Fowler is already dealing with Piaget's formal operations, and in stage 4 he has got as far as Piaget goes. The power to form abstract ideas and to use reasoning is a prerequisite condition but not a sufficient explanation for development in faith.[18] This claim is a strong one only when most factors in a situation are under control and a mysterious element or two escapes the explanation. However, when Fowler and Kohlberg refer to Piagetian theory as the basis of their theories, the case is not very strong. The second half of the scale is simply said to require Piaget's formal operations, the power to reason in abstract terms. As to where Kohlberg and Fowler wish to take their theories in advanced stages, Piaget is in fact of little help.

Fowler's relation to Kohlberg is more complicated. Both men acknowledge their debt to Piaget and then add their own conceptions at the further half of the scale. Kohlberg's addition, as I have said, is higher-level abstractions. Fowler is looking for a different movement, or perhaps it should be said he is forced by the evidence in his interviews to describe a different movement. At the first two stages we seem to have an easy correlation of Fowler and Kohlberg, at 3 and 4 they are diverging, and at 5 they are going in very different directions. Fowler can correlate some of his stage 3 with Kohlberg's stage 4 and can find Kohlberg's principled thinking within his stage

4. The power to perform accurate moral reasoning can show up in someone who gets to Fowler's stage 4. What counts is what the person does with that power in 3 and 4 in relation to the wider context of imagery, commitments, and personal character. Kohlberg's method leaves behind this context as extraneous to the high-level reasoning of 5 and 6. Fowler, on the contrary, is interested in the person's outlook on what has come to be the material of his or her life. This moment of Fowler's system would seem to offer fruitful questions for further research. Sharon Parks, for example, has distinguished two phases within Fowler's stage 4. She calls the first "young adult," a place where many college students find themselves. Parks then works out some helpful implications for people dealing with college-age students.[19]

Fowler finds that already in the first stage the child is suffused with grand pictures of the universe and also with great fears. Children can have a powerful moral/religious sensibility, a fact that is obscured in Piaget and Kohlberg. Fowler notes the significance of fairy tales in the development of young children. One has to be careful about the child's impressionability, he points out. Young children can be deeply affected by hearing preaching on the devil, sin, and hell or the way God punishes our failures. As history bears witness, if adults have the mind to do it, they can bring about dramatic "conversions" among seven- and eight-year-olds.

Fowler says he was surprised to find that anthropomorphic images of God did not emerge until the second stage. In the first stage, a clear differentiation between God and other reality was impossible. God may be imagined as "like the air—everywhere" but not imagined as another person. In stage 2, faith takes the form of story, drama, or myth. A more narrative and linear construction of meaning occurs then. I gather that is why Fowler uses the word *mythic* in the second stage. Depending on the connotations one gives to the word *myth*, I think one could also locate the word in stage 1. If myths are tales with grand conflicts of opposites, then the fairy-tale age surely qualifies as an age of myth.

Stages 3 and 4 are times of idea systems or ideologies. In stage 3 ideology is a possession not reflected upon, while in stage 4 it is a system of rules and standards consciously grasped. In stage 3 one is dependent for guidance upon external authority figures. If everyone in the same neighborhood or church holds similar ideas, then one can rest in stage 3. When there is great diversity in the environment and when the trusted institution or trusted people no longer speak with a single clear voice, then the individual is thrown back upon his or her own resources. If at that moment the personal center is strong enough, what emerges, according to Fowler, is an "executive ego." This moment is a precarious one in development. If one is thrown into a diversity that relativizes one's ideologies and there is no strong, centered ego, the person sinks into a sea of ideas. On the other hand, if the strong ego emerges without a relativizing of one's ideas, then the hard-edged ideologue may be the result.

The last two of Fowler's stages read this way:

Stage 5: Paradoxical-Consolidative; also called Conjunctive (after age 30)

Stage 6: Universalizing

In stage 5 the tension of opposites is striking, reminding one of the mature women in Gilligan's study rather than of anything in Kohlberg. The key is revealed in Fowler's description of the stage-5 woman in *Stages of Faith*: "As is characteristic of Stage 5, it was a new beginning that had to reclaim and reintegrate elements of strength from her childhood faith."[20] The spiraling effect and the process of recapitulation are apparent here. In some way one must come to terms with the unconscious—that is, with those forces in life that are outside direct awareness and conscious control. Stage 5 is therefore connected to the pre-stage as well as to stages 1 and 2.

Truth at this stage is not the view from the higher perspective but the view from multiple perspectives in one person. The mature person has to live with paradox, which can be done only if one's language and imagery are capable of supporting apparent contradictions. This statement does not imply that stage 5 is open only to the educated middle class who have high I.Q.'s Presumably many years of schooling should teach people about imagery and language; at least schooling should not obstruct the process.

What is at least as important is other kinds of experience not particularly associated with schooling. "Stage 5 requires that one know suffering and loss, responsibility and failure, and the grief that is an inevitable part of having made irrevocable commitments of life and energy."[21] One can interpret that passage to refer only to a minimum age; eventually everyone does experience suffering, failure, and grief, whatever the circumstances of his or her life. Obviously there are further questions of quality: the particular nature of one's response to failure, and how one has made those irrevocable commitments. Fowler says there is some evidence that persons who are "disadvantaged" or suffer oppression "construct Stage 5 perspectives earlier than do more advantaged persons."[22] The word *earlier* in that statement avoids a romanticism of the oppressed. Presumably many disadvantaged people are stunted in development because their suffering is unmanageable. Other suffering people, however, make progress faster than the average and become models of development for the rest of us. Lest the point be taken as an excuse for political inactivity regarding oppression of the disadvantaged, it is important to stress that the individual's response to suffering, not the suffering itself, is the reason for development.

Fowler's name for stage 6, universalizing faith, is the easiest name to remember, but the reality of this stage is the most doubtful. Perhaps a lack of clarity and a lack of persuasiveness should be expected, and they simply prove that most of us have not arrived at stage 6. Still, my question would be whether there is a stage here at all (in his meaning of *stage*). Fowler writes in *Life Maps*: "I am not sure that Stage 6 really describes or requires any basic structural advance beyond Stage 5."[23] He then proceeds to speak of the radical relativization of the self as center of the world and of self-spending action as characteristic of stage 6.

Fowler's interview data are apparently very scant for describing and illustrating stage 6. He provides one interview with a Catholic monk in *Life Maps* and no interview in *Stages of Faith*. In both places he lists names of well-known people (Mahatma Gandhi, Martin Luther King, Jr., Thomas Merton, Mother Teresa, Dietrich Bonhoeffer) as examples of stage 6. I am puzzled by this list of people that supposedly form a structural unit and puzzled by how the decision was made about each person. It is, of course, impossible to interview all (or nearly all) of them. Presumably one could identify certain characteristics from an analysis of their writings. Most of them have left a body of works, including in many cases an autobiography. *Stages of Faith* does not comment on these writings, referring instead to some of the public facts in the lives of these great people.

I do not see that these people have a "structure of faith knowing" that represents progress from stage 5. The one characteristic I see

Fowler stressing is *action:* At stage 6 one becomes an "activist incarnation" of the values of stage 5.[24] For the woman in *Life Maps* who had been described as stage 5, "the active and the contemplative must be maintained and not collapsed in either direction."[25] Fowler, if I interpret him correctly, is suggesting that the tension should be collapsed on the side of the active and that one should engage in a "selfless passion for a transformed world."[26]

I am not persuaded that all or even many of his examples illustrate this movement. One can no doubt claim that these people were passionately concerned with justice and love. However, their "actions" were often a refusal to do what most people think of as action to improve the world. Many of them took a contemplative attitude of detachment from this world. They recognized a strange paradox in the relation of contemplation and action that leads to detachment from the results of personal activity.[27] Some, such as Bonhoeffer, were forced into the situation; others, such as Merton, chose retreat. Where we have written evidence, there seems to me to have remained in the lives of these people strong tensions of interior life/external action, of powerful personal center/abandonment to providence, of intimacy with God/life in a cloud of unknowing. In short, the people Fowler cites as stage 6 seem to me excellent examples of stage 5.

I have already noted Fowler's introduction of the kingdom-of-God image into his description of stage 6. On the positive side, this metaphor should prevent us from thinking that the selfless passion he describes in stage 6 sinks us into an undifferentiated unity, what C. S. Lewis called "the great tapioca pudding of being." Kingdom of God is a reminder that all along we have been moving toward communal, social, and political unity. The personal does not disappear as it does in Kohlberg's super stage. The individual, on the contrary, becomes more and more unique by its relation to a community of persons and a "commonwealth of being" on the side of personal consciousness.

I have to admit a lack of enthusiasm for the image of kingdom of God. In fact, the phrase does not call up *any* image. That fact could be an advantage if the image is just eluding me and leading me on. But before one can transcend an image one must have an image to start with. I marvel at Christian writers using the words *kingdom of God* as if they carried an obvious image and meaning for most people. If one places kingdom of God where Fowler does, it assumes that the image is rich in paradox and tension.

Perhaps contemporary writing on this term will uncover or recover the rich possibilities of this term. Writing on the historical period of tribal federation before the kings in Israel is one rich source.[28] Writing on the parables and sayings of Jesus also promises new insight into the wildly paradoxical meaning of *kingdom of God*.[29] Modern Christianity on both the left and right collapsed the tension. The right wing of the churches used the phrase while withdrawing from political life; it did not seem to notice the anomaly of using an ostensibly political image, kingdom, in the phrase "kingdom of *God*." The left was more interested in realizing the *"kingdom* of God." While almost the whole apparatus of biblical and doctrinal Christianity seemed to be disappearing in their hands, the phrase *kingdom of God* remained preeminent. Those on the left did not seem to notice that as a simple political image, *kingdom* was as irrelevant to the twentieth century as many other doctrines discarded on the basis of irrelevancy. *Kingdom of God* in its rich biblical meaning may be recoverable by historians and exegetes, but the task for educators here is enormously difficult.

I agree with Fowler that some image, some intimation of unity, governs our assumptions about movement and development. *Kingdom of God* could be one metaphor that helps if its paradoxical meaning is attended to. I also think we should play with some other imagery to complement that of the kingdom or reign of God. One supposed advantage of *kingdom of God* is that it spans Jewish and Christian traditions. But I am *a priori* distrustful of all language that claims to include Jewish and Christian. Imagery that shapes lives and moves people has to be rooted in the particularity of a tradition. Thus, it might make more sense to use Sabbath and Body of Christ before trying to find a common image in *kingdom of God*. (It isn't even clear that *kingdom of God* sufficiently includes Christians; the image has been primary in Protestant Christianity, generally more peripheral in Catholicism.) No single image sparks the same response in everyone, which is why we need complementarity. Within Christian history a variety of images have shared center stage: redemption, salvation, resurrection, communion of saints, beatific vision. Some of them may be gone beyond revival; others may be among the most powerful images of the twentieth century.

Fowler's shift from talking of stage 6 into an explanation of *kingdom of God* indicates that the issue is not another stage but the image(s) influencing all the stages. *Kingdom of God* is not what we get to live in at stage 6; it is an image of time's end in the double sense of conclusion and purpose. The image binds our experience of ordinary time and our intimation of time's fulfillment. Fowler is right that we get intimations at every stage, including stage 5, of something greater still to come. Despite the complexity and tension of stage 5, people do act in light of images that attract them. Some people, at least at some times, do reach awe-inspiring and heroic simplicity of life.

I think, nonetheless, that there is great danger in adding a separate stage beyond the paradoxes of the religious outlook in stage 5. I mentioned that Fowler says people are always most interested in stage 6 and adds: "The more 'secular' the audience, the greater the interest."[30] The secular listener, I suspect, is anxious to leave behind all that religious imagery and finally get an explanation in simple terms of altruism over selfishness or enlightened reason over merely individual concerns.

Fowler acknowledges the problem of fanatical leaders who might be confused with stage-6 persons. He offers some helpful criteria such as inclusiveness of community and commitment to justice. Still, the problem remains when he refers to leaders who should try to create "a world made over not in *their* images, but in accordance with an intentionality both divine and transcendent."[31] The trouble is that all images *are* persons' images; humans cannot leave behind their own images for a divine intention known in a manner that avoids the ambiguities of human language and human images. If humans get *any* glimpse of divine intentionality, it is in the process of transcending human imagery for less inadequate imagery and in turn transcending that imagery. Anyone who claims to have transcended human images and have discovered what has to be done to realize divine justice is suspect. A more inclusive stage 5 might make another stage unnecessary. It might also suggest that the most spiritually or religiously developed are not necessarily famous people in the newspaper; it might be they "who lived faithfully a hidden life, and rest in unvisited tombs."

Fowler's Meaning of Faith

My comments on stages 5 and 6 lead to my final consideration in this chapter, Fowler's meaning of faith. The first section of *Stages of Faith* is called "Human Faith," and in the last chapter Fowler says: "Rather steadfastly I have kept the focus on *human* faith" (his italics).[32] Some readers may be puzzled: human as opposed to what? The next sentence begins "Except for a brief theological passage" and goes on to say that he hopes a variety of religious peoples can hear what he says, despite the temporary shift in stage 6 to (Christian) theological language. Fowler in fact makes two shifts: (1) from the first four stages, which are "human faith," to stage 5, which is "essentially religious,"[33] and (2) the further shift in stage 6 to "biblical faith," or to language that Fowler proposes is both Jewish and Christian.

The contrast between "human faith" and any other kind of faith threatens to open up the dichotomy which Fowler intends to overcome. "Human faith" is a peculiar phrase and seemingly redundant. I can only surmise that at the early stages Fowler is trying to exclude a religious meaning to faith. I think the choice is an unwise one.

Faith in its richest, most important meaning is not an object or a human possession. It is a gift to which a human being responds. As the applicability of the word *faith* widens (a movement that Fowler approves), the breadth of its meaning narrows (a movement that Fowler disregards). From the standpoint of Jewish, Christian, or Muslim traditions the most focused meaning of faith involves one simple issue: Have you accepted God's gift? Are you on God's side, or the devil's? The harsh language in each group dividing the world into "the faithful" and "the infidels" is an inevitable result of the logic of faith. The danger comes when a group presumes that it can infallibly draw the line between the faithful and the infidels. Jewish, Christian, and Muslim traditions at their most self-critical agree on this point: Only God knows for sure who is on God's side.

If one cannot even be sure of one's own faith, if faith is a disappearing point inaccessible to human view, what is Fowler studying? The answer, it seems to me, is those attitudes, expressions, symbols, and so on, which lead to and lead from that disappearing point of faith. Most people, I think, would call these things a person's religious life and the verbal part of this complex a person's religious beliefs. Strangely enough, the beliefs are just what Fowler insists he is *not* studying. He begins by opposing the word *faith* to both *belief* and *religion.* That choice may seem to work well in stages 1 to 4, but it does him in when he gets to stages 5 and 6. These last two stages reveal that from the pre-stage on, the evolution is of beliefs and other religious symbols. The biblical and Christian images at the last stage are a making explicit of what had been implicit in earlier stages. This claim is an arrogant one only if Christians suppose that development could have taken no other shape or that there are no images comparable to Christian images in their universalizing power.

James Fowler's meaning of faith heavily depends on W. Cantwell Smith's writing, especially *Faith and Belief.*[34] Fowler is attracted to Smith's meaning of faith because that meaning is so widely applicable. However, the simple structure of meaning that makes possible the wide applicability ("Are you on God's side? Yes or No") does not easily lend itself to a structure of development. Smith sets up a dichotomy between the fundamental orientation of the individual and the externals (doctrines, behavioral codes, rites) by which the same individual or other people can understand that orientation. Smith would claim that he is simply reporting what he has found in his careful and exhaustive study of the meaning of faith in ancient documents. The trouble is that since Smith must use contemporary English, he is limited by his own presuppositions and the ambiguities of the contemporary situation. Smith's thesis, beginning with the book's title, is that faith and belief are two different things. The sacred books, such as Christian, Jewish, Muslim, or Hindu, are all about faith and not at all about belief. There once was a time, Smith says, when the word *believe* could convey a sense of trusting and loving (a meaning still present in the German *belieben*); some of that meaning may have been there until the seventeenth century, but now *believe/belief* simply means the holding of certain *ideas* as true. Smith wishes to resist this reduction of faith to the holding of certain ideas, including whether or not a being called God exists.

I agree with the need to resist reducing faith to (1) assenting to truths that are not known by reason and to (2) the objects that one holds that way. Smith's solution, however, is not an improvement. He simply declares that faith is different from those meanings, whereas I would contend that in contemporary English *faith* can be more than those meanings but also includes those meanings. There ought to be an inner tension of several meanings of *believing;* there also ought to be a healthy tension between faith and the religious aspects of life. Instead, Smith collapses the tensions. He writes: "That religious people are expected to believe something is a modern aberration."[35] No doubt the statement is intended to shock, but it is not very accurate nor does it open new doors. I would reformulate the statement to read: "That only religious people are expected to believe something and that religious people are expected only to believe something is a double modern aberration." That statement would lead to an analysis of several meanings of *believe* and the relation of *believing* and *religious*.

Smith and Fowler are trying to get at activity, process, and development, as opposed to static objects. How can one do that with the word *faith*? Fowler likes to say: "Faith is not a *noun* but a verb."[36] That statement is simply not true. Everyone, including Fowler, knows that in English the word *faith* is a noun, and Fowler proceeds to use it as a noun. On occasion he suggests that we should invent a verb that does not exist—"faithing"—but he seems unwilling to lead the fight to establish it. The verbal form for the noun faith is *to believe*. Even if one were to agree with Smith that *to believe* has been reduced in meaning, it is immeasurably more likely that one can recover meaning that has been in a verb than invent a verb which no one seems willing to use.

The conclusion I draw is not that Smith should reverse sides and support *belief* instead of *faith*. Rather it is to recognize that there are several meanings of *belief* and that they are variously related to faith. What he assumes to be the "modern meaning" of belief is simply not borne out by contemporary usage. Undoubtedly in the eighteenth and nineteenth centuries the rationalistic intelligentsia were intent on pushing out the word *belief*. When everyone was enlightened, it was supposed, beliefs would disappear—at least all those superstitious, irrational beliefs of religion. Belief would then merely signify those things we hold as true but have not yet verified for ourselves. A funny thing happened on the way to this rationalistic heaven: It collapsed in the twentieth century. We have not returned to the seventeenth century, and we have not given up grabbing for rationalistic answers. The sea of belief that has been rolling in is not necessarily the one that Matthew Arnold saw retreating. Some of the beliefs are wildly irrational responses to scientific and technological reductionism. Some of the beliefs, however, are a simple return to sanity and to the recognition that the world's survival depends upon people believing. As Alexander Bickel nicely phrased it: "No one wants everyone not to believe in anything."[37]

The word *believe* is still used to mean trust, care, loyalty, and commitment. The usual sign of that usage is the construction *to believe in* followed by a person or a cause. Constructions vary, however, and sometimes no object follows or the preposition *in* is implied. A U.S. president asks Wall Street to believe in his program (economic policies, it is now widely admitted, cannot work unless people believe in them). A baseball player says: "You gotta believe!" Baseball fans need no further explanation. A labor union leader says: "We believe our cause is just"; grammatically "that our cause is just" is the object, but if the members are willing to risk their lives here, something besides holding statements as true is involved. When Ralph Nader began saying in the 1970s that "history belongs to those who believe," he was taking the same step as do innumerable other persons in the twentieth century: recognizing that facts are set within frameworks of belief. The philosophy of science is where one might expect an outpost for the defense of pure fact against mere belief. Instead, many philosophers and scientists today would grant that a fact is simply a strong case of belief. What we call a fact is merely the least inadequate model we have for a mysterious reality that is never encompassed by our rational concepts.

The contemporary world's use of *faith/believing* has only tenuous connection to the meanings in Bible and Qur'an. Still, for those who value Jewish, Christian, Muslim, or other traditions the connotations should be built upon. The opposite of faith, Smith says, is nihilism. In its own way that's what the contemporary world has been discovering. Our world needs to be linked back into religious sources through its beliefs such as the dignity of the individual or an opposition to oppression. Instead of severing faith and belief, we need to be working out the intricate web of meanings within faith.

Another statement Fowler regularly makes is: "Faith is an irreducibly relational phenomenon."[38] This statement is true only if belief is integral to faith. Smith and Fowler insist that *faith* is not a word denoting the subjective, that it is relational. The fact is that faith in the richest meaning that Smith stresses *is* subjective; it would be difficult to find a word that is more subjective. In its related meanings faith is not exclusively subjective; belief brings in the objective element. If Smith and Fowler wish to do something relational with faith, they ought to emphasize that belief is integral to faith. Instead, they work at cross purpose to their professed intention. Of course, to accept faith as necessarily embodied in a set of symbols that have verbal, political, and institutional reality is to shift a study of faith away from mental structures.

PART TWO

A Proposed Theory for Religious Educators

7

A Grammar of Religious Development

The term *religious development* meets two objections that are nearly opposite. People who take over the word *development* may object that religion is too static for development. Insofar as one believes that religion is a set of objects—a fixed code of morality and a set of truths revealed by God—then religion is an obstacle to human development, and one can become mature only by being liberated from religion's restrictions. In contrast, many people these days who are religious object to the word *development* as too fixed and pre-dictable for describing the growth, conversion, pilgrimage, or journey of religious life. The one point on which these two positions agree is that *religious development* is not a useful and accurate term.

However, my claim in this book, and especially in this chapter, is that we should not abandon the term *religious development.* To the religiously inclined I have argued in Chapter 5 and elsewhere that any substitute word (e.g., *growth, progress*) will be at least as prob-lematic as *development.* Furthermore, the word *development* is simply not going to subside in importance. Its usage is critical in the world of politics, economics, and ecology as well as in psychology. Religious people would be unwise to give up this common, useful word to people who profess to be "the developmentalists." To those who assume that development must exclude religion it is important to argue that, on the contrary, human development *requires* the reli-gious. When developmental theorists fail to be developmental enough, what is regularly lacking is the religious. A beginning way to define the word *religious* would be to say that it refers to whatever keeps open the process of development.

The meaning I have just attributed to *religious* is not some wildly inflated or vaguely generalized meaning. Of course, more needs to be said about concrete forms of religious attitude, religious experience, and religious language. Nonetheless, as a start the adjective *religious* refers to those attitudes and activities that challenge the limits of experience. In this sense "religious experience" is not a set of experiences (in contrast to non-religious experiences), nor is religious language a particular set of words or statements. Rather, the adjective involves an intended redundancy, not a reference to a particular set of experiences but to all of experience. The word *religious* should remind us that experience always includes more than we have grasped. When we think we have exhausted the resources of language, then religious use of language protests against prematurely stopping with the world as it is ordinarily named.

In the above paragraphs I have been, among other things, pointing out the distinction between the word *religion* (considered as a set of objects) and *religious* (referring to an impulse within experience, language, community, imagery, etc.). This distinction is part of what I call a grammar of religious development, my intended contribution in this chapter. A grammar is a modest but necessary contribution. Even if the data were available I could not lay out the whole story of religious development. What I can do is insist on several key distinctions that will make possible the emergence of a theory of religious development. These distinctions are denied, omitted, or at least underemphasized by many of the authors referred to in previous chapters. Besides the relation between the words *religious* and *religion* (already discussed briefly), I also want to note the relation between *religious* and *faith,* and between *faith* and *revelation.*

Before pursuing these distinctions by referring again to W. Cantwell Smith, I wish to set out a preliminary description of what I consider to be the stages of religious development. My outline is not based on the kind of empirical research done by Kohlberg, Gilligan, or Fowler. I am willing to test out what I offer against interviews or biographies, surveys of religious experience, and broad theoretical schemes of someone like Erikson.

In barest essentials, religious development of the person has three stages or periods. This pattern corresponds to a religious evolution of the race in which the first and second stages have clearly occurred; the third stage has been emerging in a precarious and fragile condition for several centuries. In most parts of the world, a person growing up today ineluctably goes through the first two stages but has no guarantee of an environment that makes the third stage a genuine possibility.

1. *The Simply Religious.* Young children are profoundly religious beings. The first part of life is one of a simple religious outlook. Moreover, what happens to them early in life affects their orientation to life as a whole and the images of life and death which they carry.

2. *Acquiring a Religion.* With the rise of reflective self conscious-ness the child's ego is now set over against a world of objects. The child at this stage begins differentiating between profane and sacred. Instead of being religious, one is now a Jew, a Buddhist, a Christian, and so forth. (Eastern religions have more fluidity here: One can be Buddhist and Confucian at the same time.) Nonetheless, some form of distinguishing "my people" and "not my people" is found around the world.

3. *The Religiously Christian (Jewish, Muslim, and so forth).* A further stage of development is demanded in adulthood. True, some people do go around the rest of their lives merely "having a religion" and professing that God is found only in that segment of reality. But the childish/adolescent attitude of having God in one's possession can be subverted by elements within religious traditions themselves (religious doctrines insist that God is free of any human control). Moreover, the twentieth century has been accelerating a process that forces people into this third stage: A modern consciousness cannot abide imagery that divides God's world from ordinary life.

What hangs in the balance is the kind of unity that the world is coming to and the kind of integrity possible in individual lives. We are all being pushed willy-nilly beyond the bifurcations of the second stage. The kind of unity I advocate—and I claim that by one's use of imagery and language everyone does advocate some kind of unity—is a rediscovery of childlike attitudes integrated with rational knowledge and technical skills. The religiously adult person is one who holds in fruitful tension the rational and nonrational, dependence and independence, action and receptiveness.

This three-stage development can be filled out with further distinctions and some descriptive material. Nonetheless, this simplest outline needs to be highlighted as the life-to-death framework of religious education. It is a framework not clear in Erikson's "eight ages" and a framework quite alien to Piaget and Kohlberg. It has some correlation to Fowler's stages of faith, though my focus of concern is not structures of faith but a complex of religious factors among which are several meanings of faith.

The tentative correlation I suggest to Fowler's stages is:

1. My first — Fowler's pre-stage and some of #1 and #2
2. My second — Some of Fowler's #1 and #2; Also all of #3 and #4
3. My third — Fowler's #5 and #6

Stage 1. Fowler's pre-stage of trust and mutuality clearly belongs with an initial stage of religiousness. Some of the things that Fowler places in his Piagetian framework of #1 and #2 also belong to early religiousness. Play, vision, fairy tale, and myth immerse the child in mystery, spontaneity, and great cosmic struggles.

Stage 2. Fowler's constructivist categories in stages 1 to 4 describe the great middle of religious development—what I call the second stage. The sense of individual ego emerges and directs the organism in its search for control. Fowler has helpful descriptions of temporal ordering, development of ideologies, and the pressures toward the relativizing of our religious convictions. The way beyond stage 4 opens as individuals discover that Piaget's formal operations are only an instrument in the search for life's deepest meaning.

Stage 3. Fowler's stage 5 corresponds to what I said is the third stage that most human beings reach, however tenuous is their hold. Some people enter it rather smoothly when they travel abroad, study at the university, start a family, or reexamine their religious life. Others may be suddenly pushed into it with their first heart attack at forty-five. Some may still be making the transition on their death-bed at eighty-five. Sufficient experience and a degree of openness bring about a reintegration of the childlike into one's attitudes and a re-imaging of one's relation to the universe. This final stage, because it is an acceptance of diversity within unity, allows unending development. Tensions of dependence/independence or action/receptivity are always capable of being worked out in richer ways. Because these relations are never an object of possession they can never be finally declared our own. The de-absolutizing of idols remains the constant religious vocation until death. The stage of religious adulthood is not a plateau or a peak but a journey toward the center of oneself and of the universe.

I have used the word *stage* with some misgivings. Like *development,* it is a good simple English word; it need not mean movement up a hierarchy of stages. Far from going straight up, the stages of religious development proceed with a circling back that creates a spiraling effect. The least inadequate image of the religious journey is that of a journey toward the exact center of a sphere. One can speak of moments, periods, phases, stages, etc., along this journey. The most explicit religious language might refer to stations on a pilgrimage. But no word or image is guaranteed to convey the synthesizing and integrating that religious development includes. All in all, it seems to me best to fight for a share of the word *stage* while supplementing that word with other words and images.

Religious and Faith

I return to James Fowler's and W. Cantwell Smith's discussion of faith. Here I am interested in how they relate the words *faith* and *religion.* Their opposition of *faith* and *belief,* which I discussed in the previous chapter, is part of their opposing *faith* and *religion.* They acknowledge, of course, that *faith* and *religion* may be connected, but they are intent on creating a distance between the two words. I agree that religion understood as a static object is a danger to faith, but I think one must make a special effort to save the living qualities in the adjective *religious.* Fowler writes: "Faith *may be* but is not necessarily 'religious' in the sense of being informed by the creeds, liturgy, ethics and esthetics of a religious tradition. Faith, rather, is a person's or a community's way of being-in-relation to an ultimate environment."[1]

Fowler in this passage gives over control of the word *religious* to the fixed forms and institutions we today call religions. That leaves him with no word for those activities, symbols, and formulas which mediate between the person and the ultimate environment. But is not "a community's way of being-in-relation to an ultimate environment" just what the term *religious* can mean and should mean? Fowler wishes to make faith the person's act of being in relation to an "ultimate environment." What that act necessarily entails is a *way,* a set of transpersonal symbols that make a relation to ultimate environment possible. That is precisely where the word *religious* belongs.

Fowler, like Smith, is fighting against a reductionism in the use of the word *faith*. He is insisting that faith is not the same as "having a religion." Faith ought to develop into something more personal and more profound than holding membership in an organization. We should note that each of the religious traditions in its own way acknowledges the same thing. The individual's faith is not a passive acquiring of creeds and practices but a means by which the tradition is re-created and transformed.

I have said that "having a religion" historically typifies one era of religious evolution and is also one stage in the individual person's religious development. The situation of "having a religion" is not bad, but it is also not good enough. Progress beyond this stage could be described in one of two ways: (1) A reduction in the significance of religion in relation to the personal act of faith. In that way religion would not obstruct the movement of faith toward the ultimate. (2) A recognition of the religious as whatever may mediate one's relation to the ultimate. Here the religious is on the side of faith as its necessary embodiment.

By always distinguishing *religion* from *religious*, I can include both of the above points in a theory of development. In fact, the two points are successive moments in the reform of religious organizations. Most likely they are also connected moments in the individual person's development. One must clear the ground of atrophied religion so that a personal religious life can blossom. The next generation, of course, has to repeat the process: A tradition while being passed on needs to be continually renewed.

In its most superficial meaning faith may not be religious at all. We sometimes say *faith* when all we mean is the holding of ideas as true—and those ideas might pertain to many areas, including religion. Smith and Fowler are interested in faith's richest meaning: a person's stance toward all reality. At this level, if the person's faith does not find expression in one of the world's great religious traditions, it will have to devise or discover religious expressions elsewhere. The more profound the act of faith, the more religious it becomes—that is, the more it finds embodiment in imagery, language and activity that reveal the ultimate.

W. Cantwell Smith makes a good point in saying that in recent Western history the struggle has not been between reason and faith but between faith in reason and faith in God.[2] I agree with his intent to strip away the illusion that one may choose either faith or reason. However, his proposed substitution of faith in reason versus faith in God is just as misleading, for it obscures the religious elements that embody faith. The conflict would better be described as between those who believed in technical rationality as the way to God and those who believed in the richest possible conception of humanity as the way to God. Both sides had their faiths; both sides had a God.

My statement of the conflict shifts and complicates the analysis. It also illustrates the importance of distinguishing *religion* from *religious*. Not everyone who belongs to a religion is religious and vice versa. In the early modern period, some of the Christian clergy were in the camp of a narrow technical rationality as the way to God. On the other side some people who were called agnostics were searching for a religious meaning beyond the limits of modern technical reason.[3] The twentieth century's choice is not between faith and reason; neither is it between reason and God. The choice, in William Lynch's terms, is either to build a human city for which an increasing use of imagination is needed, or else to build a walled-in city that excludes the nonrational part of ourselves and that part of the human race not advanced in the modern sciences and technology. Our choice of city reveals the God in whom we believe.[4]

Diagram 1

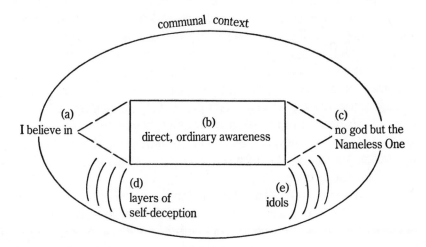

Faith and Revelation

The points made so far in this chapter can be brought together in the preceding diagram and the two diagrams on following pages that place faith within a process of revelation.

Diagram 1 represents the major elements and the main movement found in most religious traditions. (a) Faith as "a believing in" represents the attitude of the person toward the ordinary reality which is to the immediate right in the diagram and the more-than-ordinary reality farther to the right. (b) Ordinary awareness is the mundane existence in which we spend most of our waking hours. Our minds are filled with memories from the past, a jumble of present thoughts, and plans for tomorrow. (c) The point beyond the finite objects of our experience cannot be described. Religious traditions indicate it by a process of saying it is "not this, not this." (d) All the religious traditions warn us that we are deceived about our true selves. Without a discipline and transformation we cannot discover that point of "I believe in" that is deeper than our rational thinking and conscious choice. (e) The layers of idolatry to the right correspond to the layers of self-deception on the left. A lesser self sets its heart upon a lesser God; as false selves are stripped away, idols are revealed for what they are: substitutes for the Nameless One beyond all gods.

All the great traditions start with the ordinary person possessed of ordinary consciousness. All of them take their devotees on a developmental journey beyond anything these persons could have imagined at the beginning. There is a remarkable similarity of structure among the religions—a similarity that we are barely beginning to understand. Perhaps the twenty-first century will have the means to draw detailed comparisons. I am not suggesting that Yahweh, Brahman, and Nirvana are "different names for the same thing," though some writing on mysticism prematurely jumps to such conclusions.[5] Names in fact make a great difference as to where we are going and how we try to get there. Nonetheless, the writing on mysticism during the past fifty years suggests striking similarities of "developmental stages."

When we pass from early childhood into a stage of self-reflective consciousness, the religious mysteries of the universe recede. We sense that we are getting control of things by means of the systematic order that our minds impose. The possessive ego enables us to have a stable world of ordinary waking consciousness. It also cuts us off from the joys and anxieties, the spontaneity and fluidity of childhood. This developmental stage can issue in either of two attitudes that are ultimately abortive. Some people spend their lives wishing they could return to the simplicities of childhood. They try to leap out of rational consciousness into a simple faith, but they succeed only in being irrational. Other people use their energies to insist that childhood is finally behind them. They are unalterably attached to their reason, independence, and security, but *attachment* to these values does not necessarily mean attainment of them.

Religious development beyond this stage takes issue with both these attitudes. It patiently pushes back the walls of ordinary reality, thereby allowing the recovery of some childlike attitudes. Ordinary reason is not denied, but its self-sufficiency is called into question. Reason's lack of self-sufficiency is not remedied by the sudden introduction of a being called God. A God of ordinary consciousness would merely be one of those idols the mind can construct. God cannot be attained by notions of construct, make, conceive and possess. Religious traditions in a variety of ways turn the mind against itself, not in a destructive way but in a discipline of receptivity to reality. Through the use of pun, paradox, parable, and other literary devices, religious literature strains at the limits of language and prepares the mind for the One that cannot be named.

Diagram 2

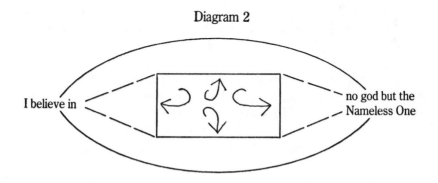

The process by which language keeps transcending itself is metaphor.[6] Religious development thus occurs by means of metaphors that are based on imagination, nourished in community, and rooted in tradition. How can we speak of a more-than-ordinary reality when in fact all our words are ordinary words? The answer is by a process of metaphor—by statements or implied statements that are literally false but which awaken the imagination to the mystery of things. In Diagram 2, statements within ordinary consciousness press at the boundaries in all directions. The religious literature of both East and West warns us not to be trapped by prepositions (e.g., God is above us, God is outside us).[7] If we wish to journey toward God, the movement is within and without, below and above, to the past and the future. The religious task is to leave nothing of our self behind even as we look for what is greater, truer, more really real.

Metaphor is the linguistic part of the religious journey. In much of recent history, metaphor was assumed to be a mere ornament of speech. Instead, it is the ground of all knowledge, and religiously speaking it is the point beyond which speech cannot go.[8] A metaphor is not just a word but an implied statement that forces together two unlike things. The well-chosen metaphor shocks us into the realization that we have settled too complacently for things as ordinarily named.

The dictionary is, to a large extent, a collection of dead metaphors; it draws all the obvious comparisons. The first time someone referred to the leg of a table, people probably saw both tables and human legs in a new light. When someone first compared sending radio messages to what a farmer does with grain (i.e., broadcast), it expanded the human imagination. A few years later, however, people are unaware of the metaphorical origin of the term they are using.

Religious literature is especially rich in metaphor because the attempt to grasp the human relation to what is ultimate necessarily strains at the limits of knowledge. The New Testament speaks of shepherd and sheep, vine and branches, head and body, father and prodigal son, owner and laborer, and hundreds of other images. Eastern religions that are more skeptical of language nonetheless deal in metaphor as well. The Bhagavad Gita, the sayings of the Buddha, or the writings of Sankara have to push at the limits of language with language itself. An empty mirror, a drop in the ocean, or a spark from metal are ways of talking about the nature of the journey and its destination.

Let me take one example from Jewish and Christian history that speaks to us today and raises a question for the future. When someone refers to God as our father, that may seem to some people a trite image. But for Pharisaic Judaism and the early Christian Church the image helped transform reality.[9] "God is our father" is a false statement in our ordinary biologically based meaning of fatherhood. Suppose, however, that the relation to the Nameless One is *something like* our relation to our father. We will then look at all reality in a different light, including the reality of ourselves and our fathers. This single metaphor did not jump out of nowhere; the ground was prepared by other images (for example, God as landlord, warrior, king, jealous husband). Even should one suppose that God as our father is the richest image that human beings can conceive, the fatherhood of God would still need a context of other images to convey its meaning.

Today the question is naturally raised: Why not "God our mother"?[10] Did not male imagery displace earlier goddess imagery? The change of imagery that took place over a period of centuries was not necessarily an unambiguous good. Undoubtedly, the metaphor of God as mother would have profound implications for individual autonomy and institutional form. Women and men would have to rethink what autonomy means in relation to a mother image; religious institutions would have to incorporate a nurturing element into their conceptions of authority. However, the difficulty of getting the metaphor heard indicates the slow process by which the metaphors of religious life change. The historic religions have both the strength and the limitation of being fixed in texts from one era; in Eric Voegelin's phrase, they have mortgages imposed on them by their historical origins.[11] Christianity, for example, cannot simply decide that Jesus should have called God mother. Nevertheless, religious development does not end with the fact that the text is fixed. Great literature is self-transcending; it unveils the authors in larger and larger contexts and challenges the reader to go deeper into himself or herself. Thus, if one could recapture the full context of the evolving Christian Church, including its origin in Judaism and Judaism's relation to competing religious forms as well as Judaism's subsequent relationship to Christianity and Islam, then the motherhood of God might emerge in the Church as a whole or in Judaism as surely as it does in the lives of individuals.[12]

The fact that it can emerge and has emerged in individuals creates a great impatience today. Must we wait a lifetime to see only glacially slow changes, particularly in Christianity, Judaism, or Islam? Some women today are trying to take a different route to traditions that preceded Judaism and Christianity or continued parallel to the dominant religious culture. There is increasing interest in witchcraft and goddess worship. A scheme of religious development has to allow for alternate journeys. However, one cannot get rid of centuries of religious development by simply stepping outside them. We have to confront in some way and at some time the historically given metaphors of our culture so that we can help to change them. Religious development does not proceed by wrenching out one idea and substituting another. Development means slowly becoming another person as the language of our community shapes and reshapes the whole of life. The rediscovery of female or feminine imagery seems to be one of the tasks to which our age is called.

Diagram 3

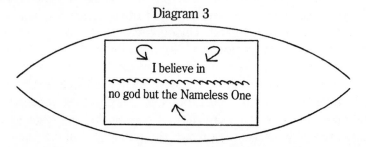

I am trying to show in this third diagram that the religious journey turns out to be simpler than first appeared. As imagination expands and the mind is quieted, we come to see the similarities among all things. Simultaneously, we become detached from superficial perceptions of the self and from the apotheosis of any object. The journey to the One beyond all names is a trip of no further distance than a coming to awareness of oneself. In the first diagram I had pictured the believing self far to the left and the Nameless One far to the right. Here I am indicating the revelation that these two converge in the depths of whatever is real. "If all things resemble one another then the pursuit of reality through metaphor becomes a whirlpool in which the poet can spin forever downward through a proliferation of resemblances."[13]

In this final state of convergence there are no longer subjects that perceive objects. Our ordinary ways of using language to name things, including the I, fail us at this point. Religious imagery that has any depth attempts to transcend the dualism of subject and object. However, as I pointed out in Chapter 4, religious traditions approach this nonduality in differing ways. Buddhism confronts in the starkest way the absence of objects, the no-thingness of a final condition. One could easily mistake that for simple nihilism, except that Buddhism plays with all final formulas to remind us that it is not making a simple denial. "Nonduality is not one, not two, not both and not neither." "The void is void also, of voidness." Hinduism is in many respects an approach to nondualism from the opposite side, developing the image of a great Brahman richer than the piecemeal of objects. As the atman or self is absorbed into that one true reality, we escape the illusions of this phenomenal world. Each of the Western religions has its own way of approaching a final nondualism. Whatever the variety in these religions, their greatest thinkers and mystics do not end with subject and object. God plus creature does not equal two. The Christian doctrine of the Trinity mysteriously says that God is numerically not one, not many, not both and not neither.

The formulas in religion are paradoxes that push our awareness back to the particular realities of everyday life. My three diagrams indicate that religious life begins with the concreteness of things and ends there as well. Religious progress comes about by an increasing awareness of the interconnections of things. [14] Imagination becomes less inadequate as we care deeply for things in their concreteness, their "suchness." One must put trust in particular words, in definite images, and in individual persons. Each of these realities is limited, but one can find that limit only by first caring for specific words, images, and persons.

The religious act of believing in is directed ultimately to the One beyond names. That no-thing can be reached only through penultimately believing in everything. Believing in is directed toward each of the things of our experience, not as a final resting place but as movement in that vortex toward a point beyond all names. Martin Buber warns that placing the word *God* as an object after *believe in* may convey a restriction of believing. We believe in everything/ nothing on the way to the One who shatters all our conceptions of God. [15]

If the I who believe in converges with the Nameless One, does that mean I believe in the self that believes? Should you "believe in yourself" as the popular self-help books urge you to do? The religious traditions advise "Yes, but. . . ." You should believe in yourself but not assume you already know what that self is. For example, the rabbinic tradition counsels: "Do not believe in yourself until the day you die."[16] That advice may seem incompatible with other religious statements like this one of Gabriel Marcel's: "At the heart of all fidelity lies the ability to be faithful to oneself."[17] My diagrams above account for both statements. We must trust in the best self we know, but the true self—the disappearing point in the diagrams—is revealed only at the end of our earthly journeys.

Religious traditions, such as Buddhist or Christian, believe in the self's convergence with the ultimate truth of the universe. Our problem while we walk the earth is that we know *neither* the self that is ours nor the One beyond names. In the confusion and fears of our ignorance we attempt to construct with words and images that are ready at hand a realm of safety for the ordinary self. Religions invite us beyond this defensive and possessive ego across a bridge of believing, trusting, and caring to wholeness, peace, and fulfillment.

Religious development in the East seems mainly directed by the image of enlightenment. Western religions have leaned toward the image of revelation. The two images have different connotations, but they do agree upon the need to reach a true self by penetrating beyond a false self. Western religion's use of the image of revelation is closely connected to its affirmation that reality is personal and personalizing, which includes the belief that the great Nameless One is accessible in ways that include speech. The image of revelation refers to what happens between persons at intimate levels of exchange. To be known, the secrets of the heart must be revealed— that is, unfolded with some degree of freedom, spontaneity, and unpredictability. Nonhuman nature can also "speak" to those human beings who are ready to hear. Revelation as a religious term is not a category confined to Judaism, Christianity, or Islam. It cannot be reduced to equivalence with a text. Revelation is a comprehensive image for the picture suggested by our Diagram 2, a pushing at the walls of ordinariness. As an image for the whole movement of religious development, revelation is the last word before silence.[18]

A weakness of modern Christianity that stymies religious development is the abandonment of the word *revelation* to fundamentalist preachers who are sure they know what God has said. The liberal branch of Christianity is embarrassed by the literal meaning of revelation. The claim that God unveiled his secrets to one group of people seems to be a primitive myth. Liberal Christianity has not developed an alternate pattern for relating rational knowledge to a kind of knowing that goes beyond human control. Christian images such as kingdom, covenant, and salvation presuppose some image in which the element of knowing is foremost. That is, how do Christians know about such things as covenant or kingdom? Modern Christianity's answer is: by faith. But faith, even if it includes the secondary meaning of beliefs, cannot carry the whole weight of religious knowledge.

The act of faith needs to be seen within a revelatory process such as described above. The religious journey will then be concerned with social, political, and institutional life. In that process, faith is a response in the deepest interior of the person. And beliefs can be situated as the least inadequate expressions of a developmental process in which the divine and human are revealed together. Just as the history of doctrine needs a larger context of church life to make the development intelligible, so a study of an individual's beliefs needs the context of the person's whole religious life.[19]

I do not see that the term *faith development* can carry the whole, even if one were to broaden the meaning of faith beyond mental structures to include beliefs. What can and should be studied is religious activity, including beliefs. Religious activities shift from one pattern to another in the course of a person's life. These patterns are visible wholes that cannot be captured in exclusively psychological terms.

By connecting religious development to metaphor I am locating the person in a social context; more than that, I am pointing to political, economic, and institutional questions. Personal theories of development, I have noted, often seem to exist outside of politics and without reference to struggles against injustice. Even the psychosocial theories transcend the psychological mainly by referring to other individuals. Psychological and psycho-social theories are mainly concerned with the inner life of the individual. As I have noted throughout the previous chapters, an obliviousness to the imagery that guides theorizing can mask sexual, economic, and other kinds of bias. Religious development, in contrast, revolves about the fundamental metaphors that relate a person to the universe. Politics in its richest meaning is the use of language for the governing of life; religion is never simply neutral in relation to politics.

I have suggested that in simplest outline, religious development includes two major shifts: (1) when the child realizes that there is an objective world and that the world includes objects that constitute "a religion"; (2) when the emerging adult realizes that the objects constituting one's religion can be an obstacle to the quest for some greater unity of life. Within the three stages so formed, the religious and the political interplay in the following ways.

At the first stage the child does not carry on any overt political activities. But the imagery one absorbs and the way in which speech is acquired set the stage for one's engagement in political and economic life. If religious activities provide a coherent way of life for the young child, religious life will be closely related to political life. Religion as "pie in the sky" is itself a political stance, a willingness to accept the lot of the oppressed as unchangeable. One should, however, be cautious about making that judgment in specific cases, for the powerful religious images of salvation, reconciliation, and righteousness can sustain an individual for years and a people for generations while political reforms are slowly realized.

Similar to what happened in world history, the child reaches a second stage in which a realm of politics is separated out from a realm of religion. One "has a religion" (or denomination) much as one might later have a Republican party affiliation. Religion becomes a complex object of study, one that can have its own realm of politics, such as ecclesiastical politics. In this stage politics means a certain breed of officials who preside over the distribution of power and wealth. As the realms of religion and politics further separate, many persons in the religious world become oblivious to political structures. However, some religious leaders try to apply their doctrines to political life. Some conservatives try to coerce the political world into submission; some liberal religionists, trying to be flexible and irenic, are forced to thin down their doctrines. In both cases the conflict of political leaders with religious spokespersons will most likely end in a standoff. Unless votes are at stake, politicians are not likely to be impressed by the doctrines, even when the doctrines are from the politicians' own denomination.

One could hope for a third stage of religious development in which current religious institutions would become more clearly distinguished from business corporations. Then we would have a kind of political-religious interplay different from that of officials making pronouncements. Religion would more directly influence personal choices in politics, and small religious communities would be influential through their teaching and example. I suspect that a transition into this third stage may be occurring today but will take generations to accomplish; institutions that include hundreds of millions of people do not change rapidly. I am suggesting, however, that individuals and small groups are already embodiments of that coming world. Groups that are concerned with saving the earth's resources or preventing nuclear war very often draw upon the historic religious traditions. To live with a religious-political integrity, groups have to resist much of today's organization. A Christian group might sometimes have to stand against the (current form of) church for the sake of the church (yet to be realized). Or, to use the distinction of *religion* and *religious*, a Christian religious movement is likely to have some conflict with the Christian religion.

The person who emerges into a rich third stage of religious development does not leave politics behind. True, such a person may become indifferent to the intramural squabbles of political factions. He or she does not trust in political solutions as the final answer to human dilemmas. Nonetheless, the religious person is at the heart of politics by protesting against imagery that narrows or demeans life: for example, imagery which assumes that all values are reducible to the exchange of the market system. Religious traditions supply poetry, narrative, and vision that keep imagination open to possibilities beyond the daily political battles.

By many common standards the third stage of religious development can be called conservative. Indeed, it not only conserves the past but rediscovers it. It does not spend its energies fighting free of doctrines; it reintegrates doctrines, rituals, and codes of behavior with an openness of mind but with passionate conviction. For example, it understands its sexual code not as threat or coercion but as an educative instrument for those who are ready. Having come this far on the journey, a religious person has a very definite orientation. One who has given a wholehearted yes to life can be quite absolute in saying no to the oppression of the poor, the destruction of beauty, and insane rationalism. Such a person may or may not take an active role in party politics, but the political effects of such a religious life can be earth-shaking. A religious community that is alive brings forth people with clear vision, steadfast character, and sustaining rituals that are the necessary context of political life.

The Three Religious Stages and Six Moments

In this section I will expand on the three religious stages previously named. Each of these stages can be divided into two moments that suggest a movement within each stage. The three stages and the six resulting moments can be labeled in the following way:

1. Simply Religious
   a. The Physical
   b. The Mythic
2. Acquiring a Religion
   a. Our People's Belief
   b. Disbelief
3. Religiously Christian (Jewish, Muslim, etc.)
   a. Parable
   b. Detachment

Simply religious

The first primordial stage of religiousness begins at birth, or some months earlier. It lasts until about five to seven years of age. Within that time two main moments are distinguishable.

Physical: One of the two greatest religious events in life is to be born. A passive attitude is suggested by that verb; not only that event but much of the first few years of life are spent in receiving. From the standpoint of rationalistic philosophy, life seems outrageously unfair in that our orientation to life so thoroughly depends on other people's action on us. We may not even be able to remember those actions that strongly influence the rest of our lives. From the religious standpoint this period of life simply manifests two connected characteristics that apply to life as a whole: (1) Whatever good we have is ours by gift, not by right, and (2) we are part of a community of persons; we do not save ourselves, but saving takes place in, with, and through other persons.

Primordial religiousness suffuses the whole physical organism. The conditions before birth, birth itself, and many experiences in the first eighteen months provide the small human being with imagery of life and death. Regular and affectionate physical contact with other human beings is indispensable. The right kinds and amounts lay the foundation for trust, care, and love. The power of the mother here can be overwhelming, especially when the mother is the exclusive caretaker of the infant. The fault is not mainly the mother's; she needs the help of other adults to share the power. Because maternal power is initially experienced as all-enveloping, many men spend their lives fleeing from the power of a great mother god. If power were first experienced as something mutually shared, it would not be grabbed for or fled from. Later the infant could experience separation as a step toward an adult interdependence of parent and son/daughter. If the child can interact with the mother and other adults, he or she is on the way to discovering that it is all right in every way to be human;[20] the child's initial experience of the mutuality of power creates a receptivity to whatever life brings.

The religious life of the small child is one of unending mystery and unalloyed wonder. The divine is everywhere, manifested in life's daily miracles. Ultimate questions of life and death, the origin and purpose of the universe, quite naturally arise for three- and four-year-olds. No one has to put religion into them, although conditions can surely abort a religious development. G. K. Chesterton captures nicely the contrast between this moment and a later moment of the first stage: "A child of seven is excited by being told that Tommy opened a door and saw a dragon. But a child of three is excited by being told that Tommy opened a door."[21]

Mythic: The second moment of this first stage when the child is delighted with dragons is an age of brilliant imagery and powerful stories. God or gods are alive in the universe. Fowler, as we saw, finds that children at five or six have not formulated the concept of a personal god. For them, the divine is a power manifest in all intense experiences. Religious experience can be joyful and also terrifying. If the child's fear can be put in the form of story and image, then the fears become bearable. Such is the function of fairy tales, a second language of children for expressing these terrors. The child of five or six knows that a great cosmic battle is raging. Stories give assurance of the triumph of good over evil.

Studies in recent years reveal that children—at least some children—have intense experiences that stay with them for life. Edward

Robinson has gathered together the testimony of people who in their 50s and 60s can remember in vivid detail the religious visions they had as young children.[22] The child with such a vision might even pity the ignorance of grown-ups. Children can have an eerie sense of death; a parent's death can be the ultimate terror. Surprisingly, however, for some young children death means that "the door of eternity is already open; for them, death stands not for frustration or annihilation but for liberation."[23] The mythic structure that dominates the child's mind is dualistic. Life and death are in a struggle; all the other powers of the universe are involved. The religious life of the child is one of wholeheartedness, the desire to be on the side of life.[24]

Acquiring a religion

The second stage in the child's religious development entails a separation of what had been united. The previous dualistic pattern of mythical thinking prefigures a growing polarity in the ways of thinking. The child gradually comes to see that some things are living and some are not, what is a person is clearly opposed to what is not, God is a person and not anything else. As we shall see, these beliefs can be subverted later in the stage.

Most educational resources in the modern world have been aimed at this stage of development, which starts at five or six and lasts through adolescence. An individual has a great capacity at this time to gather and store information. Also, he or she develops the ability for abstract thinking and so can set out to construct a system of ideas. The description of a second religious stage cannot pretend to be a description of "natural" development or one that applies to all cultures, for artificial construction surrounds this age. The obsession of the modern world to direct and control this second stage of development—while neglecting the educational possibilities of the first and third stages—is a chief concern of my last two chapters.

Our people's belief: As soon as children pass from a primordial religious immersion in the universe, specific beliefs and regulated practices are bound to arise. Historically the human race went through that development, and something similar happens to every child today. Children at this age ask questions and receive answers that begin to clear up some of the mysteries of the universe. The answers come from parents, teachers, or other trusted adults who at first seem omniscient, although that assumption is quickly overturned these days. Still, the beliefs about the way the world is are tied into assumptions about "what everyone knows to be true."

When the Lynds did their study of *Middletown,* they identified a class of statements as "of course" statements.[25] Questioning a practice that was peculiar to the United States, to Indiana, or to a neighborhood of Muncie would be met with the bemused response: "Of course, everyone knows that. . . ." The firm convictions of a group can range from "salad should be eaten before the main course" to "homosexuals are abominably evil." Every individual acquires thousands of such beliefs from the simple fact of belonging to a group that has a certain outlook on the world. Later on these beliefs can deserve the name *ideology,* but that word connotes a systematic and defensive pattern of thinking. At first the child has these ideas simply because they are "our people's beliefs."

At an earlier historical period this moment could be called the tribal phase of religious development. The child acquired knowledge of how to get along in life; included in that knowledge was the proper worship of the tribal deity. In today's world the parents bear most of the burden of the tribe, including the task of handing on religious beliefs.

The idea is widespread that the family is disintegrating and that parents have too little influence upon the child. Actually, the family remains enormously powerful as a religious influence. One could even suspect that the family is too powerful. God is still imagined as a father who has laid down clear rules, and against that powerful backdrop other religious imagery must struggle for a hearing.

A family in our culture is likely to have some religious "affiliation." A Jewish child will almost certainly have a sense of "our people" in which the Jewish family is located. Christian children are likely to have some sense of peoplehood, too. Catholics often have that sense mediated through ethnic practices and a Catholic belief system. Protestant children may acquire it directly from the Christian story in the Bible. "Our people" has to have some great past (it could be suffering as well as victories) with which the child can identify. Story can now take on the more specific characteristics of historical narrative. Early in this stage the child starts putting order into past, present, and future. If beliefs are set within the framework of an historical drama, they are not obstacles to thinking. The child has become "a Jew" or "a Christian." At its best the wording means identification with some particular people who have a past and are shaping a future. At the poorest level the wording merely means "denomination," the one among many religions I happen to hold membership in.

The beliefs of a people, its story about God and itself, are nowadays typically found in written form. At a particular historical moment the storytelling found expression in the written text. The gains in permanence, accuracy, and accessibility are obvious; the drawbacks have not always been as obvious. The sacred writings could easily be taken as truths dictated by God; the twentieth century has been recovering the artistic form of the Bible, a book whose full effectiveness is tied to its being appreciated as literary art. An earlier tendency was to see the Bible and other foundational documents as a tidy summary of what we are to believe, and the child at this stage of religious development may likewise assume that the Bible (or perhaps some other book) has the answers. Why bother with the ambiguities of religious experience and religious searching if the answer is available in a text? The apparent vagueness of being religious is replaced by the concreteness of being a Christian (a Jew, a Muslim). Other people merely have religion; our people have the faith. Thus in history the words *Christian* (or *Jewish* or *Muslim*) and *religious* become separate and opposed.

Disbelief: The title "Disbelief" is intended to be a little shocking or at least disconcerting. Current theories of development often seem to imply a steady unfolding from stage to stage, with some ripples of trouble in the transitions. Fowler, however, as I have noted, does want to include conversion and circular movement. I doubt that faith as the primary idea provides enough flexibility to trace the currents, whirlpools, and eddies of religious development. When the child of the second stage has built up a system of beliefs, more of reality intrudes and the young person must begin dismantling the system. This moment of development is not *unbelief* (a word that may not have any logically coherent meaning) but *dis-belief,* a movement guided by what the person is fighting against. One begins disbelieving the very beliefs recently acquired because both in their form and content they are too limiting for the journey toward adulthood.

Much writing on conversion errs in assuming that conversion happens but once. I think it is quite possible for the young person in this country to have three conversions: from the first to the second stage, within the second stage, and from the second to the third stage. The first of these conversions is toward being Christian (or Jewish, or whatever) and consists in acquiring a Christian language at an early age. While this conversion can be a helpful step, it is not to be greatly trusted in itself. Within the second stage there is a conversion of disbelief. It is usually a necessary prelude to asking more profoundly religious questions of one's religion. An individual who begins to disbelieve that his or her beliefs are adequate will then have to ask: What do I really believe in? The answer can bring about the beginning of adult religiousness in the third stage.

Ironically, the religious tradition sets the stage for its own problem by providing a coherent picture of the universe. Religious belief gives assurance that the world can be understood and that it is all right for the individual to trust his or her thinking. Thus the medieval Church, not only by its corruptions, but also by its high-powered thinking, gave birth to the Protestant Reformation. Just as a strong family upbringing for a child makes possible strong rebellion against the family, so a powerful Christian education can issue in later disbelief, not as a matter of statistical failure but as a next step in religious development.

Disbelief is directed at the external, verbal side of faith. Discontinuity at that level can happen even while there is continuity in the attitude of believing in, activities of care and love, and opportunities of risk and courage. The young person's character perdures and develops while a thousand confusions cloud the mind. John Henry Newman's "a thousand difficulties do not make a doubt" is true if by doubt one means a basic infidelity. More realistically, one might admit the word *doubt* and then distinguish two or more kinds of doubt. Judaism, attached to definite behavior, has more room to allow doubts in the mind. Even to the extent of doubting the existence of God, a Jewish answer is: Pray to God about that.[26]

The progress within adolescence is likely to be a movement from religious to philosophical. For many young people, Christianity having edged out the religious early in the stage, what follows is often some form of modern philosophy. Especially for the academically bright student, there is a moment at which building the philosophical system (with an accompanying anti-religious attitude) seems to be the answer to all problems. The apparent strength of the adolescent can be very misleading because this constructed system of ideas may exist separate from the emotional upheavals that so many adolescents experience. We saw that in Fowler's fourth stage the individual's executive ego needs to emerge with the relativizing of the world view; otherwise there is trouble.

The prevalence of religious cults today and society's way of coping with them can attest to the accuracy of these comments on disbelief. The young person is going through a fairly normal pattern of disbelief. Childish beliefs do not work anymore, and yet no one can live without believing in someone and something. Society provides little space for individuals to rebel against their religious upbringings and yet hold on to their underlying love of family and friends. More important, society offers few outlets for the sense of religious devotion and great commitment to causes. If no non-exploitive agency is available to receive religious devotion, then some authoritarian individuals will be very willing to use it.

The majority of young people do not seem to go through a spectacular passage of disbelief. Nor does religious devotion reach a fever pitch at this time of their lives. The childish/adolescent religion is destructured, and those who have developed a strong ego may put their energies to work at being a success in this world. Current studies of adult development support what Gordon Allport said many years ago: "There is good reason to suppose that on the average the early and middle twenties are, in fact, the least religious period of life. It is then that the alienation from parental codes has become complete. It is then that youth feels most secure in pursuing his life's ambition. He has not yet had the rude shock that comes to nearly all adults when they first realize that their abilities and probable accomplishments are, after all, not likely to equal their aims and pretensions."[27]

In the above quotation Allport's use of the masculine pronoun should warn us of a possible male bias. In the past, the pretensions and ambitions of men emphasized the value of independence and of trust in mastering the environment. In that same past, women were supposed to follow a different pattern. What the pattern for women in the future will be or should be is not clear. We do have some evidence that religious development occurs differently for a woman with a career in business and for one who is raising a family. A woman facing the questions of a four-year-old confronts religious issues that a vice president at a board meeting does not.[28]

Religiously Christian (Jewish, Muslim, etc.)

The third stage of religious development reappropriates childhood's best attitudes, providing the needed context for being Jewish, Christian, Muslim, or whatever. One no longer has a religion; one is religious in a particular way. To be religiously Christian today, one has to live in relationship, especially with an appreciation of Judaism and Islam. Someone religiously Christian recognizes someone religiously Jewish, for example, as sharing a common religious quest. Both quests can be seen as valid because the two groups are on the way even though the particularity of one's own way is what is most valued.

Parable: I call the early part of the third-stage *parable* to indicate its outlook and mode of speech. Persons in this historical era are being forced beyond the second stage. They pass beyond the negative stance of disbelief and decide to set their hearts on something. An unsuccessful religious transition leads to a continuing succession of idols or to a henotheism of several gods at once. In either case the heart is given over to a god that is too small, and no adult wholeness results. Yet, while a human being lives, the possibility remains of being awakened to the need for religious integrity. When we are young we hope to find the right principle, the right system, the right solution. Parables, such as those in the New Testament, are stories that make us reflect on life's paradoxes and inequities. A parabolic attitude is the recognition that the search for answers must go on but with a different expectation of success. We realize that we are never going to reduce life to a rational system. "In important matters we understand not as we simplify but as we can tolerate the paradoxical."[29]

The parabolic moment largely corresponds to Fowler's fifth stage, where he finds it necessary to introduce the adjective *religious*. As can be seen in Fowler's subjects, the earlier parts of life are now brought into tension within the present. The infant's sense of unity, the child's sense of duality, and the adolescent's sense of rational system all come together in adult religiousness. Religious language is now understood to be not a set of sacred words or a collection of texts or sacred objects but a process of using language to subvert our conceptions of the ordinary world and reveal deeper truth. In adolescence, the role of storyteller is diminished. Story drops to the background and we prefer the factual. In adulthood, life itself is understood as a story, and fiction is now seen as sometimes more revealing than fact.

The particular form of story that best captures the spirit of this moment is parable. Starting from some simple experience of ordinary life, parable awakens the imagination by twisting back on the premises we brought to the story. For example, the treatment of the Prodigal Son in relation to his brother is likely to run counter to our assumptions about fairness and justice. Parable, like myth, features a duality of principles. In parables no single answer issues from a problem. Rational logic turns out to be incapable of giving a solution. It is true that in much of the history of Christianity, parables were thought to be moralistic tales with instructions to behave in one way. But a contemporary understanding of the parables sees them as asking us to live within the tension of the story itself.[30]

Living with a tension of opposites does not mean the paralysis that is non-action. Life demands activity, and the religious person is engaged in acting the best way he or she can discern. The religious adult does not possess a detailed and complete plan, does not claim to know what God's justice is or what is in God's mind. But the person who is formed by parable does claim to be able to recognize blatant injustice. There are things wrong in the world, and someone must take the risk of stopping them. A parabolic outlook gives one a sense of belonging to a specific group and a particular history. The religious adult appeals to "my people" as an embodiment of "the people." The beliefs of our people can now function not as blinders to a wider truth but as powerful stimuli to act on behalf of all.

One is not likely to attain a parabolic attitude before one's thirties or forties. Physical changes may help bring on the development; the first heart attack in men is often a powerful instigator of a new look at life and death. With a different biological timeclock, women may develop this attitude earlier and with less trauma. The lack of empirical studies and the shifting position of women today make firm conclusions on the point impossible. We do know that many successful men go through a dangerous period of burnout when the thought comes to them, sometimes like a flash out of the sky, that no matter what they do, the world will not be right in their lifetime and that success leads nowhere but to the grave. If a man can be helped beyond that crushing vision, he can start acting again to reduce the sufferings of this world. And his action will now be more effective because he has discovered the humanity he shares with those who bear the heaviest burdens.

Detachment: The parabolic attitude shades off into the final moment of detachment. In the second stage the earlier and later moments are in such contrast that one might think them not a single stage. Not so in the third stage. The parabolic is never left behind. It is simply deepened and enriched by the development of a contemplative center to life. As usual, time is the necessary but not the sufficient condition for this moment of the scale. Eastern religion emphasizes this contemplative element but runs the risk of undercutting political struggles against injustice. Nonetheless, Western religions could learn from the East that one must finally be detached from everything, including one's own life.

Detachment is a peculiar moral/religious term that is easily misunderstood; however, that is true of all paradoxical religious language. The detached person may be active, but the word *action* has been transformed. One must act without looking for the "fruits of one's actions."[31] Detachment means the willingness to wait, the determination and the patience to stay at what one feels called to. Whether one's work is to design a cathedral, mop floors, govern a nation, or lie flat on one's back in pain, the human vocation is to stay at one's post and do the best one can. And after doing the best possible, the detached person takes no credit but returns glory to the source of all gifts.

I am describing here the furthest mystical stage. Meister Eckhart, for example, uses *detachment* as a favorite word to describe the mystical path.[32] I am not presuming, however, that detachment is only for a few mystical souls in the unitive way. I am assuming this characteristic to be common in later life. Those who have come to terms with life and befriended death are aware that the human being leaves this world as he or she arrived. The very old have something of the same simple vision of unity as the infant. But now the unity is a synthesis of all of life's elements, and one prepares for a new birth.

No one knows exactly what happens after earthly death. The immovable religious conviction is that death is not god, not the ultimate reality. Our lives move toward deeper communion and toward the heart of reality. The detached person knows that this movement of a lifetime is not a fraud. Belief in life beyond life is based on a lifetime of evidence. All the major religious traditions point to a unity where the dualisms of this world are overcome. The interpretation of this nondualism differs widely and the differences in doctrine deserve study. Likewise, the variety of imagery that sustains a person in old age or sickness is not insignificant. Still, those who love life and are detached from a possessive attitude toward it have a remarkably similar attitude of calm acceptance of life so long as life is offered, and a childlike acceptance of death when the time has come.

8

A Grammar of Educational Development

The same question must be raised here about the word *educational* as was asked at the beginning of Chapter 7 concerning *religious*. Is the introduction of the qualifier *educational* a faddish extension of developmental thinking into an area where it does not belong? Should developmental theory be left to the psychologists, and after they have done their work might educators decide whether to use the theory? My twofold response parallels my defense of the term *religious development*: (1) Education needs the idea of development so that we might have better educational theorizing and (2) development itself needs to be conceived of as educational or else it will not be an adequate account of human development.

On the first of these points, educational theorizing remains to this day rather thin. People have theorized about education at least since the time of Plato and probably long before that, and the educational ideas of great thinkers from the past can of course still nourish us. An adequate theory, however, would have to incorporate the complex patterns of modern life into which each person is now born. During recent centuries, especially the last, we have placed nearly all our educational eggs in the basket of the school. Our system was built on a simple premise: People of a certain age (children) should go to a certain place (school) to receive a certain package of information (education). That seemed like a reasonable way to cope with a complex world. The only problems seemed to be opening the ideal to more children, building better schools, and providing the information more efficiently.

Much of society is still intent on following this ideal. Many poor people around the world are anxious to get in on the benefits of education. For some years, however, an increasing number of people have felt that the ideal itself is in trouble. Signs of erosion pop up everywhere: decline of test scores, voting down of school bond issues, violence in school buildings, Ph.D.s out of work, and dozens of similar phenomena. The biggest problem of all is that having turned over educational language to those who train children in school, we now have no alternative language with which to ask different questions. A new language has to be created, one that rediscovers some old meanings and insists on some key distinctions. The notion of development, I will try to show, is central to that enterprise.

On the second point, we will never have an adequate meaning of development unless education is intrinsic to the notion. What distinguishes the human being is its educability. Other things in the universe grow, evolve, or develop, but the human being's special kind of self-direction requires education.

If human life is to remain always open, as the modern meaning of development requires, then it cannot simply follow preordained instincts or fulfill some set plan. The human infant starts with an astounding range of receptivity to impressions. The child could not survive the first two weeks or two years without adults directing, controlling, protecting, shaping, and inspiring it. Education begins no later than birth, but our educational language obscures that fact. Education also continues beyond the age of sixteen, twenty-one, or whatever age we tell young people to go out and face the world. Human development stops whenever education stops, but the current poverty of our educational language hinders us from seeing human development as lifelong. Bernice Neugarten, long a student of middle age and old age, says our theories of development are still "childomorphic." The compelling issues of adulthood (work, love, time, death) are not the main themes of developmental psychology.[1] I want to note three signs and symptoms of progress, however, before introducing my main distinctions:

1. Jerome Bruner's work in the 1960s was directed, he said, to a theory of instruction.[2] Previous theories of development, he claimed, were only theories of learning; they delineated what a child *could* learn. That is valuable to know, but it does not address the questions of the educable animal: What *should* the child learn out of all that it

could learn? How does one person help another person to learn so that each generation need not reinvent civilization? Bruner wrote: "The heart of the educational process consists of providing aids and dialogues for translating experience into more powerful systems of notation and ordering. And it is for this reason that I think a theory of development must be linked both to a theory of knowledge and to a theory of instruction, or be doomed to triviality."[3] I think one must broaden the theory beyond instruction to education; nonetheless the theory that Bruner described was a step in the right direction.

2. Some of the liveliest educational writing in recent decades has been in the curriculum area. Curriculum theorizing in the first half of this century did not break much new ground. Curriculum was understood in a mechanical way, and questions revolved around improving the efficiency of the machinery. That writing found a culmination of sorts in Ralph Tyler's 1950 monograph, *Basic Principles of Curriculum and Instruction.*[4] In Tyler's view there are four steps to instruction: objectives, selection of experiences, organization, and evaluation. One decides on the objectives after perusing studies of learners, studies of contemporary life, and listening to suggestions by subject-matter specialists. What Tyler called *educational* objectives, later writers called instructional, then behavioral, then performance objectives. Tyler did have a kind of instructional theory, as Bruner said we needed. However, without a real educational theory, instruction becomes narrow, impersonal, and technologized in meaning. Tyler's monograph and associated works such as Bloom's taxonomy of objectives have been the focus of reaction by other curriculum theorists.[5] They are certain that there is more to say about curriculum than "needs assessment," organization, and testing. I will presently return to what I see as a large stumbling block in this literature.

3. Kieran Egan's *Educational Development* is a provocative little book, one that the author claims is the first book on its topic.[6] The only precedent he can find for his work is Alfred North Whitehead's *The Aims of Education.*[7] Whitehead's three stages of romance, precision, and synthesis suggest there is a movement different from what we often assume must be the sequence: from easy to difficult, from simple to complicated, from concrete to abstract. Egan notes that Whitehead's scheme is so general that it provides little practical

help for teachers. Egan's own theory proposes a description of development in four stages: mythic, romantic, philosophic, and ironic. These four stages describe the way people learn best and the way education should proceed.

Egan may slightly exaggerate by claiming to have invented the field of educational development. For example, some of the writing on curriculum just referred to is surely concerned with educational development. If Egan's response is that curriculum theorizing has not created a theory to cover the whole range of development, the same would have to be said of his own book. That is, although I find his four stages very helpful and will later rely on them, I am troubled by the fact that he omits the beginning of life and the end of life. Like curriculum writers, Egan wishes to transcend the image of education as training the child for later life, but he does not entirely cut loose from modern culture's twofold assumption: (1) Education is what you get in school and (2) school is for children.

My own conclusion is that we have to stop making this twofold assumption if we are to have educational development. We have to stop saying *education* when in fact we mean *school* or *schooling*. Among writers on education one could find an apparent agreement on the legitimacy of this distinction. But in practice one finds no consistency in making the distinction. Writers on curriculum are especially striking because so many of them are intent on breaking out of the confinement of textbooks, lesson plans, and syllabuses. What they often break into, though, is heady discussions of phenomenology, existentialism, and critical theory. The indispensable distinction, which they need but do not consistently advert to, is one between *school* curriculum and *educational* curriculum. Curriculum theorizing would be much simpler and more practical if it made that distinction. Why, for example, is so little said about the family in curriculum theory? If one were clearly talking about education and not just school, the family would immediately loom large.

A Test: The Meaning of Teaching

I propose that a key test of how writers use the word *education* is their references to teacher/teaching. What do books on education mean by teacher/teaching? Nearly always, school-teaching is either the exclusive reference or at least the primary analogue. There is the real meaning of teacher—the professional schoolteacher—and then there are lesser forms of teaching found elsewhere. As the word *professional* indicates, part of the problem is simply the professionalization of every sort of specialty in the modern world. This process is particularly dangerous, however, when it means cutting loose from its roots in ordinary life a universal and fundamental activity such as teaching.[8]

We all use shorthand in an assumed world of discourse. No one reasonably objects to saying *the* sun although it is merely *a* sun, the one in the earth's solar system. Football announcers need not keep repeating the word *foot*ball (though they usually do) when everyone watching knows it is not a baseball or basketball. If one is talking about the workings of a school, one naturally says *teacher* in contrast to *administrator, student,* or *janitor.* But if one is theorizing about education one ought to say *schoolteacher* if that is what is meant. The point is not to lessen the significance of the schoolteacher's work but, on the contrary, to give it added help. The beleaguered schoolteacher will never get very far in understanding teaching if he or she reflects only on schoolteaching. If one wishes to reflect on the art of teaching, a natural place to start is to think of a parent with a child. The adaptations and qualifications of the school setting would then be included as one moved from what teaching is in more typical settings to what *school*teaching is.

Teaching is an activity that adults provide for the young and for one another. A teacher shows someone else how to do something. In the act of teaching, words are choreography for the body's movement. Good teachers have the know-how to break up a complex activity in ways that help the learner. Schoolteaching is a peculiar kind of teaching, a limit situation in which the words are mainly about words. Schoolteaching can therefore be the emptiest kind of teaching, although when the conditions are right it can be very powerful. A long-standing argument concerns whether anyone can teach if no one is learning. The answer to that question is: Yes, in the limit situation of schoolteaching. In more normal teaching situations (e.g., teaching a child to ride a bicycle) the teaching and learning are so bodily related that the question can hardly arise, for teacher and learner have a sense of mutual success or mutual failure.

Our equating teaching with schoolteaching reveals why we have progressed so little in understanding curriculum and development. If we think of teaching as what a certain group of adults are trying to tell children past the age of six, then we have an insoluble problem of "the child versus the curriculum." We don't seem to have gone much further than John Dewey's essay on the topic.[9] We go through cycles of putting the child at the center or the subject matter (as in "back to basics"). But Dewey at least tries to reconceptualize the question in relational terms, a direction more fruitful than that followed by many lesser writers after him.

Unfortunately, Dewey's language contains two fatal flaws that ought to be evident today: (1) By curriculum he means school curriculum. Although Dewey wishes to distinguish school and education, he pessimistically and inaccurately assumes that other educational agencies (e.g., family, church) are impotent. Unwittingly he collapses the meaning of education to what schools do. (2) Like writers to this day, Dewey says *child* when he should say *women* and *men*. An educational curriculum has to be for life. Dewey rightly objects to the myth that children are dependent and adults are independent; that premise identifies teaching with the authority of adults and the obedience of children. But we have not freed ourselves of that myth; indeed recent educational literature has reinforced it.[10] We cannot get free of this bind until we begin to imagine and to speak of educational development as lifelong and to speak of teaching as the specifically human help that any person can give to another.

An Image of Education

My intention in this section is to provide an image and a descriptive definition of education, a grammar that would be adequate to a developmental idea of education. Discussions of education in the modern world are remarkably tame, for the most part. Some of the literature flies off into general and global aims (the quality of life, the good life, the whole person) that no one objects to because nothing definite is proposed. Other writing descends into scientific facts and marketable skills that no one objects to because the question of value is seemingly sidestepped. We get shocked into attention only when parents in West Virginia reject the school's textbooks, a group in Arkansas wants "scientific creationism" in schools, or parents in a Long Island suburb ban certain novels from the school library.

Whatever the wisdom of such pressure groups, at least these people are aware that educational decisions are not just technical issues of "implementing" what everyone has already agreed upon. *Education* is one of a few words in the language that implies a value judgment. Descriptions of education do not long remain neutral, and if they appear to avoid debate, then the debatable issues are being hidden. Education is about what *should* be done. Elliot Eisner writes: "Unlike schooling or learning or socialization (all of which are descriptive terms), education is a process that fosters personal development and contributes to social well-being. . . One can learn to become neurotic, be schooled to become a scoundrel, or socialized to be a bigot. Education implies some personal and social good."[11]

The fact that education implies value judgments raises the very serious question that is so often avoided: How can any human being set out to educate another? Is not the role of educator an impossible presumption? Carl Bereiter, to his credit, tackles the question head-on. To the question which is the title of his book, *Must We Educate?*, he gives a negative answer.[12] Unfortunately, he is tongue-tied and mixed up in his proposals. He does want children to have a "better life," but after blasting education throughout the book his quixotic conclusion is: "I am an educationalist by trade, and the first thing that needs to be realized is that educationalists are not the people to look to for noneducational alternatives to schooling."[13] Surely, the first thing anyone who is against education must do is to stop calling himself an educationalist. What would be more helpful for him is to start distinguishing the work of schoolteaching from the whole of education. Then he could start proposing educational complements to schooling rather than the bizarre "noneducational alternatives to schooling."

Bereiter is correct in seeing education as a dangerous idea. When any group, no matter how well intentioned, defines for everybody what education is, it exercises an unwarranted power. Bereiter's solution ("Don't educate") would probably make things worse; it turns over the definition of the good life to some other group, probably those who have power, wealth, or traditional prestige. The more helpful direction is to open the idea of education to the interplay of many groups and to several well-defined forms of learning, among which is schooling. The aims and the means of education ought to be worked out in the context of scientific, artistic, philosophic, and religious life. Most of all, we need imagery and language that keep open the very meaning of education. Any end to education (in the sense of object reached or point to stop) is the end (i.e., destruction) of education.

The twentieth century glibly uses the metaphor *open-ended* but in a manner too mechanical for educational purposes. Education does not, or should not, end, because what is attained is always in relation to some greater unity of life. That unity emerges partly from our efforts and partly without our efforts. We need very definite forms of education, and I will presently describe them. The plurality of educational forms allows a give-and-take (for example, between family and schooling); what one group sees as an educational good may need to be balanced by the conviction of another group. The giving and the receiving avoid the feverish activism that may take over when education has no conclusion. Such activism can be seen in Dewey, for whom the point of learning is to learn still more. Lewis Mumford wrote: "Happiness means for Mr. Dewey what it meant for the pioneers: a preparation for something else. He scarcely can conceive that activity may follow the circle or the pendulum, rather than the railroad train."[14]

Mumford's images of pendulum and circle are scarcely better than that of the railroad train. In what I would call an aesthetic movement for describing education, the interplay of forms is best imagined as a journey toward the center of a sphere. A three-dimensional figure can include Mumford's cyclic and pendulum movements and also Dewey's railroad. In my image the center is beyond one's grasp, but directly and indirectly we can move closer to it. My image of journey toward the center has some resonance in contemporary educational writing. But the imagery in curriculum writing remains unclear.

In one proposal, curriculum can be understood according to one of three images: production, growth, or travel.[15] The third image receives considerable attention today. However, I would not wish to oppose it to production and growth. In parts of education, including school work, production is a legitimate image. Likewise, it is important to retain the organismic image of growth. I have expressed doubt about growth as a comprehensive image, but it should have a place. When people object to production I think what they mean to oppose is reducing education to a commodity. But one can connect the image of productiveness to an organism as well as to an industrial plant or a business corporation.

The educational (not just schooling) curriculum needs all three images: production, growth, and travel. My preference for journey instead of travel is an attempt to incorporate production and growth. Travel could be an image in which education means acquiring interesting information. In some elaborations of the image the teacher becomes a travel agent or a tour guide. That use of imagery trivializes the profound meaning of teaching and—in contrast to journey, production, and growth—says little of the body in its many relationships.[16] The educational journey I am trying to describe is an interplay of bodily and social forms that are always open to further development.

Four Main Forms of Education

In each of the four settings in the following diagram we have experiences that pertain to education. The experiences, in Dewey's terms, can be educational or miseducational. They are educational to the extent that the social forms are understood to embody universal values. Thus, family should be a partial embodiment of community, as should job of work, schooling of knowledge, leisure of wisdom. The embodiment in each case is partial; family, school, job, and leisure need to be complemented by other embodiments. No family exhausts the meaning of community; a family needs other families and also non-familial forms of community life. The following diagram shows this principle operating in each of the four cases.

Diagram 1

family + other forms	job + other forms
community	work
schooling + other forms	leisure + other forms
knowledge	wisdom

The word that appears on the bottom of each relation can be an image for the whole of education. One can therefore say that education is a movement toward community or work or knowledge or wisdom. Each word can convey some understanding of the universal good that cannot be expressed by any single word. The experienced tension in each case (e.g., family is an intimation of *the* community) reminds us that community, work, knowledge, and wisdom are not objects we can acquire but values that lead us on. There is always a danger that one of the elements in this diagram, if lifted out of context, can become an idol (e.g., schooling is salvation). The four pairs should themselves be kept in a creative tension so that the four parts of the diagram would flow in a circular movement that has a vortex.

Diagram 2

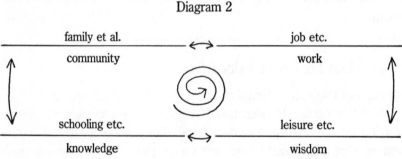

Diagram 2 indicates an interplay of the four pairs. A final diagram will indicate how this educational pattern can be shaped and reshaped. Each form is an embodiment of its universal value when the other three values are present as satellites in the background. For example, a school will succeed in being a place of knowledge only if secondarily it is a place of real work, genuine community, and quiet wisdom. The following diagram fills out all these relationships.

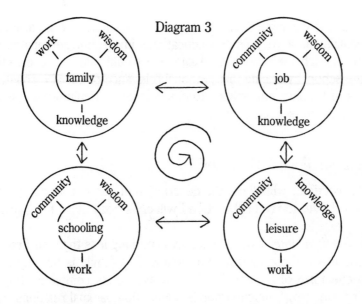

Diagram 3

As the configuration of Diagram 3 shows, one of the four comes to the center and then moves to the background. For an infant the family is indispensable as a form of learning; then the family recedes in importance though it never disappears. For most (but not all) persons it reemerges strongly in young adulthood. At the other end, the leisure of retirement is needed in old age. However, unless leisure has been appreciated throughout earlier life, then retirement may be experienced as emptiness. The same is true of schooling (emphasized but not exclusively located at one stage of life) and jobs, the main learning in the middle of adulthood.

I would propose my description of education as an adequate context for discussing curriculum. Most discussions of curriculum are not clear in whether they are referring to schooling or to the whole of education. For example, Elliot Eisner identifies five basic conceptions of curriculum: cognitive process, academic rationalism, personal relevance, social reconstruction, and technology.[17] I find it puzzling that Eisner declares "I am not taking the position that one of the five orientations is better than another."[18] Surely one must evaluate and say that one orientation is better than another. Eisner's typology doesn't lead to effective evaluation because it is not clear what curriculum is in question. Is the issue school curriculum, or educational curriculum? We might decide that a certain orientation (e.g., academic rationalism) is a very limited educational image but perhaps appropriate enough for schooling. Again, we would take some pressure off the school by seeing that personal relevance or social reconstruction is of primary importance to educational curriculum but less important to the schooling part.

The Four Forms Described

In this section I will fill out the description of the four learning forms named above. In the final section I will crisscross those four with six stages of education.

1. *Family/Community.* The family is nothing less than our first and central form of community experience. The family is nothing more than one form of community that always needs complementing by other forms (e.g., neighborhoods, clubs, homosexual relations, daycare centers). Ever since the seventeenth century in this country, people have been certain that the family is disintegrating. Ironically, almost the reverse is true. Other social forms have always had difficulty existing in this country, but the family is the one form that clearly does exist. In fact, the family may be too strong in its effects on children. It certainly is too strong as a metaphor that envelops many organizations (sports teams, corporations, law firms, parishes). Unfortunate effects of this metaphor include someone playing daddy and adults being treated like children. Concerning the family's future, the simple fact is that 97% of children under age fourteen are with one or both parents; there is not even a potential competitor to the family on the horizon.

Although the family exercises an enormous educational influence, our educational language is constructed to exclude that truth. The professional educators of the nineteenth century concluded that the family was withering away and that the only hope was the school. Michael Katz has traced that attitude back to well before John Dewey. Already in the mid-nineteenth century there was the impossible presumption that the school should educate "the whole man."[19] Occasionally we have flourishes of family education programs that are special niches in contrast to the ("real") education given by the schools. Even a writer who wishes to stress the importance of the family and the limits of schooling can say: "Current interest in the family expresses this loss of confidence in education, which in turn reflects the loss of faith in politics and government."[20] What he presumably means is a "loss of confidence in *schools*"; practically no one has lost confidence in education, the poor being almost desperately concerned with education.[21] So long as the family is by definition excluded from education, then parents and schoolteachers cannot develop a cooperative relationship *within* education, a relationship that would help both family and school.

The family teaches by its form. If an individual family is isolated it is liable to teach some authoritarian attitudes even if neither parent has that kind of personality; we need adequate form to share power. The bright side is that most parents probably do a much better job than they give themselves credit for; their attitudes to life come through with and sometimes despite their intentions to instruct. Parents who are disappointed in their children have often been programmed by society to hope for a finished product, the young person who proves they did all the right things. The expectation is unrealistic. "Every realistic mother is reminded continually as to how much her 'product' is beyond control. . . . *Outcome* is not an accurate term in reference to human beings who as long as they live provide surprises and demonstrate potentiality."[22] The limitation here—no finished product—is the best evidence that the family educates. Society, in fact, may be frightened by the suspicion that parenthood is a revolutionary kind of learning, one not pre-controlled by others' principles and precepts.[23]

Throughout life, the tension within the limits of community form is the basis of creativity. Rousseau's contrast (popular again in the 1960s) between Robinson Crusoe learning to think by experience and the unfortunate people who learn from books and authorities is really an absurd choice. Experience is always communal, at least implicitly. Individuals have to find the way to reshape traditional forms, including the family. Reform could make the experience more personally rewarding and at the same time a sharing with others. The experience of every communal form, the familial and the nonfamilial, is a step toward participation in the human community that education envisions.

2. *Schooling/Knowledge*. By knowledge in this context I mean the great achievement of the rational and speaking animal, the human

grasp of the events of the world. Knowledge can mean something less than that (the storing of information) and something more (what I refer to as wisdom). Schooling is a major way, and in the second period of life today is *the* major way, to organize and assimilate human knowledge. The human being does not have to start over in each generation. The knowledge of the human race is available, still mainly in books though increasingly in other forms.

It is helpful to distinguish schooling as a form of learning from school as the usual place where that learning finds expression. Schooling can be viewed as less than school (as something that occurs in the school building along with lunch, recess, and weekend dances) and something larger than the school (i.e., a system involving teacher unions, county administrators, and publishers). Schooling is neither a preparation for life nor life itself as the old debate had it, but an entry into a very specific form of life and learning.[24]

The distinction between place and kind of learning raises two key issues about the nature of schools, one concerning preparation for jobs, the other concerning the arts. *Schooling* is a word that strongly connotes the acquisition of "academic" learning: history, literature, mathematics, and sciences. I do not think this connotation is bad. We need to insist upon the value of literate knowledge, the kind that books, classrooms, and schoolteachers are supposed to convey.

In addition to that kind of learning we need education that prepares people more directly for their jobs. We also need education in the arts, for which the discursive language of classrooms is not best suited. The so-called work-study programs represent some evolution in fulfilling the first need; the "extracurricular" activities of schools have been a partial solution to the second need. In neither case is there sufficient clarity about distinct, balanced, and complementary forms of learning. I will return to this question in discussing work.

Schooling, it should be said without apology, is mainly concerned with the past. It cannot always be breathlessly exciting, personally relevant, and socially constructive. "The daily life of even the best of schools must be a mundane mastering of other people's reflection."[25] With that comment of Eva Brann I entirely agree, but she undercuts her case by also saying: "I think that the course of education is the course of *learning to read* and to have an education is *to know how to read.*"[26] The failure once again to distinguish schooling and education has the effect of either stunting education or else placing an impossible burden on schooling's result. Why cannot we allow to schooling its limited role of concern with speaking, reading, writing? By giving people access to language, the school can open the door to the power that accompanies a better political and economic life. Schooling can also be a training in and expansion of imagination if school people do their part of the whole and allow the term *education* to encompass other people and institutions.

3. *Job/Work.* My uses of the word *work* as central to education is no faddish invention. Work is what life is concerned with, and in the richest meaning of the word, work is the aim of all education. Our hesitation to praise work springs from strong pressures to reduce the universal value of work to one of its forms. In the ancient world, work was often thought bad because it entailed labor—that is, physical exertion, repetition, and suffering. Nevertheless, all the European languages retain a distinction between labor and work that allows work to refer not only to daily toil for survival but to great religious and artistic endeavors.[27]

In the modern world, as machinery has replaced much of the labor, we have a related problem: the reduction of work to job—or to even narrower twentieth-century terms like *employment* or *occupation.* Most often these terms connote earning a salary. Job needs the complement of work that is not salaried (though it may be recompensed in some way). Play, art, and childcare may involve money, but they cannot be reduced to the market system without being undermined.

Education includes the shaping of the job and the shaping of the relation of job and non-job work. The form of a job teaches us what the world is like. To work within a bureaucratic pattern, for example, shapes one's whole outlook on hierarchy, competence, and secrecy. Most jobs can be improved to a degree if the mind and the imagination are not dulled. That is why work-study (or more exactly, job-study) programs are important in bringing knowledge and perspective to the tasks we perform for earning a living. A closer relation between schools and jobs is desirable but only on the condition that the industrial world is willing to be changed. The relation has to be mutual or else the business world could increase an already-swollen power over schooling.[28] Some people (e.g., counsellors or musicians) have the great fortune that their jobs are also real personal work. The best course available to bank tellers or street cleaners may be to develop non-job work that sustains them in their off-job hours.

In the first two decades of this century, much of educational writing dealt with this topic of work. The unfortunate resolution of the issue was a two-tier system of schooling in which the academically proficient get little orientation to the job world and other students get little intellectual stimulation. John Dewey's idea was that everyone needs both academic education and job experience. Dewey lost his argument with David Snedden and others who constructed the tiered system we have had since then.[29] We need to reopen the badly-named issue of vocational education. One place today where that may happen is feminist issues concerning work.

What had been named women's work is a litmus test of whether our ideas on work are changing. The first and most obvious need is that activities like child care and care of the home be recognized as work. Men as well as women need to look again at "women's work" (e.g., birthing, feeding, clothing, cleaning, healing, burying) as the primary meaning of work or at least the human foundation for the meaning of work. The adage "woman's work is never done" is both a sorrowful and a hopeful note. The toilsome part must be repeated, and it is subject to very little technological substitution. On the positive side, any genuine work is never finished; it stays with us from birth to grave.

4. *Leisure/Wisdom*. Continuing our line of thought, we can say that men and women should retire from jobs but not from work. In the last part of life our main education is in learning to let go of some preoccupying tasks so that we can dwell on issues of more lasting worth. Retirement that brings leisure ought not to be a form of life sprung on us at age sixty-five or seventy. The attitude should be growing in men's and women's lives when they are in their fifties or forties. Indeed, the attitude should take root in childhood.

For a short time in the 1960s researchers spoke of "disengagement" as a characteristic of later life. The word was later judged to be misleading as a description of a process of interiorization.[30] The old do not or should not disengage from life, though they do tend to take a more detached view of the possessions, ambitions, and accomplishments that moved them at an earlier age. One caution in the generalization: Women and men seem to move differently, whether for biological or cultural reasons. The shift toward a contemplative attitude and quieter life has been found in studies of men.[31] Women at that same time may be discovering the other side of their lives; in many cases that means taking a more aggressive and active role. Women may discover contemplative wisdom starting at adolescence and not abruptly at forty-five or fifty. In old age men and women continue to differ on this attitude, but the difference usually narrows after middle age.[32]

Leisure in any case is not the exclusive domain of the old; the retirement leisure of the old needs complementing by other forms of contemplative wisdom. The old can teach the young the need for periodic rest within each day, each week, each year. On this issue of rest, quiet, and peace, religious devotion has an important part in education as a whole. The exclusion of artistic and religious activity from education breeds a narrow and feverish activism in which knowledge is reduced to technical data. The retirement of the old, situated at the center of community, knowledge, and work, should remind us that we do not so much acquire an education as grow into it.

Wisdom is one of the four names I have used for the aim of education. The ancient word that would have gone here was *leisure*, a word difficult to salvage from its twentieth-century meaning as time off the job. Aristotle's saying that "the aim of education is leisure" or "we are unleisurely in order to have leisure" does not make much sense in contemporary language.[33] Far from disparaging work, this use of *leisure* is a test of whether we are concerned with mere occupation or with forms of work that educate. An ultimate test for our conception of education is whether it is oriented to bring forth wise men and wise women who in the later years of life can be sources of wisdom for the whole community.[34]

Six Stages of Education

In this final section I will crisscross the socially-oriented forms of learning described above with the educational material that the individual meets at different ages. I rely here on Egan's *Educational Development,* although, as I indicated, his stages are missing a first and a last. With those two added the resulting six stages are:
1. Physical
2. Mythical
3. Romantic

4. Philosophical
5. Ironic
6. Leisurely

In an adequate developmental theory any one stage implicitly contains the others. What is most prominent at one stage recedes but does not disappear in another stage. Thus, physical education applies throughout life; no stage of education can simply neglect the body. However, the first five years, and especially the first two years, are the foundation of all devlopment for physical education. So also the word *philosophical* shows up at #4 because that is when the philosophical mind becomes explicit. Stages 5 and 6 are also philosophical, but this attitude is not the dominant concern at these stages.

This principle makes intelligible a famous statement of Jerome Bruner's: "Any subject can be taught effectively in some intellectually honest form to any child at any stage of development."[35] The statement provoked controversy and at times ridicule. To give any practical meaning to the claim one has to use the word *subject* with a broad meaning. For example, one can teach mathematics to a person at any stage, but one cannot teach differential equations. In giving a dramatic expression to the developmental principle, Bruner may have obscured the principle by stimulating argument about his formula. Whitehead had made the same basic claim: "The problem of curriculum is not so much the succession of subjects; for all subjects should in essence be begun with the dawn of mentality."[36]

I would also note that in talking about "subjects" both Bruner and Whitehead seem to have schooling in mind. If one were to talk about the curriculum of *education* rather than of schooling, it would be clear that we do not move by mastering easy subjects and moving on to difficult ones (we learn to walk and to speak very early in the curriculum). We progress by sometimes getting a sense of the whole and then filling in the details. Or we build up the pieces and arrive at a system. Either of these movements may be found at any stage of education. Whitehead used the cycle of romance, precision, and synthesis to describe not only a single movement but movement within that movement. For example, we are entertained by a Greek epic, settle into the hard work of Greek grammar, and emerge with a detailed appreciation of the literature. However, even at the second stage of precision we can get a sense of elegant structure to the grammar before going into precise details of the grammatical rules.

"Education should consist in a continual repetition of such cycles. Each lesson in its minor way should form an eddy cycle issuing in its own subordinate process. Longer periods should issue in definite attainments, which then form the starting-grounds for fresh cycles."[37]

The six educational stages, therefore, are not a straight-line sequence from one to six. Like the religious stages of Chapter 7, the movement from one stage to the next can vary in rhythm. Sometimes the movement is a matter of emphasis (mythic to romantic, ironic to leisurely); sometimes it is one of reaction (physical to mythical, romantic to philosophical). At all transitions between stages there is some continuity, although the reactive movement may be so strong that for a while only the discontinuity is evident. In light of Whitehead's principle we should also see each stage in relation to more than just the preceding stage. The philosophical stage is reacting not only against the immediately preceding romantic but against the mythical and physical as well. In this larger cycle the adolescent is trying to become an adult by leaving childhood behind. At the ironic, and more so the leisurely, stage one realizes that to be adult one must also be childlike. As a result, #6 is not only continuous with #5 but is also a recapitulation of #1 to #5.

1. *Physical.* The first educational stage, which I have named physical, is in many ways the most important. Our educational language, however, usually does not include it. Adults are educating a child from the first moment of life. In its turn the child is absorbing far more than we can imagine. We used to think, Montessori says, that the child did not have intelligence; now we know the child is almost nothing but intelligence.[38] Montessori is here referring to the total receptivity of the infant organism. What was said of the poet is true of every infant: "His intellect was at the tip of his senses."[39]

Because of this extraordinary receptiveness to physical stimuli, the small child needs protection against excessive stimulation. Because of rationalistic assumptions and a school mentality, we assume that disadvantaged children lack external stimulation. Usually, the reverse is true; undereducated children are those who cannot escape a constant background noise. For the educationally advantaged child the parent provides important education by creating a zone of quiet and safety. A mother gently rocking a child is conveying that sense of quiet and safety to the infant. The adults are protective filter so that the child can take in physical stimulation at its own pace.[40] We can hardly be said to teach children how to speak; what we do is provide sounds of human speech in a manner that infants can respond to.

Adults build rituals with small children. These gestures, even before the advent of speech, deserve the name education. Repetition, as both Piaget and Montessori stressed, is important for the child's development, even if the child's "do it again" can be wearying for the adult.[41] Adults don't always have to be "intending" education or deliberately inventing the forms of learning. The ordinary family life holds many of the forms within itself, and in a secure environment children should be left to invent their own. One author on fatherhood says, "The one thing I do not want to deprive my children of is boredom. For that's their main chance to find out what they have in them. If necessity is the mother of invention then boredom is the mother of creativity and resourcefulness."[42]

Play begins in the first few months of life. It gradually finds expression in rituals and games. Most parents go through a quite elaborate game when the child of three or four gets ready for bed.[43] Play is the child's work, the child's contribution to a better world. In later life play becomes a test of whether a job is genuine work (scientists play with their data, novelists play with their characters, investors play in financial markets). Play is also a complement to schooling as a form of knowledge. Ideas are things to be played with: Their limits are to be tested, and occasionally the ideas fail. Nothing is more important to adults than to be able to play with ideas, to contest other people's ideas and not feel destroyed on discovering that one's own ideas are limited.

2. *Mythical.* At the mythical stage the child embodies in language the contesting, the repetitive, and the wondering. A modern view of myths is to see them as stories of binary opposites: good and evil, light and darkness, heaven and earth. Myths are repetitive in the structuring of their content. Like the infant playing patty-cakes or peekaboo, the myth-teller structures the universe on the basis of repetition. "The function of repetition is to render the structure of the myth apparent."[44]

A child who has been read to at home or has been told stories probably grasps already this mythical structure. In families where literature is valued the child may teach himself or herself to read. (Many children show up for the first day of school expecting good books to read and are given the letters of the alphabet.) The cooperation of home and school from the first moment is crucial for this relation *within* education. When a "reading problem" exists it is not likely to be overcome by hammering directly at the surface problem.

One of Egan's most important comments refers to this educational moment when the child is in touch with the whole cosmos through mythical stories. The "professional educator" may assume that the child is acquainted with only the family and that the next educational step is to the neighborhood, the supermarket, and the town hall. Egan protests: "What children know best when they come to school are love, hate, joy, fear, good and bad. That is, they know best the most profound human emotions and the bases of morality."[45] Here we have a key moment of moral education even though Piaget and Kohlberg treat the child as "pre-moral." Their blindness on this point is not an error in calculation but a revelation of fundamental deficiency in their image of development and their meaning of morality.

3. *Romantic.* Starting in the mythical and continuing into the romantic stage, the child has to make a commitment to language. Oral language has to be complemented by written language. Some children make the transition smoothly, while others find the step very difficult. We do not know all the things that contribute to this ability, but part of it is physiological. If the commitment to language is not made at this stage, it will be difficult and nearly impossible later.

In this regard, Marie Winn and others have argued that too much television harms a child's educational development.[46] The point here is simply *quantity*; whatever the quality of the programming, large amounts of television-watching interfere with physical and social conditions of language development. If that is the case, then television will forever remain a dangerous instrument for children and a great test of parent-child attitudes in the home. Television is still a puzzling toy to the human race. It has the potential for being the most revolutionary advance in education during this century. Its political implications, especially when it becomes a two-way system, are beyond the scope of the present discussion. The developmental point is that television is a potent and dangerous medicine. For the young, television within careful limits can be a way into myth, romance, and philosophy, a way of learning that can complement the child's reading.

For adults the possibilities are even greater. Adults who read the most also watch a lot of television. In hospitals, nursing homes, and apartments that have shut-ins, television (especially when accompanied by a video recorder) can be a great educational help. A condescending attitude toward this mysterious new power is unwarranted and impractical.

The romantic stage involves a fascination with whatever exists, with names of things, with dates of all kinds of events, and with startling information of any sort. The romantic stage is in continuity with the mythical, but there is a reversal of method. "Instead of projecting opposites from within, the romantic mind searches outside itself to the limits of the world for external binary opposites within which reality exists."[47] A child at this age—upper elementary, junior high—is immature intellectually, but that is not bad. Egan says the immature require immature concepts: "This romantic engagement with the awesome, the wonderful, the different is not only acceptable but *necessary* for students' educational development."[48] The romantic mind should be allowed to roam over a wide field of interest. Egan suggests that scholars who were pushed through the romantic stage too quickly got locked into their academic disciplines. Such experts hardly deserve to be called "well educated," even if they have Ph.D.s. "They know only that beyond these secure boundaries there be dragons and monsters."[49]

One aspect of this stage is the value of developing a memory that can hold a mass of information. Modern education has few good words for the value of memorization and the storing of facts. Psychologists interested in learning capacity seldom discuss the memorizing of poetry. Even Whitehead's philosophical essays hit hard at inert knowledge. Whitehead ridicules a concept of education as "watching the open pages of all the books which we have ever read, and then, when occasion arises, we select the right page to read aloud to the universe."[50] I think this question needs situating within the four forms of learning and the six stages of educational development. Granted, memorizing poetry or studying the details of a science-fiction odyssey are not the whole of education or even a great educational accomplishment. Yet, within schooling and within schooling for children of a certain age, such things should be encouraged rather than discouraged. The fact that excites a ten-year-old is not a useless fact, and lines of poetry barely understood at twelve can be a great comfort at eighty-two.

4. Philosophical. The philosophical stage is the time of the young person's fascination with ideas as building blocks of an ideology. The use of the word *philosophical* can be very misleading here; the young person's fascination with ideas has to be distinguished from "being a philosopher." Being interested in philosophy at twenty is fine so long as this interest is situated in a developmental process that will keep reshaping the philosophy for decades to come. The ancient and medieval worlds thought a man could become a philosopher only at about age fifty. John Henry Newman, combining the ancient view and his own developmental thinking, wrote: "It would appear that a boy may be a mathematician, but not a philosopher, or learned in physics, and for this reason—because the one study deals with abstractions, while the other studies gain their principle from experience, and in the latter subjects youth do not give assents, but make assertions, but in the former they know what it is they are handling."[51]

Piagetian studies account for the young person's ability to engage in philosophical thinking. Beyond describing a prerequisite for the young person's education, Piaget has little to offer in educational directions at this stage. Erikson's stage of identity does not seem to correlate very well with the philosophical. However, the emotional side and the insecurity behind the philosophical exterior are important considerations for anyone involved with the education of youth. Fowler, as we saw, does have both the ideological side and the precarious ego in his fourth stage.

Teachers of youth, whether in school or elsewhere, need patience and understanding to cope with the philosophical stage. Those who seemingly worshiped hard facts a few years previous may now be enthralled with grand systems of ideas. Boys have traditionally been more enraptured by this phase, though the supposed difference between boy and girl here is probably only a matter of emphasis. In any case, with the image of movement assumed here, a more pronounced philosophical stage does not necessarily mean greater progress. Too strong a reaction against physical, mythic, and romantic may be difficult to overcome later. Since people can stunt educational development by identifying education with the ideas they left school with, an intense attachment to the philosophical stage is a special danger.

The strategy of those who are older and presumably wiser should be to guide the young discreetly at the time when ideologies develop.

If an eighteen-year-old boy says he is a Marxist, there is not much point in either ridiculing the claim or making a frontal attack on the system. But an adult can gently restrain the overconfidence of the young in their new-found answers to the world's problems. The sympathetic adult might gradually introduce anomalies and dissonances into the cherished system of ideas. Adults can thus provide a safety zone where ideas can be played with (again) rather than overpowering the young with an alternate ideology.[52]

5. *Ironic.* The passage to irony is a kind of conversion, a willingness to circle back and pick up elements kicked out of the ideological system. In particular, irony reappropriates the binary opposites of the mythical stage chastened by the world limits of the romantic stage and clarified through the rational analysis of the philosophical stage. Egan fails to develop this connection with the prior stages, and his discussion of this stage is far sketchier than for the previous stages. Two reasons account for his brevity here: (1) There is an unavoidable religious element in the ironic stage which Egan does not introduce; (2) Egan's focus has been on the schooling part of education, and by the thirties and forties schooling plays a small part in most people's education.

Here is where one must shift attention to the second cycle of family/community patterns. Now the education is one of being "childed" rather than parented.[53] The relation to children and the relation to adults we love dearly teach us how important we are and how fragile our lives are. Irony in this context is the holding together of two attitudes: that human beings are the greatest thing in the universe, and that human beings are ridiculously small and vulnerable. At this stage people also realize that their jobs may be important but that a job will not transform the universe. By staying at our life's work even as we become aware of its limitations, we make our jobs an education in irony.

Humor is an indispensable part of an ironic outlook. The humor needs to be tied to a sense of place, of tradition, of community. Ironic thinking becomes possible when we can play with contrasting ideas and frightening hypotheses. Such play requires a feeling of security. The individual can loosen his or her grasp upon the idea system because there is a community and a tradition to give support. That stance is particularly important at times of sickness, when our great plans are upset by the body's illness. Unless we live in a context where we are playfully buoyed up by vision, story, and ritual greater than ourselves, our irony can quickly turn to bitter cynicism.

When the philosophical stage has been transcended, philosophical ideas can now return at the service of life. The limits of any philosophical system can now be seen as the system is tested against the concrete particularities of everyday existence, including job and family. Story comes back into prominence after having been banished as a distraction from factual truth. At the ironic stage we recognize that the way to ultimate truth is by story and that the way to deal with life is to tell a story that includes ourselves. If someone else has a different story, that person's truth does not have to be seen as a contradiction of or a threat to our own. A large part of an adult's education is through novels, plays, movies, and television; at their best these forms throw light on the family/community and job/work ironies of life.

6. *Leisurely.* Egan's description of the ironic stage as "forgetting the self" and getting closer to the objective and the real seems to me a distortion of irony.[54] One must know where irony goes, just as *romantic* or *philosophical* would be distorting without a next stage. Egan lacks a last stage. I have called it the leisurely, despite the limitations of this term today. *Leisurely* here names the stage at which we situate a fully developed self in a calmly accepted cosmos. The paradoxical tensions of irony are still there, but they are accepted with more equanimity. The last educational stage is preeminently a stage for the religious question of life and death. Once again, because of our identifying school and education, we thoroughly underestimate the significance of education in old age.

Schooling, of course, plays a secondary role in old age. But perhaps we should today stress that schooling in old age could take on greater significance than it has had during the ironic stage. A newly conceived idea of schooling is awaited by many people who have retired or partially withdrawn from their jobs.[55] They are ready now for the books and ideas to clarify their fund of experience. They deserve educational centers that are adapted to their limitations—temporal, spatial, visual, and auditory. *School* comes from the Greek word for leisure. While schooling is not entirely wasted on the young and while the old will not sit in classrooms five hours daily, the leisurely-stage older population would like their fair share of schooling.

The third main cycle of the family/community relation is also a powerful educational force. Freedom from the pressing responsibility of being a parent and from the subjection that goes with being a son or daughter makes the grandparent/grandchild relation a revolutionary force. The relation between grandparent, natural or adopted, and grandchild comes closer to a mutually beneficial education than parent-child or most adult-child relations. The very young and the very old are co-conspirators in a world obsessed with rational productivity. Beneath the differences in the number of wrinkles and the amount of physical energy, the old and the young, if given half a chance, discover a common good. Anyone whose theory of education does not include a grandparent sitting quietly in the sunlight does not have an adequate theory.[56] If the world has a future at all, that future largely depends upon the child a few years from birth and the old person a few years from death speaking, in their own secretive way, of mysteries that the rest of the race is too old or too young to comprehend.

9

A Theory of
Religious Education Development

What remains to be done in this final chapter is to reassemble the pieces of the picture given in Chapters 1 through 8. That is, religious education development as presented here is not still another theory of development that parallels or substitutes for previous theories. Rather, I have tried to show that the modern idea of development contains within itself a religious meaning and an educational meaning. This chapter on the religiously educational meaning of development is mostly an integration of the previous material and a summary of my own ideas.

I wrote in Chapter 1 that the sequence of chapters in this book would follow from and embody the meaning of development that I advocate. That meaning is not a straight line toward a final point but a constant circling back. Here in the last chapter I am back with the fundamental concerns of the first chapter: What imagery is assumed with the word *development*? What kind of language is needed to prevent closure of human development? How can one bridge the two bodies of development literature, the one controlled mainly by psychologists and the other by economists? The answer to these concerns of Chapter 1 can be found in a religious educational meaning of development, the basis of which has been laid in Chapters 2 through 8.

Chapters 2 and 3 describe contrasting schools of developmental writing. Chapter 4 follows from Chapter 3 and deals with Kohlberg's attenuation of Piaget's development. Chapter 5 on an alternative understanding of moral development is in conflict with Chapter 4 and provides a transition to the chapters that follow. Chapter 6 on Fowler's faith development recapitulates Chapters 2 through 5. Chapter 7 on the religious and Chapter 8 on education draw upon Chapters 2 through 6. This present chapter deals with the relation of Chapters 7 and 8, offering not so much a resolution of their differences as a statement of their troubled but nonetheless necessary relation.

I have often compared religion and education to a bickering couple who do not get along well when they are under the same roof but who are much worse off when they go entirely separate ways. Put in starkest contrast, education is concerned with finding or creating order in this world, while religion is a going beyond this world. Given the obvious potential for conflict in that formulation, the structural similarities that Chapters 7 and 8 reveal are quite remarkable.

Abstractly defined, religion and education collide. But placed in relation to the idea of development, the educational and the religious achieve a working relationship. Education needs a religious impulse, or else its concern to put things in order closes off further development and thereby undoes the meaning of education. Religion needs educational restraint and challenge so that its impulse to transcend the world does not lose touch with the world to be transcended. Otherwise, religious activities are not a going beyond but a gone beyond, leaving us with a sphere called religion which no longer transforms our lives together.

The idea of development, I suggested in the first chapter, is the linchpin to the existence of a field of religious education. Since the seventeenth-century colonies in North America, religious education has been struggling to come into its own. Education in religious matters was central to life in the seventeenth century. The family, church, and school combined to see that the child knew his or her Bible, doctrines, and morals. The Puritan church ideal was someone who had experienced the truth and been converted by the word of God.[1]

The eighteenth and nineteenth centuries did not develop the religious education adequate to a new society. The culture, with its Catholic, Jewish, and widely diverse Protestant groups, became religiously complex. Education became more secularly oriented, and after the adoption of the U.S. Constitution religion was nearly excluded from the idea of education. Where certain groups had the power to enforce their ideas, prayer, Bible-reading, and religious viewpoints were kept in public schools. But these efforts were mainly to stem the tide of modernity rather than to provide an educational approach to religious life. The Sunday School in the nineteenth century was thought to be the complement of the weekday public school. Despite valiant efforts by its supporters, the Sunday School could hardly do more than provide basic Bible knowledge.[2] The Catholics, objecting to religious bias in the public school, established their own school system. These schools gave religious instruction an educational context but at the cost of separating Catholics from some of the culture's main institutions.

During the nineteenth century, religion and education went their separate ways. Without a sufficient educational context, religious experience was always at the edge of the irrational and in danger of turning fraudulent. Religious movements swept across the country in the form of the revival. Life's complexities could be resolved by a single conversionary crisis in which one would pass from sinner to saved. The great preacher would boom: "It all resides in the will. For every man in the house tonight it's 'I will' or 'I will not.'"[3] Those who were ready to repent came down the aisle and made their commitment to the Lord.

As an alternative to this revivalism, Horace Bushnell offered his *Christian Nurture*, an early intimation of religious education development. For Bushnell the child does not grow up a sinner and then, perhaps at adolescence, become a Christian. In Bushnell's phrase, "The child was to grow up a Christian and never know himself as being otherwise."[4] Bushnell could accept a great deal of the sin rhetoric, but he saw the church's power, especially transmitted through the parents, as a means of grace overcoming sin. Bushnell in opposing any "spiritual torments" and in proposing instead "little conversion-like crises all the time" was implying a developmental theory for religious growth. Education was *in* conversion rather than *to* conversion.[5]

Horace Bushnell opened the door on development and offered many insights that are still worth considering. However, two serious flaws in his work must not be overlooked: one educational, the other religious.

Educationally, Bushnell contrasted family nurture and revivalist preaching. In itself that is not a bad choice unless nurture is made into a complete educational model. Bushnell, along with Catherine

Beecher, Horace Mann, and others of the time, stamped the emerging public school as a place of nurture and moral training.[6] What disappeared in the choice between nurture and revivalism was a conception of the school as an educational place that dealt in solid intellectual inquiry. The church school tended to be a place for nurturing the faith of the child. The early nineteenth century's harsh rhetoric of sin gave way to a soft sentimentalism in the latter part of the century. Neither outlook saw a need for complex educational forms that would provide for lifelong religious inquiry.

Bushnell's *religious* flaw lay in equating *religious* and *Christian,* or, perhaps more exactly, substituting *Christian* for *religious.* In the language of his alternatives, one passed from being a sinner to being a Christian. That assumption excludes Jews and other non-Christians from religious education. Interestingly, the nineteenth century usage of the word *Christian* also excluded Catholics. Indeed, Bushnell's usage of *Christian* included a virulent anti-Catholicism.[7]

What is called *the* religious education movement of the twentieth century had some continuity with Bushnell, although it attempted to be more liberal. *Religious* usually meant Protestant Christian, a Protestantism going easy on doctrines that seemed outdated or controversial. While the revivalists were still preaching the reality of sin and the need for conversion, the new religious educators were enamored of psychology, progress, and social harmony. George Albert Coe, the greatest theoretician of the movement, wrote: "The constant aim of elementary religious education should be to make conversion unnecessary."[8] Coe affirmed with Bushnell that the child should be brought up Christian and that conversion, if useful at all, should describe a reverence for life in all its twists and turns.[9]

While this movement advocated an education more solidly based than Bushnell's nurture, its meaning of *religious* was thinner. The attenuation of biblical and doctrinal specificity was not accompanied by dialogue with Catholics, Jews, and others who might have added substance to the meaning of *religious.* Inevitably, the main forces of the Protestant denominations rose up against the thin liberal content, no longer recognizably Christian. The Catholics and Jews continued on their own paths of education. If they took notice at all of a movement in the 1940s and 1950s from religious education to Christian education, they viewed it as a move from liberal Protestant to conservative Protestant education.

The last thirty years have seen progress toward Catholic-Protestant conversation and Jewish-Christian dialogue. In addition, religion has achieved a place in many college curricula, although attempts to address religion in elementary and secondary schools have been politically volatile and very slow going.[10] After some fashionable talk in the 1960s about the death of God, religious fervor was again in the news throughout the 1970s. Religion at the same time has been a central element in conflicts around the world. Unfortunately, we still do not have a well-developed field of religious education to channel, restrain, interpret, and criticize religious experience.

Three Stages of Religious Education

From the brief survey above and drawing from Chapters 7 and 8, I will propose a way of looking at religious education developmentally. In the later part of this chapter I will fill out in more detail the moments that make up these three stages. Those details must not be allowed to obscure the simplest pattern of a field of religious education conceived developmentally.

Simply religious

Up to the age of reflective self-consciousness the child's education and religious education are not distinguishable. Whatever contributes to the child's education also provides the necessary foundation for a more complex form of religious education in later life. One reason for raising the question of development is to stress the reality of education/religious education in early childhood.

Our educational language is dominated by the language of school, and more specifically school as an age-specific place ("He is of school age"). We can hardly avoid the significance of the family and early experience, but we translate that into "pre-school" concepts. That is, with education conceived as a commodity available in school, the consumer can be well or ill prepared on reaching "school age." With this attitude we can nullify much of the significance of early education. Our culture fails to acknowledge the profound educational meaning of childhood precisely because that education is religious—that is, it deals with fundamental orientation to life and death, ultimate mysteries, and visions of unity.

The Piagetian wing of developmental studies did not help to clarify this first stage of religious education. It gave the impression that the limited mind of the small child makes it a pre-moral, pre-religious being. That judgment follows from the Piagetian equivalence of morality with rules and of religion with beliefs. "Having a religion" may indeed only be recognizable in the upper years of elementary school, but being religious is a condition known to every child. Religious education of the young has little to do with instruction in belief; it has much to do with providing aesthetic form, stable environment, and personal warmth that protect the religiousness of the child's experience.

The severe limitations of a Piagetian approach to religious education were demonstrated by the work of Ronald Goldman in the 1960s. Goldman's books had a brief run of popularity; they perhaps clarified some issues of curriculum in elementary and secondary schools.[11] Goldman advocated "life themes" when the child is seven or eight; the treatment of historical material was to come only after age thirteen.

The troublesome or even shocking thing was Goldman's use of the word *religious*. The child of five to seven was called pre-religious; seven to eleven was the sub-religious phase.[12] Up until adolescence, religious education was still something that children were being prepared for. "The change from concrete to abstract modes of thought appears to become possible in religious thinking about the age of thirteen years. The adolescent is now in what I would call his religious stage of development, in which he is intellectually ready to apprehend what is the Christian faith."[13] Evident in that statement is the conflating of *Christian* and *religious*. Related to that problem is the assumption that religious education means apprehending the "Christian faith" by abstract modes of thought.

Christian or Jewish or Muslim

Goldman's reductionism is not uncommon in Christian writing. The level I am calling intermediary, where a child should learn Christian beliefs, is made to bear the whole burden of a religious education. At an earlier time in history a Christian (Jewish, Muslim) education may have worked quite well. What preceded and what followed the period when the child could "apprehend what is the Christian faith" did not seem to require much attention. The surrounding culture was assumed to be Christian (Jewish, Muslim). For better or for worse, religious education cannot be so conceived for Christians or Jews or Muslims or any others today. One has to direct attention both to early childhood and to the adult years.

By calling Christian (Jewish, Muslim) education an intermediary stage of religious education, I am not disparaging its importance. To be religiously educated, one must get this solid substance of a particular religious tradition. Biblical, doctrinal, historical material was what the religious education movement of the early twentieth century rebelled against. But rebellion against something does not necessarily produce a new framework. The movement's result was not a new religious education so much as a thin Christian education. Most school people would have no part of it. School curriculum, as part of educational curriculum, needs intellectual content. If and when religion is taught in the school it needs more, not less, intellectual substance than it has had in most of its educational history.

Elementary and secondary schools are places for becoming literate, knowledgeable, and scientifically informed. Children growing up in our culture ought to have the chance to acquire a knowledge of the nature and influence of religion in their lives. The opportunity should be available in the public school, especially in literature and social-studies curricula. This knowledge should be complemented by additional conceptual learning provided by one's own group as well as by another kind of knowledge, the experiential. Experiential forms of religious learning, including participation in worship services and holyday observances, belong to settings of Jewish or Christian or other people. Children ought to get a thorough immersion into the documents concerning the history of their people. Even if they wish to reject religious practice later, they ought to have an elementary knowledge of what they are rejecting.[14]

Religiously Christian (Jewish, Muslim)

Adulthood, from both a religious and an educational perspective, involves a reappropriation of childhood. With the advent of self-reflective consciousness, childhood's naiveté is forever lost. Adolescence pushes aside the magical, superstitious, and religious in favor of calculative and instrumental rationality. The adolescent is looking for measurable things and reasonable explanations. Adulthood is the discovery that childhood was not all in error and that rational control needs a religious context of mystery and wonder. The "second naiveté" (Ricoeur) of adulthood is a complex phase in which the simple genius of childhood reappears in chastened form. A religious education should now regain its prominence.

My use of the awkward phrase religiously Christian (Jewish, Muslim) is to indicate that religious education in adulthood is different from the global experience of childhood. Adulthood needs a definite content and set of practices. There should be no attenuating of the doctrines and codes learned at the second level. The point at this third level is to give the specific religious form a richer context of understanding. The Christian way, to be more fully intelligible to an adult, needs to be put in relation at least to Judaism and Islam. The world has been hovering on the threshold of a volatile but potentially fruitful conversation involving all the religious ways. If such dialogue is preceded by solid grounding in one's own tradition, then the result is usually an enrichment for everyone concerned. Jews become more Jewish, Christians more Christian. An added benefit, sometimes the most important, is that differences *within* each group also get illuminated by conversation beyond the group.

A 1980 book by Thomas Groome has the interesting title of *Christian Religious Education*.[15] It attempts to break an impasse between those who use the term *Christian education* and others who insist on *religious education*. Partisans of *Christian education* see an awkwardness or even redundancy in Groome's title. The question has been raised: Is there any Christian education that is not religious? To which one can answer: Yes, indeed there is. The Christian education movement in the twentieth century was very much a reaction against the religious element that had been emphasized in the religious education movement. The reaction of the 1940s and 1950s replaced the ambiguities of the word *religious* with *Christian* answers. It followed in the wake of Karl Barth's "religion is non-faith." People who had much to say about (Christian) faith had little to say about religious experience or religious symbols.

My own reservation about Groome's title is that I think one of the adjectives should be an adverb. It is not that a set of things called religious educations exist and that one of the set's elements can be qualified by the adjective *Christian*. Rather, the adjective *religious* qualifies education; however, when the religious reemerges in adulthood it is now itself qualified and specified by Christian, Jewish, or Muslim elements. One could therefore speak either of a "Christianly religious" stage, or a "religiously Christian" stage. The former phrase would stress the reemergence of #1 in #3; the latter phrase would emphasize the continuity of movement from #2 to #3 in which a narrowly defined set of beliefs and practices are placed in an ecumenical setting of religious conversation.

The Four Social Forms

In Chapter 8 I described an interplay of educational forms. The question now is, What happens to the movement of education when one asks about the explicitly religious in education? The answer is not to add religion to family/community, job/work, schooling/knowledge, retirement/wisdom; rather, religious education transforms these elements. When people talk about church (synagogue, mosque) and home as agents of education, they are usually trying to break the hegemony of the school. Religious education is then the education given by the school plus something else. I fear that the result may be to trivialize the church (synagogue, mosque) by viewing it as a place that offers a special kind of education for those people who want an extraneous addition to the (real) education of the school.

Synagogue, mosque, and church do have a specific contribution to make, but not mainly as suppliers of additional content. Rather, together with any other interested parties, they should challenge the meaning of education from within education itself. The adjective *religious* does not so much add to education as resist the tendency of modern education to close in upon itself. Much of modern education is idolatrous; it offers the false hope that, if only you can acquire an education, then you can settle down safely and securely, with the world under control.

A first way to bring out the religious dimension of all education is to notice the four educational values: community, work, knowledge, and wisdom. Each of these values is implicitly religious and is open to a religious interpretation. If one wishes to render these values more explicitly religious, then one might name them communion, vocation, vision, and contemplation. For example, when one is talking to a Christian audience in the intimate language of Christian doctrine, then it makes sense to talk of the communion of saints, the work of Christ, mystical contemplation. A Jew might instead speak of Sabbath or holy people. The language differences remain, but an educational context would allow for exploring differences without rancor or threat.

The second and more important way in which these four educational forms can be religious is by the tension they create betwen partial embodiment and universal value. That is, the religious outlook is aware both of the goodness of all creation and of the limitation of everything earthly. Education easily succumbs to idolatry when it overvalues the family, the job, or the conceptual knowledge given by the school. Religious traditions value family, job, or schooling, but always in a relativized way: The best of families is not the kingdom of God; the most brilliant scientist does not have a vision of God. Religious traditions, because they are aware of the limitations of every created thing, are not surprised by society's periodic discoveries that one of its idols has clay feet. Some reformers would like to replace the family or to "deschool" society. Religious traditions take a more balanced view of family, work, school, and leisure, as the following comments about these four forms suggest.

1. Religious education is a clear-eyed affirmation of the ordinary, finite family in relation to something greater than the family. One definition of religious education could be: It is whatever affirms the family while at the same time reminding the family that it is not the final community.[16] That principle offers very specific directions to religious educators. Whatever in the environment destroys the family should be resisted (e.g., the dangerous and destructive aspects of the multi-billion-dollar toy industry). The use of the double negative is crucial to religious education: Negate what negates. Religious education does not invent the family or even have a proper description of family life. It is not the role of the religious educator to offer a blueprint for how the ideal family should live. Too often family education in the broader society has meant (male) experts telling women how to raise their children. Religious education affirms the *form* of family by resisting what interferes with men, women, and children

responding to their own best lights.

The individual family is relativized (that is, affirmed but not as an absolute) toward the greater community by its being in relation both to other families and to nonfamilial communal forms. Here there is an obvious and important role for church, synagogue, and other religious bodies. Our society tends to isolate families (one-family home, one-family car) and to make cooperation difficult. Anything that creates cooperation between or among families (a neighborhood skill bank, childcare exchange) can without the slightest inflation of the term be called religious education.

A religiously educating body must also demonstrate that many people live fruitful and holy lives outside of the family. Stanley Hauerwas has described the two communal vocations in the early Church, family and singleness, as having been valued in relation to each other.[17] I would only add that the category "singleness" needs spelling out today in the many communal forms in which people live, including homosexual relations.[18] When a religious body does provide a setting for the diversity of communal forms, then people discover community across their categories: two-parent and one-parent families, divorced and married, gays and widows, nursing homes and youth centers. Religious education begins by naming the ways people live and then it attempts to give them a richer communal meaning for working out their lives.

2. Religious education in a second formulation is the relativization of one's job or ordinary tasks toward one's work or vocation. On the one hand, no task that human beings have to perform in the ordinary course of affairs need be demeaning. On the other hand, no job, however exalted in human eyes, is more than a tiny contribution to the human vocation. Religious education from the standpoint of work is whatever affirms our job while reminding us that there is something greater to be accomplished in our lives.

Every job can be improved, and a specific concern of religious education is resistance to the noise, dirt, pressure to produce, underpayment, and so on, that demean the worker. Religious bodies can sometimes exert political and economic power against degrading jobs or at least expose them to the light. Religious bodies can also be a main source of non-job work, things that people do for the love of the work or the importance of the results instead of exclusively for the salary. This area can include forms of work that have turned into mere occupations but can use the challenge of those who do the work for religiously motivated reasons. The moment of birth and preparation for death are two dramatic examples of where a different approach to work is being reintroduced after the work had been made into a salaried job.

I am adverting here to a rediscovery of the older meaning of *professional*, a meaning that traditionally included some kind of religious commitment.[19] A professional once was someone who was dedicated to a work that transcended money exchange. Over the past century *professional* has come to mean almost the opposite; that is, it now refers to someone whose specialized talent can bring higher pay as well as control over working conditions. The rhetoric that speaks of service to the client taking precedence over personal gain can still be found in the professions, however, especially the oldest ones of law, medicine, and ministry. Therefore, if religious educators wish to call themselves professionals, they need to examine their relation to education on one side and to religious ministry on the other. The work has to be designed and executed in a way that restores the place of some non-professionals, especially the family. It also has to embody the belief that work is not reducible to money values. This principle is not an excuse for failing to pay a living wage to teachers, parish directors, or religious personnel. The question here is how religious bodies as a whole, including the people who pay salaries, can challenge and complement the jobs of today's secular society.

The most explicit challenge that the religious body makes to the idea of work is prayer, worship, or liturgy. Etymologically, *liturgy* means "public work (of the church)"—that peculiar kind of work that reminds us that our job is not our whole vocation. We step back from ordinary busy-ness into comfortable rituals that involve awareness, bodiliness, and community. The religious attitude toward the "service of God" is a combination of seriousness and play, or better, a regaining of that seriousness we had in play as children.[20]

A weekend visitor to the planet earth might get the impression that the effective liturgies are in sports stadiums. The weekly services of church, mosque, or synagogue seem unable to match the attractiveness of sports. The religious groups, however, have the centuries on their side. Without getting panicky over numbers, they could profitably examine other "liturgies" of society to see what uplifts the spirit. For many people in this country, baseball is their closest approach to mystical experience—not only interest in the single game but daily interest that stretches across years and decades. That is not a bad thing; spectatorship is a valid role in ritual. Sport as a religious phenomenon can be thought of as an ally rather than a competitor to religious bodies, part of whose religious education should be to resist what destroys sport: for instance, the existence of prize fighting, the violence of football and hockey, the continuing discrimination against women, the domination by large corporate interests. Keeping sport playful is a concern of adult religiousness.[21]

3. With reference to schooling/knowledge, religious education includes, of course, the knowledge gained in school. I have said that whenever religion becomes part of a school curriculum it should be treated in a rigorously academic, scholarly way. A religious outlook, however, has a reserved enthusiasm for schooling, the part of education that appropriately deals in rational concepts and discursive language. Religious education respects other kinds of learning that do not come from books. Thus it is always pushing at the walls of the school system to let counseling, the arts, or simple friendship be a source of education.[22]

Whatever opens reason in relation to some greater intelligence or understanding is part of religious education. Education cannot be irrational (a word connoting violence and chaos), but it must often be nonrational. Even for the sake of rationality we need a ground, context, and interpretive approach not reducible to reason in its modern instrumental meaning. Religious education cannot dismiss out-of-hand claims to charismatic gifts, visions, or powers beyond scientific explanation. Without being gullible or naive, the religious educator has to keep his or her mind open to new possibilities. As is well known, sometimes people who claim to be religious turn out to be mentally unbalanced. Religious inquiry is a dangerous undertaking, and the dangers cannot be entirely eliminated. A tradition of religion can protect people against exploitation and develop criteria for distinguishing religious passion from sick obsession.

4. The relation between leisure and wisdom is in many ways the most obviously religious of the four forms. Wisdom or contemplation has been associated with religious traditions throughout the centuries. My concern here is to relate the leisure that is possible in

retirement to the religious concern for wisdom. The leisure of retirement ought to be one form for wisdom. It needs to be protected from external assault such as government's cutting back on its financial commitment to the old. Leisure in old age needs to be complemented by other forms of contemplative quiet. Times of reflective disengagement are not just for the elderly. As mentioned earlier, the parent has to provide a zone of calm for the infant. The student, the laborer, the parent all need times and places to be quiet. The retreat experience can be an explicit form of contemplative quiet in Christian churches. And the Sabbath in Judaism remains a striking reminder of the value of stopping and becoming aware of who we are.[23]

Every major religious tradition has a central place for personal prayer or meditation. Bodily posture, repeated formulas, and discipline of the imagination may accompany the prayer. The limitations of schooling and instruction are particularly clear in reference to prayer. No one really instructs us in prayer. Someone can train us in posture or teach us words with which to pray. Or we can study and improve environmental conditions. But ultimately, we pray because we are at the still point of the soul. Prayer is not an instrument that teachers use, is not a part of school curriculum. It can be a criterion to test whether retirement is contributing to wisdom. Prayer's ultimate educational meaning is as a test of whether the vortex of social forms is truly educational by always being open to further truth.

Six Moments of Religious Education

In this last section I will expand on the three stages of religious education, dividing each of the three into two moments:
1. Simply Religious Education
   a. Physical
   b. Visional/Mythical
2. Christian (Jewish, Muslim) Education
   a. Narrative
   b. Systematic
3. Religiously Christian (Jewish, Muslim) Education
   a. Journeying/Inquiry
   b. Centering

Simply religious education

Physical: In this first moment of religious education the concern is to provide environment and personal care that will make the infant's experience educational rather than miseducational. At this time, whatever is education is religious education. The reason for the adjective *religious* is to stress the peculiar qualities and characteristics of the small child's education. The infant's possibilities are almost unlimited, and by the same token the child is precariously exposed to detrimental influences whose effect can be lifelong. Hidden beneath everyone's consciousness are memories of near-death experiences that we underwent at birth and in early months of life.

No educational system can be devised that will eliminate the risks and anxieties of infancy. "You're on earth and there's no cure for that" (Beckett). Nevertheless, the human race can certainly reduce some of the traumas of pregnancy and birth. What may be the greatest single scandal of human history—the astounding incidence of child abuse throughout the centuries—is finally beginning to be acknowledged. A great amount of time, energy, and money is expended on later education that cannot be very successful if the infant has been maltreated. Educational language has to include the preservation and development of the physical organism in infancy. Most obviously, the verb *to teach* should include what parents do with infants; all the elements of feeding, clothing, caressing, disciplining, and conversing are educative for the child.

The religious education principle, once again, is to destroy the destroyer. In this case, that means being attentive to environmental conditions that harm family life and lessen the infant's chances of physical health. Some of these dangerous influences are unfair tax and welfare rules, inadequate legal services for children, exploitative advertising, and poor-quality foods. To complement the family, a religious body can remove some of the parental burden. As Sidney Callahan notes, when a religious purpose disappears, the responsibility of the parent increases; the success or failure of the child's life when he or she is removed from relation to God is thrown back upon the parents.[24] A church can be a big help simply by its presence. As a place of meeting and consolation, the church puts the responsibility back into context. Often what is needed is not an expert on children so much as a kindred soul who shares the feeling of responsibility.

Education in bodily skills is rooted in the bodily experiences of childhood. The care of plants and animals, the care of diet and cooking, the care for clothes and the home all have a religious import. Each form of bodily care is a reaching out beyond the closed ego that tries to save itself by its own unaided efforts. Bodily movements, especially proper breathing and dancing, are intimately connected to being religious. One cannot transcend the body unless one has come to feel it as one's own. If we have lost the connection between the body and religious activity, that is because we are not attentive to the (religious) education of the young child.

Visional/Mythical: There is usually no sudden jump into this second moment. As early as a few months after birth, a child exercises imagination and can begin to visualize reality. The child can also pick out sounds, especially the human voice, to which it responds. The infant's impulse to play matures into rituals and games. Play, as I have noted, embodies the child's attitude to the sacred. As the child's capacity to hear language develops, storytelling becomes central to the child's (religious) education. Once again, resisting whatever smothers the child's imagination or obstructs its involvement in story listening is religious.

Edward Robinson, as I previously noted, has gathered some extraordinary data on the religious visions of young children.[25] If these accounts are at all typical, the religious life of many children is both intense and indelible. Here are sixty-year-old people who can recount the details of visions that they had at four or five years of age and that left a permanent impression upon their lives. Robinson is critical of Piaget and of Goldman's use of Piaget to construct a curriculum of "religious thinking." Such a curriculum could deal only with the child's abstract conceptions about religion. Robinson writes that "'thinking directed toward religion' doesn't get at what one respondent calls 'that deepest part of me which was always hidden from others who never suspected its existence.'"[26]

Robinson is also critical of David Elkind's saying that religion provides "ready-made solutions" to the child's problems.[27] The religious experience, both men agree, is one of inevitable conflict. Robinson would acknowledge that when one tries to articulate the vision in story form, some stories do attempt ready-made solutions, while other stories are profound enough to let the child bear with inevitable conflict, the story having made anxiety bearable.

Bruno Bettelheim has studied fairy tales from that latter standpoint and has found that traditional stories allow the child to accept the dark side.[28] In Bettelheim's view, children of different ages can respond to different levels of the fairy tale. Most modern attempts to invent fairy tales turn out to be moralistic or overly cheery; the tales do not usually survive long. Bettelheim classifies Bible stories with moralistic stories that merely tell people how to lead a good life.[29] While no doubt that has often been the fate of Bible stories in the hands of ill-equipped teachers, Bettelheim seems unacquainted with other possibilities—for example, the modern understanding of parables.[30] Children may not understand every parable and will not grasp the full significance of any parable. Nonetheless, they can be introduced to Bible stories, including parables, as Jerome Berryman has shown in his "materialization" of the Good Shepherd.[31]

Bettelheim in *The Uses of Enchantment* is very critical of modern attempts at sex education, a topic I would see as intimately related to religious education.[32] The mysteries surrounding birth and death are the test of the religiousness at this age, and a child's questions about sex and death are often very profound. The adult may become unsettled by the questions, especially if they were snuffed out when he or she was a child. The adult is sometimes more confused than the child, who is simply looking for the meaning of things. As Ernest Becker warned about missing the point of a boy's question on sex: "He wants to know why he has a body, where it came from, and what it means for a selfconscious creature to be limited by it. He is asking about the ultimate mystery of life, not about the mechanics of sex."[33] Bettelheim castigates the rationalistic and antiseptic approach to sex education in school curricula today. He thinks that fairy tales, especially those in what he calls the animal-groom cycle of stories, are a more realistic, human way to sex education. I think it is rather amusing that David Elkind, with all of the Piagetian apparatus at hand, concludes that questions of sex and origins might often best be referred to God. He says that many children arrive spontaneously at this answer in any case and that at this stage a mythical tale of origins is preferable to biological data delivered by anxious adults.[34]

Christian (Jewish, Muslim) education

Narrative: The movement from stage 1 (simply religious) to stage 2 (Christian, Jewish, Muslim) is a kind of conversion in the form of a reversal of perspective. In the first stage the gods are everywhere and are manifest in the sky, trees, rocks, flowers, and myriad other forms. God may be a great impersonal force or in mythical terms a light overcoming darkness. When the child's individual ego emerges and when the child becomes aware of his or her own people, then the time for historical narrative and traditional practices has arrived.[35]

The Jewish, Muslim, or Christian child should acquire a sense of the past through the scriptures and their commentaries as well as through a behavioral code that includes ancient rituals. Such specific teachings and behavioral disciplines are by definition conservative. Many liberal-minded adults find the restrictions of doctrine and moral prohibition distasteful. They forget that they became liberal by defining their positions in relation to set beliefs and codes. As a certain stage within a larger development everyone can use a definite religious position from which to define his or her personal religious stance.

The teacher of religion at this point is neither indoctrinator nor someone simply sharing or holding a discussion. Rather, the attitude of the teacher of religion is in effect the following: "I and my people are not wrong. My way is not a false way. I know it is true for me because I have experienced it. I am going to show you a world that does exist. I want you to see that world because it is worth seeing. I want to invite you to join that way. You can help this people by discovering ways to resist the inevitable bias that is part of every tradition. There is an adventure to join in finding closer approximations to the truth." Whether the child becomes fully engaged in this adventure is a decision only he or she can make, and the final decision is years in the future. At every step toward a full commitment, the child's freedom to get out of the way or to raise other issues must be respected.

Is it still possible in a pluralistic society to create the sense of "my people" and "our beliefs"? Many things, including television, create an overwhelming sense of pluralism that can leave young children at sea. Nevertheless, today's means of communication and transportation could with the right context widen the child's appreciation of place, people, and history. A child who visits other places and meets other people could have an increased sense of "my people" and "our beliefs." Much depends on the capacity of family, school, and local religious community to root the child somewhere, to give a sense of belonging to something—almost anything—as a point of reference.

One indispensable root for a child of Christian education is Judaism. The relation is not the same in the opposite direction. Judaism does not theoretically depend on Christianity, although the Jewish child can hardly avoid an explicit relation to Christian culture. Christians often think they have a neutral stance toward Judaism, but I offer the thesis that nearly every Christian formula is either pro-Jewish or anti-Jewish. The ways in which Christians relate Jesus to messiah, Word of God, or Son of God either continue a line of history in the Hebrew Bible or abruptly terminate that historical development. Many Christians still do not grasp the fact that their language is subtly anti-Jewish. Yet whatever subverts the autonomy of Judaism and fixes it as a preparation for Christianity is inimical not only to Jewish education but to Christian education.

Dialogue does not fit, at least not yet, the relation of Christians and Jews. The first step from the Christian side is a kind of repentance, not mainly in the form of breast-beating for history's persecutions, but in the form of intellectual conversion. The Christian has to start taking the Hebrew Bible on its own terms and get a sense of post-biblical Judaism. Don Browning writes: "He who would claim to be a Christian must have been first a Pharisee—at least in spirit."[36] That formula has the advantage of reversing the negative meaning of *Pharisee* common in Christian books. Someone might still think that this statement means that one becomes a Pharisee and then sees the true light. What Browning means, though, is that Christianity without an inherent relation to Pharisaic Judaism is dangerous or nonsensical. This fact has definite implications for the Christian education of children. We need to immerse our children in the narrative of the Hebrew Bible. Both Pharisaic Judaism and the Christian movement were reform movements of one era that have come down to our own. The child's study of the New Testament, doctrine, and church history would be different—and richer—if Judaism were respected as an autonomous way in God's providence.

The word that Roman Catholics use for this process of immersion in scripture and liturgy is *catechetics*. It is a good ancient word with a specific connotation, a word that should be considered by all Christian groups. Catechizing refers to working with converts, new members, and revivified old members according to particular teachings, rituals, and practices. The word *catechetics* describes well this stage of religious education when the child of Christian parents is given solid food on which to test his or her membership in the church. A Protestant use of *catechetics* would connect Protestants to the early church and to the early history of Protestantism when the words *catechesis, catechetical,* and *catechism,* were commonly used. [37] Many Protestants have been leery of these terms, perhaps because Catholics often use them to cover the whole field of religious education. Catholic writers, for their part, are often unaware of how foreign their language sounds to some Protestants.

Among Protestant writers the term *Christian education* in the U.S. has usually been interchangeable with *Protestant education.* By naming the second stage of religious education Christian education I am narrowing the meaning in one direction and widening it in another. Some people will no doubt object to my making Christian education an intermediary level, but they cannot logically object to the term's including Catholics. If the term *Christian education* is ever fully to include Catholics, Protestants will have to listen to their own usage and make some fundamental changes.

Systematic: By systematic here I refer to the elaboration of scripture and doctrine into philosophical and theological categories. This systematizing can take several forms and degrees. An historical ordering is one kind of system. In Christian history it held sway until the theological revolutions of the twelfth and thirteenth centuries. Judaism has never developed the same interest in a philosophical ordering of doctrine. The term *Jewish theology* is not common. There are great Jewish philosophers, but that term doesn't really express the systematization either. The ordering is in categories closer to biblical text and schools of commentary. Maimonides, whom Aquinas quotes as a philosopher, is honored in Judaism more for his collection of the Talmud than for his *Guide for the Perplexed.* [38]

The term *theology* expresses the presumptuous claim to have words directly from or about God. As first used in Greek thought, theology was a branch of philosophy. In Christian history theology achieved a separate and preeminent position founded on the claim that Jesus of Nazareth is the Word of God and that the Bible as testimony to that person can also be called God's word. Christian theology assumes rather than tries to prove that God is revealed in the Bible. From

Anselm and Aquinas to Barth and Rahner, theology has proved to be an extraordinary mental exercise in which human reason stretches beyond itself into ineffable mysteries. While much of modern philosophy is unsure what kind of enterprise it itself is, theology can still offer the adolescent and post-adolescent mind solid substance on which to cut its teeth.

There is an obvious danger here if one stops with the construction of the grand system which purports to explain God and the universe. Christian history has sensed that danger and has had periodic rebellions against theology, as in the late fouteenth century. However, anti-theology quickly becomes a new kind of theology. An important task today is to locate theology within a developmental and ecumenical context. For now I would stress the advantages of theology and its near inevitability for any young person with intellectual appetite. If the Bible does not form the basis of one's theology, then Talcott Parson's sociology or Milton Friedman's economics is liable to play the part. The advantage of Christian theology is the length, breadth, and depth of the intellectual tradition it encompasses. In the hands of a good teacher, theology ought to be more intellectually stimulating than any modern ideology (e.g., Marxism or secular humanism) that competes with it.

While one side of adolescence goes the way of rational systems, the other side cries out for something to which one can give wholehearted devotion. These two sides are not so separated as the surface evidence suggests. The emotional life cannot keep pace with the power of rational abstraction. The young person's behavior is subject to wildly shifting moods, and as a result he or she may be ripe for conversion. Religious groups that imagine conversion to be a single leap into the faith are dangerous to the health of the adolescent, and people who undergo that kind of conversion that stops religious growth develop nearly impenetrable theologies.

I have tried to indicate that the religious life can be a continual conversion in which three or four spots stand out as potential places for more dramatic turns.[39] One such change is from first to second stage when the child becomes a practicing Jew, Muslim, or Christian. If that has happened to any degree, then the conversion of adolescence is *away from* Christianity, Islam, or Judaism. Earlier I used the term *disbelief* to characterize this religious period. Even the best of theological systems finally fails to provide the young person with the answers, that is, whom to love, what to choose as a life's work, and how to live with a sense of wholeness. The next conversion, most likely a short time after adolescence, is to a definite religious way in which the attitudes, beliefs, behavior, and ritual of earlier years resurface.

Religiously Christian (Jewish, Muslim) education

Journeying/Inquiry: A single dramatic conversion in early adolescence can lock a person into a set system of beliefs. Even if that system has the most beautiful ideas the world has ever heard of, the effect on a young person can be detrimental. A young adolescent cannot have more than a superficial knowledge of the ways men and women have searched for truth and goodness. I said that Bible and/or theology can be helpful because they link the youngster into centuries of religious life. If there is an adult community as the human context of the written text, then Bible, doctrine, and theology will point beyond themselves. The important problems that take over are the struggle against injustice and the search for peace and love.

As we pass from stage 2, Christian (Jewish, Muslim) education, to stage 3, Religiously Christian (Jewish, Muslim) education, the religious education principle reemerges in full paradox. Religious education is a process of de-absolutizing answers, even the best of religious answers that can be learned in school. The school learning is nonetheless important, because only if the mind is stretched to its limits does it make sense to describe a transcending of limits.

For most people the relativizing of academic knowledge comes with leaving school or having school take a much smaller role. The other forms of learning, namely family, job, and leisure, come to the forefront. People who have lifetime careers associated with schools are in danger of reducing education to school knowledge. Their family/community involvements and their use of leisure are especially important for religiously situating school learning. Nearly everyone finds out, whatever his or her station in life, what it means to love someone dearly, what the death of a loved person means, and what it means to get old without fulfilling one's early expectations. As in childhood, one does not have to inject religion into adult life. Questions of origin, destiny, and deepest meaning are there at every turn of life's journey.

The combative stance of "revealed religion" and its theological system gives way in the post-adolescent period often to a seeming religious indifference. If earlier stages of religious education have given the person a good foundation, then religious attitudes in young adulthood are embodied in the way people act as parents, workers, friends, and citizens. Their conversion to being "Christianly" religious may stretch over several decades. A little schooling often helps, but it usually has to be integral to family and work life. Conversations with friends, books, and magazines, or weekly instruction within religious services may suffice for the schooling part of religious education at this age.

I think the special test in our era for this age of life is a growing understanding of nonviolence. I noted in Chapter 5 the significance of work like Carol Gilligan's for a modern understanding of prudence and justice. The virtues need to be situated within a religious vision and a disciplined community that sustain people in the face of violence. Christians, Jews, Muslims, and others who are committed to non-violence are usually rooted in firm beliefs and a code of conduct transmitted from the past. A positive meaning of tolerance requires an appreciation of what it means to have beliefs. The realization of a life of nonviolence depends upon being tolerant of other views and being willing to learn from enemies. Otherwise, grim attempts to refrain from violence are sure to be exhausted sooner or later. Young children usually have a remarkable attitude of nonviolence until they learn otherwise from grown-ups.[40]

A life of religious inquiry and political nonviolence involves a poetic approach to truth. The poetic use of language, which incorporates the tension of imagination and the conflicts of history, is dismissed by hardheaded realists. From the standpoint of adult religiousness it is the poetic imagination that is tough-minded and realistic, concerned not merely with the heresies of someone's ideological system but with the agonies of a suffering world. In comparison with the might of armies and nature's violent uprisings, the imagination does not look very powerful. Nevertheless, to dwell in parable and to protest the closing of human possibilities can be the main ground of hope for us all. Religious education at this stage is not the building of one's case to score against one's adversaries. It is a journey of compassion for every human being who, no matter what his or her beliefs, is recognized, accepted, and loved as a fellow traveler on this earth. My use of the word *inquiry* at this stage is an echo of John Henry

Newman's line: "I wish to deal not with controversialists but inquirers."[41]

Centering: The second moment of this stage is usually a shifting or refocusing of the elements already there in inquiry. For acquiring human wisdom and religious holiness there is no substitute for age. Life teaches much, if religious education can simply keep the door open on human development. The latter part of life combines the religious detachment of Chapter 7 and the educational leisure of Chapter 8 to suggest a religious education moving toward a final recapitulation at life's center.

The image of center is found throughout religious history, both Eastern and Western. The religious journey can be called a centering. The developmental image I have used throughout this book is conversion toward the center of a sphere. James McDonald has used this imagery for discussing curriculum, not to push religious concerns but *despite* the imagery's religious connection. "It is important we do not turn away from examining the idea of centering simply because it is connected with spirituality. This term simply is the best one available in the attempt to focus our fundamental educational concerns."[42] We need not have his reservation if our concern is religious education.

What McDonald is discovering through the image of centering is that, in the end as in the beginning, education and religious education coalesce. In the intermediate stage it would be dangerous to collapse the difference between *education* and *religious.* That is what the religious education movement early in the century unwisely tried to do; the religious tended to disappear. In his *Aims of Education,* A. N. Whitehead offers the rhetorical flourish that all education is religious education. He then explains by saying that education should inculcate duty and reverence.[43] I am afraid words like *duty* and *reverence* can sound bloodless to an adolescent. They need embodiment in the sense of duty of Moses or the reverence of the Buddha. When an older person has done the best he or she could, receiving life gratefully at each step of the way, then indeed religious life can be simply put as duty, reverence, patience, or abandonment to divine providence.

Whatever destroys the destroyers of old age is part of religious education. Studies show that the chief fear of old age is not death but isolation from the human community. Religious educators can make an immense contribution to this age by being the connecting links, those who make sure that the old are not segregated. No great academic skills are required for this educational task, though care and sensitivity are prerequisites. Any religious group ought to value the wisdom of the old and provide a setting in which the young give one kind of help and the old another kind. Henri Nouwen has written beautifully of this exchange: "The ministry of the old to the young is no different than the ministry of the young to the old, because real healing takes place when they are no longer separated by the walls of fear, but have found each other on the common ground of the human condition, which is mortal, but, therefore, very, very precious."[44]

We seem to be entering a new era of discovering that most older people are very alive intellectually. If one has had intellectual stimulation and discipline earlier in life, then old age can be a time to bear fruit. Schooling during the early phase of stage 3 usually recedes in importance, competing as it does against kids, job, mortgage, travel, promotion, and so on. At the later moment of detachment from many tasks, schooling can increase in significance. Of most importance here, no topic will be of greater interest than religious writing. The old don't necessarily want to take courses on death. Many of them are interested in theology, now as an aesthetic rather than as an ideological work, biblical exegesis which the old now have a greater capacity to understand, and mystical writing which testifies to a final integrity. And the Christian story of the death/resurrection of Jesus can have great meaning to older people while it has only very limited meaning to people of the intermediary stage who get most of the religious education attention.

The final moment of religious education development includes the waiting and the help we can give, mainly by our presence, to those who wait. The human situation is stripped of illusion by those who wait in hospice and hospital, in nursing home and private home, for a birth into a new heaven and a new earth. One can despair that life has come to such an empty end. If, however, development has included the religious and the educational, then the final moment can be imagined as deeper communion, fulfillment of one's vocation, attainment of vision, and instruction in divine wisdom. Any theory of human development that offers less will not see us through the dark night. Religious education development is the inner/outer journey that leads to the center where peace and justice reside.

Notes

Introduction
1. Gail Sheehy, *Passages* (New York: Dutton, 1976).
2. Gail Sheehy, *Pathfinders* (New York: Morrow, 1981).
3. Ibid., p. 9.

Chapter 1
1. G. K. Chesterton, *Orthodoxy* (Garden City, N.Y.: Image, 1959), p. 81.
2. See Gabriel Moran, *Interplay* (Winona, Minn.: St. Mary's Press, 1981).
3. Erik Erikson, *Identity and the Life Cycle* (New York: Norton, 1980), p. 53.
4. See Jacques Monod, *Chance and Necessity* (New York: Random House, 1972), p. 21: "The cornerstone of the scientific method is . . . the systematic denial . . . of final causes."
5. See Denis Goulet, *The Cruel Choice: A New Concept in the Theory of Development* (New York: Atheneum, 1971).
6. Herman Daly, "Ethical Implications of Limits to Global Development," in *The Morality of Scarcity,* ed. William Finnin and Gerald Smith (Baton Rouge, La.: Louisiana State University, 1979), p. 47.
7. Sheehy, *Passages.*
8. James Drever, *A Dictionary of Psychology* (Baltimore: Penguin, 1952), p. 65.
9. Horace Bushnell, *Christian Nurture* (New Haven, Conn.: Yale University, 1967).
10. George Albert Coe, "Religious Education as a Part of General Education," in *Who Are We?* ed. John Westerhoff III (Birmingham, Ala.: Religious Education Press, 1978), pp. 15-16.
11. Evelyn Eaton Whitehead and James D. Whitehead, *Christian Life Patterns* (Garden City, N.Y.: Doubleday, 1979), p. 34.
12. Lawrence Kohlberg, "Continuities in Childhood and Adult Moral Development Revisited," in *Life-Span Developmental Psychology,* ed. P. B. Baltes and K. W. Schaie (New York: Academic Press, 1973), p. 201.
13. Jean Piaget, *Main Trends in Psychology* (New York: Harper and Row, 1973), p. 35; see also a later interview in which Piaget calls Erikson

"a nonorthodox psychoanalyst, but one with whom I fully agree" in Jean-Claude Bringuier, *Conversations with Jean Piaget* (Chicago: University of Chicago, 1980), p. 122.

14. Erik Erikson, *Insight and Responsibility* (New York: Norton, 1964), p. 135.
15. Ibid.
16. Ibid., p. 136.
17. John Peatling, *Religious Education in a Psychological Key* (Birmingham, Ala.: Religious Education Press, 1981), pp. 99-100.

Chapter 2

1. John Watson, *Behaviorism* (Chicago: University of Chicago, 1924), p. 104.
2. Alexander Thomas and Stella Chess, *Temperament and Development* (New York: Brunner/Mazel, 1977), pp. 193-211; see also Jerome Kagan, *The Growth of the Child* (Cambridge: Harvard University, 1978), p. 44.
3. Erikson, *Insight and Responsibility*, p. 229.
4. Charles Kao, *Psychological and Religious Development* (Washington, D.C.: University Press of America, 1981), p. 1.
5. Erikson, *Insight and Responsibility*, p. 132.
6. Erik Erikson, *Childhood and Society*, 2nd ed. (New York: Norton, 1963), pp. 247-274.
7. Erikson, *Insight and Responsibility*, pp. 111-157.
8. Erik Erikson and Joan Erikson, "On Generativity and Identity," *Harvard Educational Review* 51 (May, 1981):254.
9. Erik Erikson, "Dr. Borg's Life Cycle," *Daedalus* 105 (Spring, 1976):19.
10. Erikson, *Childhood and Society*, p. 250.
11. Ibid., p. 251.
12. Ibid., p. 269.
13. Ibid., p. 268.
14. Erikson, *Insight and Responsibility*, p. 133.
15. See Bernice Neugarten, "Personality Change in Late Life: A Developmental Perspective," in *The Psychology of Adult Development and Aging*, ed. C. Eisdorfer and M. P. Lawton (Washington, D.C.: American Psychological Association, 1973), pp. 327-331; see also Elaine Cumming and W. E. Henry, *Growing Old: The Process of Disengagement* (New York: Basic Books, 1961).
16. Erikson, *Insight and Responsibility*, p. 126.
17. Erikson, *Childhood and Society*, p. 266.
18. Erikson, "On Generativity and Identity," p. 269.

19. Ibid., p. 263.
20. Erikson, *Insight and Responsibility*, p. 131.
21. Ibid.
22. Erik Erikson, "On the Generational Cycle," in *International Journal of Psychoanalysis* 61 (1980):213.
23. Erikson, *Insight and Responsibility*, p. 132.
24. See Maureen Green, *Fathering* (New York: McGraw Hill, 1977); Henry Biller and Dennis Meredith, *Father Power* (New York: McKay, 1974).
25. Eliot Daley, *Father Feelings* (New York: Morrow, 1978), p. 65.
26. See Moran, *Interplay*, pp. 79-91.
27. Erikson, *Childhood and Society*, pp. 255-256.
28. Erikson, "On the Generational Cycle," p. 228.
29. Jean Baker Miller, *Toward a New Psychology of Women* (Boston: Beacon, 1976), p. 77.
30. Erikson, *Insight and Responsibility*, p. 235.
31. Ibid., p. 236.
32. On the meaning of *unique*, see Moran, *Interplay*, pp. 46-52.
33. Erikson, "On Generativity and Identity," p. 262.
34. Ibid., p. 266.
35. Erikson, *Insight and Responsibility*, p. 133.
36. George Vaillant, *Adaptation to Life* (Boston: Little, Brown, 1977); Daniel Levinson, *The Seasons of a Man's Life* (New York: Knopf, 1978).
37. Roger Gould, *Transformations* (New York: Simon and Schuster, 1978); Bernard Boelen, *Personal Maturity* (New York: Seabury, 1978).
38. Roger Gould, "The Phases of Adult Life: A Study in Developmental Psychology," *American Journal of Psychiatry* 129 (Nov., 1972):521-531.
39. Gould, *Transformations*, pp. 321-334.
40. Boelen, *Personal Maturity*, p. 12.
41. Bernice Neugarten et al., *Personality in Middle and Later Life* (New York: Atherton, 1964); Marjorie Fiske Lowenthal et al., *Four Stages of Life* (San Francisco: Jossey-Bass, 1976).
42. Lowenthal et al., *Four Stages of Life*, p. 244.
43. Ibid., p. 134.
44. Ibid., p. 222.
45. See Matilda Riley et al., *Aging and Society: An Inventory of Research Findings* (New York: Russell Sage Foundation, 1968).
46. Levinson, *The Seasons of a Man's Life*, pp. 84-90.
47. Ibid., p. 144.
48. Ibid., p. 197.
49. Ibid., p. 193.
50. Kao, *Psychological and Religious Development*, p. 2.

Chapter 3

1. See John Flavell, *The Developmental Psychology of Jean Piaget* (New York: Van Nostrand Reinhold, 1963); Margaret Boden, *Jean Piaget* (New York: Viking, 1980); Robert Kegan, "The Unrecognized Genius of Jean Piaget," in *The Evolving Self* (Cambridge: Harvard University, 1982), pp. 25-45.
2. Jean Piaget, *Insights and Illusions of Philosophy* (New York: New American Library, 1971), pp. 3-38.
3. Ibid., p. 5.
4. Ibid., p. 5.
5. Ibid., p. xiii.
6. Ibid., p. 232.
7. Ibid., p. 42.
8. Ibid., p. 209.
9. Ibid., p. 230.
10. Ibid., p. 16.
11. Ibid., p. 16.
12. See Howard Gardner, *The Quest for Mind* (New York: Knopf, 1974), pp. 57-59.
13. Jean Piaget and Barbel Inhelder, *The Psychology of the Child* (New York: Basic Books, 1969), p. 157.
14. Jean Piaget, *Psychology and Epistemology* (New York: Grossman Books, 1971), p. 24.
15. Piaget and Inhelder, *The Psychology of the Child*, p. 157.
16. Piaget, *Insights and Illusions of Philosophy*, p. 202.
17. Jean Piaget, *Origins of Intelligence in Children* (New York: International Universities Press, 1952), p. 68.
18. Piaget and Inhelder, *The Psychology of the Child*, p. 159.
19. Jean Piaget, *Biology and Knowledge* (Chicago: University of Chicago, 1971), p. 356.
20. Quoted in Erikson, *Insight and Responsibility*, p. 135.
21. Jean Piaget, *The Growth of Logical Thought from Childhood to Adolescence* (New York: Basic Books, 1958), pp. 334-350.
22. Piaget and Inhelder, *The Psychology of the Child*, p. 21.
23. Ibid., pp. 27, 114, 150.
24. See Gabriel Moran, "Social Reform: On the Way to Justice," in *Education for Peace and Justice*, ed. Padraic O'Hare (New York: Harper and Row, 1983).
25. Piaget, *Insights and Illusions of Philosophy*, p. 142.
26. See Piaget, *Insights and Illusions of Philosophy*, p. 143.

27. Margaret Donaldson, *Children's Minds* (New York: Norton, 1978), p. 148.
28. Piaget, *Origins of Intelligence in Children*, p. 150.
29. For a summary see John Bowlby, *Child Care and the Growth of Love*, 2nd ed. (Baltimore: Penguin, 1965).
30. See Jerome Kagan et al., *Infancy: Its Place in Human Development* (Cambridge: Harvard University, 1978); Michael Rutter, *Maternal Deprivation Reassessed* (Baltimore: Penguin, 1972).
31. See Rudolph Schafer, *Mothering* (Cambridge: Harvard University, 1977), pp. 38, 57; Robert May, *Sex and Fantasy* (New York: Norton, 1980), pp. 98-99.
32. Boden, *Jean Piaget*, p. 40.
33. Piaget and Inheider, *The Psychology of the Child*, p. 99.
34. Ibid., pp. 58-62.
35. See Charles Taylor, "What Is Involved in a Genetic Psychology?" in *Cognitive Development and Epistemology*, ed. Thomas Mischel (New York: Academic Press, 1971), pp. 410-415.
36. See Bruno Bettelheim, *The Uses of Enchantment* (New York: Knopf, 1976); Maria Montessori, *From Childhood to Adolescence* (New York: Schocken, 1974).
37. Flavell, *The Developmental Psychology of Jean Piaget*, p. 21.
38. Howard Gardner, "Developmental Psychology after Piaget," *Human Development* 22 (1979):73-88; Peter Bryant, *Perception and Understanding in Young Children* (New York: Basic Books, 1974).
39. See Linda Siegel, "The Relationship of Language and Thought in the Preoperational Child: A Reconsideration of Nonverbal Alternatives to Piagetian Tasks," in *Alternatives to Piaget*, ed. Linda Siegel and Charles Brainerd (New York: Academic Press, 1978), pp. 43-67.
40. See Donaldson, *Children's Minds*, p. 17; P. C. Wason, "The Theory of Formal Operations: A Critique," in *Piaget and Knowing*, ed. B. A. Geber (London: Routledge and Kegan Paul, 1977), pp. 119-135.
41. See David Elkind, *Children and Adolescents* (New York: Oxford, 1970), p. 99.
42. Jean Piaget, *Six Psychological Studies* (New York: Random House, 1967), p. 64.
43. Jean Piaget, *The Growth of Logical Thought from Childhood to Adolescence* (New York: Basic Books, 1958), p. 245.
44. David Elkind, *The Child and Society* (New York: Oxford, 1979), p. 93.
45. Edith Neimark, "Current Status of Formal Operations Research," *Human Development* 22 (1979):60-67.

46. Piaget, *Psychology and Epistemology,* p. 61; Flavell, *The Developmental Psychology of Jean Piaget,* p. 114.

Chapter 4

1. Jean Piaget, *The Moral Judgment of the Child* (New York: Collier, 1962), p. 13.
2. Alasdair McIntyre, *A Short History of Ethics* (New York: Macmillan, 1966), p. 190.
3. Ibid., p. 193.
4. Piaget, *The Moral Judgment of the Child,* p. 352.
5. Piaget, *The Psychology of the Child,* pp. 123-124.
6. Thomas Lickona, "Research on Piaget's Theory of Moral Development," in *Moral Development and Behavior,* ed. Thomas Lickona (New York: Holt, Rinehart and Winston, 1976), pp. 219-240.
7. Piaget, *The Moral Judgment of the Child,* p. 191.
8. Ibid., p. 363.
9. Lawrence Kohlberg, "Stages of Moral Development as a Basis for Moral Education," in *Moral Development, Moral Education and Kohlberg,* ed. Brenda Munsey (Birmingham, Ala.: Religious Education Press, 1980), p. 85.
10. See David Shawver, *Character and Ethics: An Epistemological Inquiry with Particular Reference to Lawrence Kohlberg's Cognitive Theory of Moral Development,* Ph.D. diss., McGill University, 1979.
11. Piaget, *The Moral Judgment of the Child,* p. 196; Kohlberg, "Stages of Moral Development as a Basis for Moral Education," p. 51.
12. Lawrence Kohlberg, "Moral Development, Religious Education and the Public Schools: A Developmental View," in *Religion and Public Education,* ed. Theodore Sizer (Boston: Houghton Mifflin, 1967), p. 70.
13. Herbert Reid and Ernest Yanarella, "The Tyranny of the Categorical: On Kohlberg and the Politics of Moral Development," in *Moral Development and Politics,* ed. Richard Wilson and Gordon Schochet (New York: Praeger, 1979), pp. 107-132.
14. Lawrence Kohlberg, "The Future of Liberalism as the Dominant Ideology of the West," in *Moral Development and Politics,* p. 62.
15. Kohlberg, "Stages of Moral Development as a Basis for Moral Education," p. 61.
16. See Lawrence Kohlberg, "Moral Education Reappraised," in *The Humanist* 38 (Nov., 1978):13-15; James Rest, "Basic Issues in Evaluating Moral Education Programs," in *Evaluating Moral Development,* ed. Lisa Kuhmerker et al. (Schenectady, N.Y.: Character Research Press, 1980).
17. See Michael Katz, *The Irony of Early School Reform* (Boston: Beacon, 1968); Carl Kaestle, *The Evolution of an Urban School System: New*

York City 1750-1850 (Cambridge, Mass.: Harvard University, 1974).
18. "The Thirteenth Annual Gallup Poll of the Public's Attitude Toward the Public Schools," *Phi Delta Kappan* 63 (1981):33-47.
19. Lawrence Kohlberg, *The Philosophy of Moral Development* (New York: Harper and Row, 1981), p. 312.
20. Ibid., p. 313.
21. Ibid., p. 315.
22. Ibid., pp. 336-337.
23. Lawrence Kohlberg, *The Development of Modes of Thinking and Choice in the Years 10 to 16.* Ph.D. diss., University of Chicago, 1958.
24. Kohlberg, "Moral Development, Religious Education and the Public Schools: A Developmental View," pp. 71-72.
25. Kohlberg, "Continuities in Childhood and Adult Moral Development Revisited," p. 182.
26. For examples of misunderstanding, see Edward Wilson, *On Human Nature* (Cambridge: Harvard University, 1978), pp. 166-167; Biller and Meredith, *Father Power,* p. 147.
27. Kohlberg, "Stages of Moral Development as a Basis for Moral Education," p. 27.
28. Ibid., p. 81.
29. Lawrence Kohlberg, "Educating for a Just Society: An Updated and Revised Argument," in *Moral Development, Moral Education and Kohlberg,* ed. Brenda Munsey (Birmingham, Ala.: Religious Education Press, 1980), p. 466.
30. Lawrence Kohlberg et al., *The Just Community Approach to Corrections* (Cambridge: Educational Research Foundation, 1973).
31. Kohlberg, "Stages of Moral Development as a Basis for Moral Education," p. 63.
32. Ibid., p. 81.
33. Ibid., p. 78.
34. Lawrence Kohlberg, "Education, Moral Development and Faith," *Journal of Moral Education* 4 (1974):15.
35. See John Eusden, *Zen and Christian* (New York: Crossroad, 1981), p. 49.
36. Kohlberg, *The Philosophy of Moral Development,* p. 367.
37. Pierre Teilhard de Chardin, *The Divine Milieu* (New York: Harper and Row, 1960), p. 44.
38. Ibid., p. 114.
39. Ibid., p. 73.
40. Ibid., p. 116.
41. Ibid.

42. See E. L. Simpson, "Moral Development Research: A Case Study of Scientific Cultural Bias," *Human Development* 17 (1974):81-106.
43. Kohlberg, "Moral Development, Religious Education and the Public Schools: A Developmental View," p. 79.
44. Lawrence Kohlberg, "Educating for a Just Society: An Updated and Revised Argument," p. 457 referring to the author's "The Cognitive Developmental Approach to Moral Education," *Social Education* 40 (April, 1976):213-216 and "Meaning and Measurement in Moral Development," *Heinz Werner Memorial Lecture* (Worcester, Mass.: Clark University, 1979).
45. Kohlberg, "Educating for a Just Society: An Updated and Revised Argument," p. 459.
46. Ibid.
47. Lawrence Kohlberg, "High School Democracy and Educating for a Just Society," in *Moral Education,* ed. Ralph Mosher (New York: Praeger, 1980), pp. 20-57; Thomas Lickona, "Democracy, Cooperation, and Moral Education," in *Toward Moral and Religious Maturity,* ed. Christiane Brusselmans (Morristown, N.J.: Silver Burdett, 1980), pp. 487-515.
48. Kohlberg, "Continuities in Childhood and Adult Moral Development Revisited," pp. 191-192.

Chapter 5
1. William Bennett and Edwin Delattre, "Moral Education in the School," *The Public Interest* 50 (Winter, 1978):97.
2. Craig Dykstra, *Vision and Character* (New York: Paulist, 1981), pp. 1-4.
3. Carol Gilligan, *In a Different Voice* (Cambridge: Harvard University, 1982).
4. Sigmund Freud, *The Standard Edition of the Complete Psychological Works of Sigmund Freud,* ed. J. Strachey (London: Hogarth Press, 1961), 19:257-258.
5. *Ms.* Magazine, Dec., 1981, pp. 63-66.
6. John Stuart Mill, *On the Subjection of Women* (Greenwich, Conn.: Fawcett, 1971), p. 99.
7. Lawrence Kohlberg and Carol Gilligan, "The Adolescent as a Philosopher: The Discovery of the Self in a Postconventional World," *Daedalus* 100 (1971):1051-1056.
8. See Howard Muson, "Moral Thinking: Can It Be Taught?" *Psychology Today,* Feb., 1979, p. 57.
9. Kohlberg, *The Philosophy of Moral Development,* p. 354.
10. Gilligan, *In a Different Voice,* p. 73.

11. Ibid., p. 75.
12. Ibid., p. 77.
13. Ibid., p. 79.
14. Ibid., p. 82.
15. Ibid., p. 101.
16. Ibid., pp. 104f.
17. Stanley Hauerwas, *A Community of Character* (Notre Dame: University of Notre Dame, 1981), especially chapters 5, 6, 7.
18. Ibid., p. 132.
19. Ibid., p. 151.
20. Ibid., p. 131.
21. Dykstra, *Vision and Character,* p. 90.
22. Ibid., p. 68.
23. Kohlberg, "Stages of Moral Development as a Basis for Moral Education," p. 81.
24. See James Loder, *The Transforming Moment* (New York: Harper and Row, 1981), pp. 79-91.
25. Paul Philibert, "Kohlberg's Use of Virtue," *International Philosophical Quarterly* 15 (Dec., 1975):462.
26. David Harned, *Faith and Virtue* (Philadelphia: Pilgrim Press, 1973), p. 125.
27. Dykstra, *Vision and Character,* pp. 84-85; see also Abraham Heschel, *The Insecurity of Freedom* (Philadelphia: Jewish Publication Society of America, 1966), p. 144: "Be eager to do a minor *mitzvah* and flee from transgression; for one *mitzvah* leads to another *mitzvah,* and one transgression leads to another transgression."
28. Josef Pieper, *The Four Cardinal Virtues* (New York: Harcourt, Brace and World, 1965), p. 146; see also Harned, *Faith and Virtue,* p. 126: "Temperance is essentially a form of justice, as Plato recognized. Even though it is directed toward the self, it tutors the individual in what justice toward others involves, so that justice will not be confused with indulgence and thoughtless gratification."
29. Pieper, *The Four Cardinal Virtues,* p. 183.
30. *Kiddushim,* 4:12.
31. Kohlberg, "The Future of Liberalism as the Dominant Ideology of the West," p. 63.
32. See Daniel Maguire, *A New American Justice* (Minneapolis: Winston Press, 1982).
33. Michael Walzer, *Radical Principles* (New York: Basic Books, 1980), p. 242.
34. Kohlberg, "Stages of Moral Development as a Basis for Moral Education," p. 59.

35. Thomas Aquinas, *Summa Theologica,* I-II, q. 58, aa. 4 and 2.
36. For a rejection of the emotivist as the only alternative to the cognitivist, see Alasdair MacIntyre, *After Virtue* (Notre Dame: University of Notre Dame, 1981).
37. Pieper, *The Four Cardinal Virtues,* p. 14.
38. See Lawrence Blum, *Friendship, Altruism and Morality* (London: Routledge and Kegan Paul, 1980), pp. 43-83.
39. For the emergence of a religious element within community experiments, see Rosabeth Moss Kanter, *Commitment and Community* (Cambridge: Harvard University, 1972).
40. MacIntyre, *After Virtue,* p. 206.
41. See John Howard Yoder, *The Politics of Jesus* (Grand Rapids, Mich.: Eerdmans, 1972).
42. See Kenneth Smith and Ira Zepp, *Search for the Beloved Community* (Valley Forge, Pa.: Judson, 1974); Herbert Richardson, "Martin Luther King—Unsung Theologian," in *New Theology No. 6,* ed. Martin Marty and Dean Peerman (New York: Macmillan, 1969), pp. 178-184.
43. On the distinction between the United States and America, see Gabriel Moran, "The American Experience," *Religious Education* 76 (May/June, 1981):243-257.
44. Hauerwas, *A Community of Character,* p. 44.
45. See William Johnston, *Christian Zen* (New York: Harper and Row, 1971), p. 92.
46. Basil Mitchell, *Morality: Religious and Secular* (New York: Oxford, 1980), pp. 152-153.
47. Robert Coles, "How Do You Measure a Child's Level of Morality?" *Learning,* July/August, 1981, pp. 71-73; and the same author's "The Faith of Children," in *Sojourners,* May, 1982, pp. 12-16.
48. Thomas Aquinas, *Summa Theologica,* I-II, q. 73, a. 10; and in Jewish tradition, *Sukkah,* 52a: "The greater the man the greater his *yetzer." Yetzer* does not mean evil but it is the basis of evil inclination. See Robert Seltzer, *Jewish People, Jewish Thought* (New York: Macmillan, 1980), p. 292; Heschel, *The Insecurity of Freedom,* p. 142.

Chapter 6
1. Sharon Parks, *Faith Development and Imagination in the Context of Higher Education,* Ph.D. diss., Harvard University, 1980; Eugene Mischey, *Faith Development and Its Relationship to Moral Reasoning,* Ph.D. diss., University of Toronto, 1976; Richard Shulik, *Faith Development,*

Moral Development and Old Age: An Assessment of Fowler's Faith Development Paradigm, Ph.D. diss., University of Chicago, 1979; Romney Moseley, *Religious Conversion: A Structural Developmental Analysis*, Ph.D. diss., Harvard University, 1978.

2. James Fowler, *Stages of Faith* (San Francisco: Harper and Row, 1981), p. 102; the language of convictional experience comes from Loder, *The Transforming Moment.*
3. Kohlberg, *The Philosophy of Moral Development*, p. 335.
4. Fowler, *Stages of Faith*, p. 101.
5. Ibid., p. 49.
6. Ibid., p. 110.
7. Walter Conn, "Affectivity in Kohlberg and Fowler," *Religious Education* 76 (Jan./Feb., 1981):44-45.
8. Fowler, *Stages of Faith*, chapter 23.
9. Fowler, *Life Maps* (Minneapolis: Winston Press, 1978), p. 134.
10. Fowler, *Stages of Faith*, p. 199.
11. Ibid., p. 293.
12. Fowler, *Life Maps*, p. 38.
13. Fowler, *Stages of Faith*, p. 114.
14. Ibid., p. 164.
15. Ibid., p. 211.
16. Fowler, *Life Maps*, p. 24.
17. Fowler, *Stages of Faith*, p. 121.
18. Ibid., p. 40.
19. Parks, *Faith Development and Imagination in the Context of Higher Education*, pp. 94-209.
20. Fowler, *Stages of Faith*, p. 194.
21. Fowler, *Life Maps*, p. 81.
22. Ibid., p. 80.
23. Ibid., p. 90.
24. Ibid., p. 88.
25. Ibid., p. 86.
26. Fowler, *Stages of Faith*, p. 201.
27. On the relation of contemplation and action, see David Burrell, *Aquinas* (Notre Dame: University of Notre Dame, 1979), pp. 162-175; Matthew Fox, *Breakthrough* (Garden City, N.Y.: Image Books, 1980), pp. 42-49.
28. George Pixley, *God's Kingdom* (New York: Orbis, 1981); Norman Gottwald, *The Tribes of Yahweh: A Sociology of the Religion of Liberated Israel, 1250-1051 B.C.E.* (New York: Orbis, 1979).
29. See J. Dominic Crossan, *Cliffs of Fall* (New York: Seabury, 1980); G. B. Caird, *The Language and Imagery of the Bible* (Philadelphia: Westminster, 1980), pp. 11-12.

30. Fowler, *Stages of Faith*, p. 211.
31. Ibid., p. 201.
32. Ibid., p. 292.
33. Ibid., p. 293.
34. W. Cantwell Smith, *Faith and Belief* (Princeton: Princeton University, 1979).
35. Ibid., p. 38.
36. Fowler, *Life Maps*, p. 18.
37. Alexander Bickel, *The Morality of Consent* (New Haven: Yale University, 1975), p. 25.
38. Fowler, *Life Maps*, p. 18.

Chapter 7
1. Fowler, *Life Maps*, pp. 23-24.
2. W. Cantwell Smith, *Toward a World Theology* (Philadelphia: Westminster, 1981), p. 52.
3. A. N. Whitehead, *Science and the Modern World* (New York: Macmillan, 1948), pp. 12-14.
4. William Lynch, *Images of Hope* (New York: Mentor Books, 1966), p. 26.
5. For example, Walter Stace, *Mysticism and Philosophy* (Philadelphia: Lippincott, 1960).
6. See Paul Ricoeur, "The Metaphorical Use of Language," in *Philosophy of Religion*, ed. David Stewart (Englewood Cliffs, N.J.: Prentice-Hall, 1980), pp. 226-238; Caird, *The Language and Imagery of the Bible*, pp. 131-159.
7. William Johnston, ed., *The Cloud of Unknowing* (Garden City, N.Y.: Doubleday Image, 1973), p. 113.
8. See Ninian Smart, *Philosophy of Religion* (New York: Oxford, 1979), pp. 41-72.
9. See Ellis Rivkin, *The Shaping of Jewish History* (New York: Scribner, 1971), pp. 57-58; John Pawlikowski, *Christ in the Light of the Christian-Jewish Dialogue* (New York: Paulist, 1982), pp. 88-89.
10. See Charlene Spretnak, ed., *The Politics of Women's Spirituality* (Garden City, N.Y.: Doubleday, 1981); Christine Downing, *The Goddess* (New York: Crossroad, 1981).
11. Quoted in Robert Bellah, *Beyond Belief* (New York: Harper and Row, 1970), p. 33.
12. See Caroline Walker Bynum, *Jesus as Mother: Studies in the Spirituality of the High Middle Ages* (Berkeley, Calif.: University of California, 1982).

13. Joseph Miller, *Poets of Reality* (Cambridge: Harvard University, 1966), p. 244.
14. Gershom Scholem, *Jewish Mysticism* (New York: Schocken, 1954), p. 27; Charles Cummings, *The Mystery of the Ordinary* (New York: Harper and Row, 1982).
15. Martin Buber, *Two Types of Faith* (London: Routledge and Kegan Paul, 1951), p. 23.
16. Norman Lamm, *Faith and Doubt: Studies in Traditional Jewish Thought* (New York: KTAV, 1971), p. 4.
17. Gabriel Marcel, *Homo Viator* (Chicago: Regnery, 1951), p. 131.
18. Gabriel Moran, "Teaching within Revelation," in *The Aesthetic Side of Religion*, ed. Gloria Durka and Joanmarie Smith (New York: Paulist, 1979), pp. 153-164; Gershom Scholem, *Jewish Mysticism*, p. 9.
19. Gabriel Moran, "From Obstacle to Modest Contributor," in *Religious Education and Theology*, ed. Norma Thompson (Birmingham, Ala.: Religious Education Press, 1982), pp. 42-70.
20. Gabriel Moran, "The Strengths and Limitations of Brotherhood," in *Women Today: A Reader for the Clergy*, ed. Regina Coll (New York: Paulist, 1982), pp. 27-42; Dorothy Dinnerstein, *The Mermaid and the Minotaur* (New York: Harper and Row, 1976).
21. Chesterton, *Orthodoxy*, p. 54.
22. Edward Robinson, *The Original Vision* (Oxford: Manchester College, 1977).
23. Ibid., p. 109.
24. Ibid., p. 133.
25. Robert Lynd and Helen Lynd, *Middletown* (New York: Harcourt, Brace and World, 1929). Something similar is discussed by Alfred Schutz and Thomas Luckmann as the "and so forth idealization" in *Structures of the Life-World* (Evanston: Northwestern University, 1973), pp. 7, 241.
26. Lamm, *Faith and Doubt*, pp. 20-21.
27. Gordon Allport, *The Individual and His Religion* (New York: Macmillan, 1950), p. 37.
28. See Angela Barron McBride, *The Growth and Development of Mothers* (New York: Harper and Row, 1973).
29. E. R. Goodenough quoted in Robinson, *The Original Vision*, p. 144.
30. John Dominic Crossan, *The Dark Interval: Toward a Theology of Story* (Chicago: Argus Books, 1975), pp. 63-87; Jan Lambrecht, *Once More Astonished: The Parables of Jesus* (New York: Crossroad, 1981).
31. See *Bhagavad Gita*, trans. Swami Prabhavananda and Christopher Sherwood (New York: Mentor Books, 1956).
32. Matthew Fox, "Meister Eckhart on the Fourfold Path of a Creation Centered Spiritual Journey," in *Western Spirituality*, ed. Matthew Fox

(Notre Dame: Fides, 1979), pp. 224-233.

Chapter 8

1. Bernice Neugarten, "Adult Personality: Toward a Psychology of the Life Cycle," in *The Human Life Cycle,* ed. William Sze (New York: J. Aronson, 1975), pp. 381-382.
2. Jerome Bruner, *Toward a Theory of Instruction* (Cambridge: Harvard University, 1971).
3. Ibid., p. 21.
4. Ralph Tyler, *Basic Principles of Curriculum and Instruction* (Chicago: University of Chicago, 1950); see also Herbert Kliebard, "Persistent Curriculum Issues in Historical Perspective," in *Curriculum Theorizing,* ed. William Pinar (Berkeley, Calif.: McCutchan, 1975), pp. 39-50.
5. Benjamin Bloom, *The Taxonomy of Educational Objectives; Handbook I: Cognitive Domain* (New York: Longmans Green, 1956). *Handbook II: Affective Domain* (New York: David McKay, 1964).
6. Kieran Egan, *Educational Development* (New York: Oxford, 1979).
7. Alfred North Whitehead, *The Aims of Education* (New York: Free Press, 1967), pp. 15-142.
8. Jane Martin, "Excluding Women from the Educational Realm," *Harvard Educational Review* 52 (May, 1982):133-148.
9. John Dewey, *The Child and the Curriculum* (Chicago: University of Chicago, 1902).
10. See my criticism of the ideal of adulthood as independent, rational, and productive, *Education Toward Adulthood* (New York: Paulist, 1979).
11. Elliot Eisner, *The Educational Imagination* (New York: Macmillan, 1979), p. 209.
12. Carl Bereiter, *Must We Educate?* (Englewood Cliffs, N.J.: Prentice-Hall, 1973).
13. Ibid., p. 103.
14. Lewis Mumford, *The Golden Day* (New York: Dover, 1968), p. 132.
15. See Herbert Kliebard, "Metaphorical Roots of Curriculum Design," in *Curriculum Theorizing,* ed. William Pinar (Berkeley, Calif.: McCutchan, 1975), pp. 84-85.
16. The danger is evident in this kind of statement by R. S. Peters, *Authority, Responsibility and Education* (New York: Paul Eriksson, 1973), p. 107: "To be educated is not to have arrived at a destination; it is to travel with a different view."
17. Eisner, *The Educational Imagination,* pp. 50-73; see also *Conflicting Conceptions of Curriculum,* ed. Elliot Eisner and Elizabeth Vallance (Berkeley, Calif.: McCutchan, 1974).

18. Eisner, *The Educational Imagination,* p. 72.
19. Katz, *The Irony of Early School Reform,* p. 125.
20. Joseph Featherstone, "Family Matters," in *Harvard Educational Review* 49 (Feb., 1979):35.
21. See Sara Lawrence Lightfoot, *Worlds Apart: Relationships between Families and Schools* (New York: Basic Books, 1978).
22. Barbara Myerhoff, *Number Our Days* (New York: Dutton, 1978), p. 267.
23. Miller, *Toward a New Psychology of Women,* p. 55.
24. Jerome Bruner, *On Knowing* (New York: Atheneum, 1967), p. 118.
25. Eva Brann, *Paradoxes of Education in a Republic* (Chicago: University of Chicago, 1979), pp. 16-17.
26. Ibid., p. 17.
27. Hannah Arendt, *The Human Condition* (Chicago: University of Chicago, 1958), p. 80.
28. John Dewey, *Democracy and Education* (New York: Free Press, 1966), pp. 194-206; Arthur Wirth, "Issues Affecting Education and Work," *Teachers College Record* 79 (Sept., 1977):55-67.
29. Arthur Wirth, *Education in the Technological Society* (San Francisco: Intext, 1972), pp. 214-215.
30. Neugarten, "Personality Change in Late Life: A Developmental Perspective," pp. 327-331.
31. Levinson, *Seasons of a Man's Life,* p. 220.
32. May, *Sex and Fantasy,* p. 148.
33. Aristotle, *Metaphysics,* chapter 1; *Politics,* 8, 3 (1337 b).
34. Heschel, *Insecurity of Freedom,* p. 84.
35. Jerome Bruner, *The Process of Education* (New York: Vintage, 1963), p. 32.
36. Whitehead, *The Aims of Education,* p. 27.
37. Ibid., p. 19.
38. Maria Montessori, *Education for a New World* (Madras: Kalakshetra, 1959), p. 31.
39. T. S. Eliot of the poet John Donne.
40. Schafer, *Mothering,* pp. 57-58.
41. Elkind, *The Child and the Adolescent,* p. 113.
42. Daley, *Father Feelings,* p. 143.
43. See the study of Elizabeth Newson as cited in Green, *Fathering,* p. 206.
44. Crossan, *Dark Interval,* p. 50.
45. Egan, *Educational Development,* p. 10.
46. Marie Winn, *The Plug-In Drug: Television, Children and the Family* (New York: Viking, 1977).

47. Egan, *Educational Development*, p. 31.
48. Ibid., p. 48.
49. Ibid., pp. 132-133.
50. Whitehead, *The Aims of Education*, p. 27.
51. John Henry Newman, *Grammar of Assent* (Garden City, N.Y.: Image Books, 1955), p. 322.
52. Egan, *Educational Development*, pp. 60, 72.
53. Green, *Fathering*, p. 159.
54. Egan, *Educational Development*, p. 159.
55. Abraham Heschel, *Insecurity of Freedom*, p. 78: "What the nation needs is senior universities, universities for the advanced in years where wise men should teach the potentially wise, where the purpose of learning is not a career but where the purpose of learning is learning itself."
56. See Margaret Mead, "Grandparents as Educators," in *The Family as Educator*, ed. Hope Jensen Leichter (New York: Teachers College, 1974), pp. 66-75.

Chapter 9

1. See Edmund Morgan, *Visible Saints* (New York: New York University Press, 1963).
2. Robert Lynn and Elliot Wright, *The Big Little School* (New York: Harper and Row, 1971).
3. Dwight Moody as described by Bernard Weisberger, *They Gathered at the River* (Boston: Little, Brown, 1958), p. 211.
4. Bushnell, *Christian Nurture*, p. 4.
5. Ibid., p. 329.
6. See Catherine Beecher, *A Treatise on Domestic Economy for the Use of Young Ladies at Home and at School* (Boston: Marsh, Capen, Syon, Webb, 1841); Redding Sugg, *Motherteacher: The Feminization of American Education* (Charlottesville: University of Virginia, 1978).
7. Much of the anti-Catholicism had been edited out but is restored in the text of the 1979 edition from Baker Book House, Grand Rapids, Mich.
8. George Albert Coe, *A Social Theory of Religious Education* (New York: Scribner, 1920), p. 181.
9. Coe, "Religious Education as a Part of General Education," p. 22.
10. See Claude Welch, *Religion in the Undergraduate Curriculum* (Washington: Association of American Colleges, 1972); Nicholas Piediscalzi and William Collie, eds., *Teaching About Religion in Public Schools* (Niles, Mich.: Argus Books, 1977).
11. Ronald Goldman, *Readiness for Religion* (New York: Seabury, 1968); Ronald Goldman, *Religious Thinking from Childhood to Adolescence*

(London: Routledge and Kegan Paul, 1964).
12. Goldman, *Readiness for Religion*, p. 196.
13. Ibid., p. 49.
14. Abraham Heschel, *Insecurity of Freedom*, p. 237: "The unique attitude of the Jew is not the love of knowledge but the love of studying. . . . According to Rabba 'when man is led for judgment, he is asked . . . did you fix time for learning?'"
15. Thomas Groome, *Christian Religious Education* (San Francisco: Harper and Row, 1980).
16. Sidney Callahan, "Family Religious Education," *Living Light* 11 (Summer, 1974):235-264.
17. Hauerwas, *Community of Character*, pp. 186-195.
18. Gabriel Moran, "Education: Sexual and Religious," in *A Challenge to Love: Gay and Lesbian Catholics in the Church* (New York: Crossroad, 1983).
19. See Moran, *Interplay*, chapter 5; also "The Professions and the Family: Healing the Split," in *Family Ministry*, ed. Gloria Durka and Joanmarie Smith (Minneapolis: Winston Press, 1980), pp. 94-113.
20. Josef Pieper, *Leisure the Basis of Culture* (New York: Mentor Books, 1963), pp. 54-64; John Westerhoff III and Gwen Kennedy Neville, *Learning through Liturgy* (New York: Seabury, 1978).
21. Even in Christopher Lasch's bleak view of U.S. culture a glimmer of light comes through in the chapter on sport: *The Culture of Narcissism* (New York: Norton, 1979); see also Johan Huizinga, *Homo Ludens* (Boston: Beacon, 1950).
22. Seymour Fox, "Toward a General Theory of Jewish Education," in *The Future of the American Jewish Community*, ed. David Sidorsky (New York: Basic Books, 1973), p. 269.
23. Abraham Heschel, *The Earth is the Lord's and the Sabbath* (New York: Harper Torch, 1962).
24. Sidney Callahan, *Parenting* (Baltimore: Penguin Books, 1974), pp. 27-28.
25. Robinson, *Original Vision*.
26. Ibid., p. 80.
27. Ibid., p. 96.
28. Bettelheim, *The Uses of Enchantment*.
29. Ibid., p. 52.
30. Crossan, *Dark Interval*.
31. Jerome Berryman, "Being in Parables with Children," *Religious Education* 74 (May/June, 1979):271-285.
32. Bettelheim, *The Uses of Enchantment*, p. 291.
33. Quoted in Paul Vitz, *Psychology as Religion* (Grand Rapids, Mich.: Eerdmans, 1977), pp. 109-110.

34. Elkind, *Child and Adolescent,* p. 29.
35. Barry Chazan, *The Language of Jewish Education* (Bridgeport, Conn.: Hartmore House, 1978).
36. Don Browning, *The Moral Context of Pastoral Care* (Philadelphia: Westminster, 1976), p. 102.
37. In this regard, John Westerhoff's recovery of the word *catechetics* is helpful; see John Westerhoff III and O. C. Edwards, *A Faithful Church: Issues in the History of Catechesis* (Wilton, Conn.: Morehouse-Barlow, 1981).
38. Heschel, *Insecurity of Freedom,* pp. 285-298.
39. In advocating "daily conversion" rather than one great event of change, I am emphasizing a kind of Christianity that is closer to Judaism where no one is "born again"; see Seltzer, *Jewish People, Jewish Thought,* p. 294: "Let him repent today lest he die tomorrow; let him repent tomorrow lest he die the day after. Thus all his days will be spent in repentance."
40. See James Douglass, *The Non-Violent Cross* (New York: Macmillan, 1968); on the absence of vengeance in children, see the remarkable study of Roger Rosenblatt, "Children of War," *Time Magazine* (Jan. 11, 1982).
41. Newman, *Grammar of Assent,* p. 336.
42. James MacDonald, "A Transcendental Developmental Ideology of Education," in *Curriculum,* ed. James Gress and David Purpel (Berkeley, Calif.: McCutchan, 1978), p. 114.
43. Whitehead, *The Aims of Education,* p. 14.
44. Henri Nouwen, "Aging and Ministry," *Journal of Pastoral Care* 28 (Sept., 1974):182.

Index

A

Abraham, 93
Adult: development, 3, 4, 20-21, 40-46, 152; education, 14; religiousness, 153-56
Aesthetic: 58, 84, 164, 188, 207
Affective: in Fowler, 109-110; in Kohlberg, 76; in Piaget, 56
Ageist, 43
Allport, Gordon, 152, 221
Anselm, 202
Arendt, Hannah, 223
Aristotle, 15, 18, 19, 23, 173, 223
Arnold, Matthew, 124
Attachment, 59, 137
Authority, 68, 139

B

Barth, Karl, 190, 202
Beckett, Samuel, 197
Beecher, Catherine, 186, 224
Behaviorism, 30
Belief, 122-26
Believe in, 141
Bellah, Robert, 220
Bennett, William, 80, 90, 216
Bereiter, Carl, 163, 222
Bergson, Henri, 80
Berryman, Jerome, 199, 225
Bettelheim, Bruno, 199, 213, 225
Bhagavad Gita, 138, 221
Bible, 13, 14, 125, 149, 150, 184, 201, 202, 204
Bickel, Alexander, 125, 220
Biller, Henry, 211, 215
Birth, 146, 194, 197
Bloom, Benjamin, 159, 222
Blum, Lawrence, 218
Boden, Margaret, 212
Body of Christ, 120
Boelen, Bernard, 42-43, 211
Bonhoeffer, Dietrich, 118-19
Bowlby, John, 59, 213
Brahman, 136, 141
Brann, Eva, 170, 223
Browning, Don, 201, 226
Bruner, Jerome, 158, 174, 222, 223
Buber, Martin, 141, 221
Buddha, 131, 138, 206
Buddhism, 46, 141, 142
Burnout, 154
Burrell, David, 219
Bushnell, Horace: anti-Catholicism, 186; on conversion, 22-23; on nurture, 185
Bynum, Caroline Walker, 220

C

Caird, G. B., 219
Callahan, Sidney, 197, 225
Camus, Albert, 102
Care, 38, 92
Catechetics, 12, 201-02
Catholicism, 120
Catholics, 149, 185, 186
Centering, 111, 164, 207
Character, 101
Chazan, Barry, 220
Chess, Stella, 30, 210
Chesterton, G. K., 11, 147, 209, 221
Child: abuse, 197; as pre-moral, 68, 85, 105; religious education of, 197-99
Childlike, 41, 131, 132, 137
Christ, 192; body of, 120
Christian: beliefs, 74; church, 12, 13, 14, 21, 139, 145, 194; education, 12, 13, 188, 189, 190, 199-202; family, 149; imagery, 120; language, 148, 151; mysteries, 12, 203
Coe, George Albert, 21, 22, 23, 186, 209, 224
Coles, Robert, 105, 218
Collie, William, 224
Communion, 80, 155
Community, 101-03, 119, 145, 146, 165-66
Conn, Walter, 219
Conversion, 22-23, 95, 106, 115, 150, 151
Courage, 98

Crossan, John Dominic, 219, 221, 223, 225
Cummings, Charles, 221
Curriculum: of education, 162; images of, 164-65, 167

D

Daley, Eliot, 211, 223
Daly, Herman, 209
Dancing, 198
Death, 21, 102, 148, 155, 156, 181, 182, 194, 206
Death of God, 187
Decentration, 57-58, 110-11
Delattre, Edwin, 87, 90, 216
Denomination, 150
Detachment, 119, 155-56
Determinism, 26, 27, 32-33
Development: adult, 20, 21, 40-46; conversion, 95; economic, 5, 19, 20, 93; faith, 10, 107-21, 143; and growth, 3, 4, 16, 95; human, 3, 5, 6, 21, 23, 24, 94, 158, 183; images of, 10, 26-27; psychological, 4, 5, 19, 20, 21; in religious education, 21-23; research and, 2; two families of, 23-26
Dewey, John, 79, 162, 164, 165, 172, 222, 223
Dinnerstein, Dorothy, 221
Disbelief, 150-51
Discipleship, 104-05
Discipline, 101, 136, 137

Disengagement, 35, 172
Donaldson, Margaret, 213
Douglass, James, 226
Drever, James, 209
Dykstra, Craig, 88, 94, 95, 216, 217

E

Eckhart, Meister, 155
Economists, 4, 19, 183
Eddington, Arthur, 52
Egan, Kieran, 159, 160, 173, 177, 178, 222, 223, 224
Egocentric: in Fowler, 111; in Piaget, 57; in religion, 136
Eisner, Elliot, 163, 167, 180, 181, 222
Elkind, David, 64, 198, 199, 213, 223, 226
End point, 26, 95, 112, 113, 164
Enlightenment, 142
Environment, 113, 133, 192
Epigenetic cycle: in Erikson, 31-32, 39; in Piaget, 55
Equilibrium: in Aristotle, 98; in Kohlberg, 71; in Piaget, 53-54
Erikson, Erik: attitude to religion, 34-35; childlike and childish, 41; eight ages, 32; feminist criticism of, 36-39; and Freud, 30; imagery, 39-40; life-cycle, 31; limits of generativity, 35-36; and Piaget, 23-27; and virtue, 33

Erikson, Joan, 39
Ethics: judicial and visional, 88; and religion, 68
Executive ego, 117

F

Fairy tales, 61, 147
Faith: and beliefs, 122-26; biblical, 112; development, 10, 107-21, 143; and reason, 133-34; and religion, 133; and revelation, 136
Family, 160, 165-66, 168-69, 192-93
Fatherhood of God, 138-39
Fathering, 37
Feminist: criticism of Erikson, 36-39; imagery, 139-40; movement, 100
Finalism: in Fowler, 112-13; in Kohlberg, 72
Fowler, James: conversion, 115; and education, 112; faith development, 10, 107-21; faith and religion, 133-34; faith as relational, 125-26; faithing, 124; human and religious faith, 122; kingdom of God, 119-21; and Kohlberg, 108-09; 115; and Piaget, 110-11; and Smith, 123-26; stages, 114, 117; structure and content, 110
Fox, Matthew, 219, 221
Franklin, Ben, 78

Freud, Sigmund, 23, 30, 58, 88, 89, 216
Friedman, Milton, 203
Friendship, 195

G

Gandhi, 31, 118
Gardner, Howard, 212, 213
Gautama, 104
Generativity, 35-36
Genetic epistemology, 47, 52
Gilligan, Carol: care, 89; criticism of Kohlberg, 88; principled nonviolence, 92-93; stages, 91; study of abortion, 90-93
God: as father, 138-39; as mother, 139, 147
Goldman, Ronald, 188, 198, 224, 225
Good Shepherd, 199
Goodenough, E. R., 221
Gottwald, Norman, 219
Gould, Roger, 42, 43, 211
Goulet, Denis, 209
Grandparent, 34, 182
Green, Maureen, 211, 224
Groome, Thomas, 190, 191, 225
Growth, 2, 3, 4, 17, 95, 96, 164, 165

H

Harned, David, 217
Hauerwas, Stanley, 94, 95, 217, 225
Heschel, Abraham, 217, 223, 224, 225, 226
Hinduism, 141
Homosexual relations, 168, 194
Human development, 3, 5, 6, 21, 23, 24, 46, 94, 95, 157, 158, 183
Humor, 180

I

Identity crisis, 39, 44
Ideology, 116, 149, 180
Idols, 27, 132, 136, 153, 166, 191, 192
Imagery: of development, 10; of education, 164
Indoctrination, 70, 73, 82
Inquiry, 204-05
Instruction, 73, 84, 159, 205, 207
Interdependence, 147
Irony, 180
Islam, 139, 142, 153, 190, 203
Israel, 120

J

Jesus, 22, 104, 105, 120, 139, 201

Jewish: beliefs, 74; education, 12, 188, 189, 201; faith, 123; family, 149; history, 138-39; imagery, 120; religion, 131; Sabbath, 102, 120, 192, 196; tradition, 99, 101, 122, 125
Jews, 186, 205
Johnston, William, 218, 220
Journey, 94, 138, 143, 204-05
Judaism, 139, 203
Jung, C.G., 45
Justice: and Kohlberg, 72; as religious virtue, 99; in religious development, 154

K

Kaestle, Carl, 214
Kagan, Jerome, 213
Kant, Immanuel, 48, 67, 73, 79, 105
Kanter, Rosabeth Moss, 218
Kantian formula, 99
Kao, Charles, 31, 46, 210, 211
Katz, Michael, 168, 214, 223
Kegan, Robert, 212
King, Martin Luther, Jr., 103, 118
Kingdom of God, 110, 113, 119-21
Kliebard, Herbert, 222
Kohlberg, Lawrence: affective, 76; behavior, 70; bias against women, 81, 88; civic education, 83; content and structure, 72; criticism

of, 85; education, 70, 73; equality, 71; finalism, 72; indoctrination, 70, 73, 82; just community, 83; justice, 72, 77, 78; liberal faith, 72; misunderstanding of, 76; mysticism, 79-80; problems with, 81-84; reaction to Gilligan, 89; religion, 74, 78-81; retrenchment, 82; role taking, 77, 84; seventh stage, 74, 80-81; social, 71; stage 4½, 83-84; stages, 75

L

Lambrecht, Jan, 221
Lamm, Norman, 221
Language: discursive, 61; Piaget, 52; poetic, 205; sexist, 40, 43
Lasch, Christopher, 225
Leisure: and school, 181; and wisdom, 172-73
Levinson, Daniel, 41, 42, 44, 45, 46, 211, 223
Lewis, C. S., 119
Lickona, Thomas, 214, 216
Lightfoot, Sara, 223
Liturgy, 189, 194
Loder, James, 217, 219
Loevinger, Jane, 108
Logic of conviction, 107
Lowenthal, Marjorie, 43, 44, 211
Luckmann, Thomas, 221
Luther, Martin, 31
Lynch, William, 135, 220

Lynd, Robert and Helen, 149, 221

M

Maguire, Daniel, 217
Maimonides, 202
Mann, Horace, 186
Marcel, Gabriel, 142, 221
Martin, Jane, 222
Marx, Karl, 23, 38
Marxism, 38, 180, 203
May, Robert, 213, 223
McBride, Angela, 221
McDonald, James, 206, 226
McIntyre, Alasdair, 67, 214, 218
Mead, Margaret, 224
Meaning: criteria of, 17; and definition, 16; obvious and hidden, 16; systems, 13
Mentor, 45
Meredith, Dennis, 211, 215
Merleau-Ponty, M., 57
Merton, Thomas, 118, 119
Metaphor, 137-40, 143
Middle-aged, 44
Mill, John Stuart, 89, 216
Miller, Jean Baker, 39, 211, 223
Miller, Joseph, 221
Mischey, Eugene, 218
Mitchell, Basil, 105, 218
Mohammed, 104
Monod, Jacques, 209
Montessori, Maria, 175, 176, 213, 223

Moral: atrophy, 106; dilemmas, 84; judgment, 65, 108
Morality, 2, 45, 67, 87
Morgan, Edmund, 224
Moseley, Romney, 219
Moses, 20, 206
Mosque, 194
Mothering, 37, 147
Mumford, Lewis, 164, 222
Muson, Howard, 216
Myerhoff, Barbara, 223
Mysticism, 80, 113, 136
Myth, 116, 148, 176
Muslim: education, 188, 205; faith, 123; religion, 131; tradition, 122, 125, 189; way, 12

N

Neimark, Edith, 213
Neugarten, Bernice, 43, 45, 158, 210, 211, 222, 223
Neville, Gwen, 225
Newman, John Henry, 151, 179, 206, 224, 226
New Testament, 93, 153
New York Times, 19
Nirvana, 46, 136
Nondualism, 79, 141, 156
Nonviolence, 92-93, 95, 205
Nouwen, Henri, 207, 226
Nuclear war, 36, 145

P

Parable, 153-54
Parent, 34, 149, 161, 196
Parks, Sharon, 116, 218, 219
Pawlikowski, John, 220
Peatling, John, 26, 210
Peter the Apostle, 105
Peters, R. S., 222
Pharisaic Judaism, 139, 201
Pharisee, 201
Philosophy: Greek, 17; history of, 48; medieval, 17, 151; and Piaget, 48-51; and theology, 202
Physical contact, 147, 197
Piaget, Jean: action, 52-53; adaptation and assimilation, 60; cognitive and affective, 56; concrete operational, 62-64; criticism of, 62-64; decentration, 57-58; equilibrium, 53; and Erikson, 23-27; formal operational, 64-65; knowledge and wisdom, 49-50; levels of development, 58; metaphors, 52-58; moral judgment, 67-69; sensori-motor, 58-60; play, 60-61; social, 54; two moralities, 68-69
Piediscalzi, Nicholas, 224
Pieper, Josef, 217, 218, 225
Pilgrimage, 94, 96, 133
Pixley, George, 219
Plato, 15, 23, 76, 77, 97, 98, 157
Play, 60-61, 176, 194, 198

Poetry, 61, 140, 145, 178
Political: in Piaget, 52; and religious, 144-45
Prayer, 196
Prodigal Son, 154
Professional, 16, 161, 194
Progress, 17, 18, 19, 55, 96
Protestant, 49, 151, 184, 186
Prudence, 100
Psychoanalysis, 24, 30
Psychology, 2, 13, 20-21, 26, 40, 93, 143
Puritan, 184

Q

Qur'an, 125

R

Rahner, Karl, 202
Reid, Herbert, 214
Religion: biblical, 103; Christian, 131; Eastern, 79, 138, 142, 155, 206; Indian, 17; Jewish, 131; Western, 79, 138, 142, 155, 206
Religious: cults, 152; development, 131; doctrine, 144; and religion, 130, 135, 145; stages, 146-56; tradition, 104, 137, 145, 156, 192, 195
Religious education: movement, 12, 21, 190; stages, 187-91

Responsibility, 90, 91
Rest, James, 214
Resurrection, 120, 207
Revelation, 80, 114, 142-43
Revival, 185
Ricoeur, Paul, 190, 220
Riley, Matilda, 211
Rivken, Ellis, 220
Robinson Crusoe, 169
Robinson, Edward, 148, 198, 221, 225
Role taking, 77, 84
Rosenblatt, Roger, 226
Rousseau, J. J., 169
Rutter, Michael, 213

S

Sabbath, 102, 120, 192, 196
Samsara, 46
Sankara, 138
Schafer, Rudolph, 213, 223
Scholem, Gershom, 221
Schooling: and education, 160, 186; and knowledge, 169-70; and school, 170
Schoolteaching, 160
Schutz, Alfred, 221
Seasons of life, 45-46
Selman, Robert, 109
Seltzer, Robert, 218, 226
Sex education, 199
Sexist language, 40, 43
Shawver, David, 89, 214
Sheehy, Gail, 3, 4, 20, 209
Shulik, Robert, 218
Siegel, Linda, 213
Simpson, E. L., 216

Smart, Ninian, 220
Smith, Kenneth, 218
Smith, W. Cantwell, 123-26, 130, 133, 134, 220
Snedden, David, 172
Sports, 194-95
Spretnak, Charlene, 220
Stace, Walter, 220
Stochastic process, 26, 33
Story, 61, 101, 147, 154, 176, 181, 198
Sugg, Redding, 224
Sunday school, 185

T

Talmud, 99, 202
Taylor, Charles, 213
Teacher: religious, 104; and schoolteaching, 160-61
Teilhard de Chardin, Pierre, 80-81, 113, 215
Television, 177-78
Telonomy, 54
Temperance, 98
Teresa, Mother, 118
Theology, 14, 112, 202-03
Thomas, Alexander, 30, 210
Thomas Aquinas, 97, 98, 202, 218
Tillich, Paul, 111
Trinity, 141
Tyler, Ralph, 159, 222

U

Unbelief, 150
United States: constitution,
184; government, 16; and
progress, 18, 19; in relation
to America, 103

V

Vaillant, George, 41, 44, 211
Virtue: cardinal, 97-103; in
Erikson, 33; in Hauerwas,
94; in Kohlberg, 78
Vitz, Paul, 225
Vocational education, 172
Voegelin, Eric, 139

W

Walzer, Michael, 98, 217
Wason, P. C., 213
Watson, John, 210
Way, 12, 13, 133
Weisberger, Bernard, 224
Westerhoff, John, 226
White, Burton, 30
Whitehead, A. N., 80, 159,
174, 178, 206, 220, 222,
223, 224, 226
Whitehead, Evelyn and
James, 209
Wilson, Edward, 215
Winn, Marie, 177, 223
Wirth, Arthur, 223
Wisdom, 172-73, 195-96, 207

Work: and care, 38; job and,
171; labor and, 171;
woman's, 38, 172

Y

Yanarella, Ernest, 214
Yoder, John Howard, 218

Z

Zepp, Ira, 218